The Archaeology
of the
Montgomeryshire Canal

Fig. 1. The Welshpool Aqueduct Warehouse in the late nineteenth century.

Fig. 2. Carreghofa Locks in decay, 1979.

The Archaeology
of the
Montgomeryshire Canal

Stephen Hughes

The Royal Commission on Ancient and Historical Monuments in Wales

ACKNOWLEDGEMENTS

My friends and mentors Graham Deamer and Peter Wakelin have contributed sections to this book: Graham has written the gazetteer of the Llanymynech Branch of the Ellesmere Canal and Peter has written most of the section on the river-trade carried on from the port at Pool Quay, based on his Ph.D. research on the trade of the River Severn. Their help has been equally valuable throughout the enterprise. Charles Hadfield has generously loaned all revelant notes from his invaluable files on canal engineering. My sincere thanks to my able colleague Iain Wright for taking most of the modern photographs illustrating this book, and to my colleagues Jane Durrant, Charles Green, John Johnston, Denise Long, Ian Scott-Taylor and Geoffrey Ward for producing much of the artwork. The over-all book design has been undertaken by John Johnston. Others helped on the survey work needed including my colleagues Brian Malaws and Tony Parkinson, who also helped supervise the survey and recording training schools for the Ironbridge Institute of Industrial Archaeology that made it possible to record the canal monuments at Belan, Garthmyl Canal Port and the Powis Estate Sawmill and Timber-yard. My thanks also to my colleague Richard Suggett who read the unedited text and made many helpful suggestions. An M.S.C. team was also trained in surveying both at Garthmyl and the Welshpool Canal Depot and then recorded other features along the canal. The drawings of the Canal Depot are by Kenneth Cole and David Gepp and several of those of the Powis Estate Castle Sawmill are by former students of the Ironbridge Institute. My thanks both to Dr. Michael Stratton and to all the students of the Institute who helped in surveying.

I must also thank the successive project managers of M.S.C. Community Programmes on the canal: Ann Wells, Andrew Guest and Graham Deamer. The schemes have been sponsored or run by the Countryside Commission, Prince of Wales Committee, Powys County Council and the British Waterways Board. The photographic and documentary work undertaken by these have been equally valuable, especially the study carried out by Philip Horsley on the Montgomeryshire Canal Report Books and that organised by Graham Deamer. Melissa Daniels, formerly Curator of the Powysland Museum, also helped in finding documentary material, including the timber sale poster reproduced from the Museum's fine collection.

The photographs captioned 'Community Programme' were kindly provided by workers on the Powys Jobs Community Programme Scheme and its predecessors, those captioned 'Ironbridge' were taken by Dr. Michael Stratton of the Ironbridge Institute.

The surveys of the Welshpool Canal Yard Warehouse and the Vyrnwy Aqueducts are provided by courtesy of Powys County Council and the British Waterways Board respectively. The help of the Powis Castle Estate management has been invaluable, particularly that of Mr. Brian Barker, the Head Forester and Sawmill manager, and his workforce who have afforded every co-operation during this recording work. Mr. H. Clayton, a director of Thomas Robinson & Son PLC of Rochdale, has kindly supplied pages of their various early catalogues of sawmill machinery.

The staff of the Department of Maps and Prints at the National Library of Wales have, as always, been a great help.

Last, but not least, my thanks to my colleague Lilwen Jones for typing this book.

Contents

During the time that material has been collected for this volume (1979-1987) the following have served as commissioners.

Preface.

The Montgomeryshire Canal has frequently been called the most beautiful canal in southern Britain. Its superb position amidst the verdant pastures and steep wooded hills of the Severn Valley is matched and complemented by a wide range of very attractive structures connected with the canal itself. It is hoped that this publication can help visitors travelling by car, on foot, or by boat, to appreciate the richness and fascination of the structures on and alongside the waterway. This book also forms an introduction to the canal's heritage for the interested archaeologist or historian and aims to place the remains in the context of other contemporary structures.

The Royal Commission on Ancient Monuments in Wales first became involved with the archaeology of the Montgomeryshire Canal when asked to evaluate the significance of the monuments remaining along its length. This was done, drawing upon the experience of the study of the remains of other canals and contemporary railway systems in Wales. A policy of selected survey and photography has since been pursued using both the Commission's own resources and as survey training exercises for both the Ironbridge Institute of Industrial Archaeology and for Powys County Council's M.S.C. scheme on the canal. It has thus been possible to survey the complexes of buildings and structures at Belan, Garthmyl Canal Port, the Powis Estate Timber-yard, Welshpool Canal Yard and Maintenance Depot prior to the redevelopment of this attractive canal as a cruiseway for modern pleasure boats.

As this book goes to press a comprehensive programme of 'listing' canal monuments is being completed after joint work between *Cadw*: Welsh Historic Monuments and the Royal Commission on Ancient and Historical Monuments in Wales.

Joint discussions between the Commission's staff, the Powys County Council task force and the British Waterways Board have also taken place concerning the consolidation and development of the major remaining limekiln-bank at Belan. The kiln-bank at Buttington and the canal-powered mill at Wern have been laid out as picnic sites. The Powis Estate is also considering the restoration to water-power of the unique sawmill at Welshpool and taking steps to conserve the remarkable Powis Castle Estate collection of architectural drawings discovered during the course of the Commission's work. It is to be hoped that the rash of concrete-block walls and perspex porches breaking out along the canal can be terminated and a return made to the pleasant and more compatible materials traditionally used on the canal in its 150 years of commercial life.

Glanmor Williams (Chairman)

Fig. 3. Stone-breaker on the limestone quarries' wharf at Llanymynech. (Community Programme)

Introduction

The 'Montgomery Canal' of today—that is the cruising waterway now being restored to navigation—consists of a continuous line of waterway stretching south-westerly from the Llangollen Canal at Welsh Frankton through Llanymynech and Welshpool to Newtown. In fact, this 56 kilometre length consists of four distinct canal schemes which have only been linked together in name under modern ownership. The objectives of three of these four canals[1] (making up no less than 55 of the 56 kilometres) was to carry and distribute lime for agricultural purposes from the lucrative quarries at Llanymynech Hill, the carriage of this lime substantially outstripping any through-traffic likely to emerge. The canal-line stretched out on either side of a junction near Llanymynech quarries. It is with the two south-west of the quarries—the Eastern and Western Branches of the Montgomeryshire Canal—that this discussion of canal archaeology concerns itself (the archaeology of the rest of the newly named 'Montgomery Canal' is summarised in the second part of the gazetteer).

What became a subsidiary traffic on the Montgomeryshire Canal—timber—had earlier been conveyed down the Severn River navigation from Pool Quay (near Welshpool) and this separate navigation continued in use during the earlier life of the canal. More of its quite separate history is described in chapter six of this book.

The original Montgomeryshire Canal was intended to run from Porth-y-waen lime rocks, north of Llanymynech, up the Severn Valley to Newtown. In the event, however, at the north-eastern end a junction was agreed with the Llanymynech branch of the Ellesmere Canal just above Carreghofa Top Lock, while to the south-west construction was stopped a few kilometres beyond Welshpool at Garthmyl, all sources of capital having run out. This 26 kilometre length and a 3½ kilometre branch to Guilsfield were constructed between 1794 and 1797. Renewed interest in canal building allowed the remaining 12 kilometres of the line, from Garthmyl to Newtown, to be built between 1815 and 1819-21 under the new and separate Montgomeryshire Canal (Western Branch) Company; the original canal then became known as the Eastern Branch. The Montgomeryshire Canal was thus in the unusual situation of being owned by two different companies and consisting of an eastern and western branch of a shared main line.[2]

The first part of this book explains and interprets the construction and line of the Montgomeryshire Canal, looking at six different aspects of its archaeology and history in turn. The second part forms a guide to the remains to be seen along the whole 55 kilometres of the Montgomery Canal.

The archaeology of a transport feature such as this canal is concerned not only the remains of the waterway itself but with the archaeology of a much larger and dependent economic system. The artery of this archaeological landscape was the canal itself—providing transport and sometimes power to an interdependent series of industrial and agricultural installations. Branching out from the waterway into the surrounding rural hinterland were the routes of the carters and waggoners busying themselves with delivering lime for the fields and collecting the harvest of fine Montgomeryshire oak.

[1] The fourth canal-line incorporated in the present 'Montgomeryshire Canal', and not discussed in the text, was a short section of the original intended mainline of the Ellesmere Canal. This had been planned to run from Ellesmere Port on the Mersey Estuary through Chester and on to the River Severn at Shrewsbury but reached no further than Pontcysyllte to the north and Weston Wharf on the south before this line was abandoned as the arterial waterway. The intermediate Frankton Locks then in effect became part of the Llanymynech and Weston branch-canals at their junction with the revised Llangollen to Hurleston Junction Ellesmere Canal mainline (C. Hadfield, *The Canals of the West Midlands*, (Newton Abbot, 2nd. ed., 1969), 167-79).

[2] For a fuller history of the canal, drawn from documentary sources, see Hadfield, *Canals of the West Midlands* and A. Howell, 'Roads, Bridges, Canals and Railways in Montgomeryshire', parts II, III & IV, *The Montgomeryshire Collections, IX* (1876), 177-92; *XIV* (1881), 89-106 and *XV* (1882), 91-116.

The seal of the Montgomeryshire Canal Company.

The Construction and Line of the Canal

The formation of the waterway consists of the excavated trough of the canal and its bed of puddled clay. Various civil engineering constructions are required in order to facilitate the passage of a level waterway through an undulating landscape: cuttings, embankments, tunnels, locks, aqueducts and also bridges to reconnect bisected roads and farmland.

The main line of the Montgomeryshire Canal follows an almost level course along the Severn Valley as a simple, lateral waterway for 29 of its 38 kilometres. Thus on three-quarters of its length the need for tunnels, cuttings and embankments is greatly reduced. On the remaining quarter of the canal, including its 3½ kilometre branch to Guilsfield, there are two substantial embankments and a deep cutting, though even in this area of more uneven relief, near the confluence of the rivers Severn and Vyrnwy, no tunnels were required.

A Earthworks

The most substantial earthwork is the great embankment carrying the bottom level of the canal over the valley of the Bele Brook at Wern. This 1,130 metres-long embankment was originally flanked by large pits (called 'borrow-pits' in nineteenth-century civil engineering parlance), made by the extraction of earth for its construction.[1]

In height this bank is surpassed by that over the floodplain of the Vyrnwy: 6m (metres) high, 30m wide at its base and 15m wide at canal level, it extended for 350m from the north end of the Vyrnwy Aqueduct to Carreghofa Locks. In its line are two groups of arches, three and four in number, to let the occasional large floodwaters of the Vyrnwy pass harmlessly through the bank.

On the Guilsfield Branch is to be found a 189m-long cutting alongside the appropriately named 'Deep Cutting' Farm. Despite its name, this cutting is relatively shallow by the standards of later railways, being only about 6m at its deepest point.

B Aqueducts

All four aqueducts crossing rivers and larger streams on the line of the original Montgomeryshire Canal failed and had to be partially or totally rebuilt during the early nineteenth century. A similar fate later befell the additional aqueduct designed by Josiah Jessop for the later Western Branch of the canal between 1815 and 1819-21. Why were these structures so unsuccessful? After all the first substantial masonry canal aqueduct in Britain over the Irwell at Barton was constructed by James Brindley in 1760-61, some thirty years before these aqueducts of similar construction were built on the Montgomeryshire Canal. Large multi-arched water-power aqueducts in Britain preceded even that.[2] In addition the high rainfall of Wales necessitated the construction of many other substantial aqueducts on contemporary Welsh canals, but no other waterway required the wholesale rebuilding of all aqueducts as was the case on the Montgomeryshire canal. The shorter Swansea Canal, for example, had no less than ten substantial aqueduct structures but there is no evidence for the early failure of any of these and the largest was built over a very large and unpredictable mountain river (the Afon Twrch). The only other failure recorded on the substantial length of canals constructed in Wales was the Afon Lwyd Aqueduct at Pontymoile on the Brecknock and Abergavenny Canal. Here, William Crosley, formerly engineer to the

---

[1] Clearly shown on 'Shropshire Union Railway and Canal, Plan and Section of a proposed railway from Newtown in the County of Montgomery to the Grand Junction Railway at Crewe in the County Palatine of Chester with Branches, 1845', National Library of Wales M.C.C. 82. All succeeding references in the text to information current in 1845 or shown on the 1845 canal plan refer to this excellent deposited plan and its book of reference.

[2] The Llangyfelach Copperworks, built near Swansea in 1717, had a very large six-arched feeder aqueduct (S. R. Hughes, 'Landore: a Study of the Use of Water Power during the Industrial Revolution', *Melin* 3 (1987), 43-59).

Fig. 4. Old photograph showing the upstream (western) face of the Vyrnwy Aqueduct with the large embankment crossing the adjoining flood-plain. The now-demolished buildings of Williams Bridge Wharf and the southern flood-arches are also visible.
(Community Programme)

Rochdale Canal Company, built an aqueduct some 4.6 metres in span and height in 1810. There were problems with the scouring of the foundations of the aqueduct at Pontymoile and it had to be demolished and rebuilt before the canal was opened in 1812.[3] Even so, the other thirteen aqueducts on that canal (the largest of which were built by Thomas Dadford junior in the 1790s—at a time when he was also nominally one of the two Montgomeryshire Canal engineers) did not fail or collapse.

Why then, by contrast, were the Montgomeryshire Canal aqueducts so inadequate for the task for which they were built? Part of the answer may be that much of the canal is built in the broad valleys of large rivers (the Severn and Vyrnwy) with deep alluvial de-

posits unsuitable for establishing stable foundations for such huge structures. This surmise is confirmed by some of the visible evidence. One horizontal timber beam or baulk upon which the central masonry pier of the Berriew Aqueduct was supported was exposed until recently. This was a rarely visible example of early engineering practice in which the beams would provide a building-platform founded on timber stakes or piles driven vertically into the soft river-bed. This also indicates that solid bedrock at a shallow depth did not exist. The Severn, Vyrnwy and their tributaries are also

---

[3] R. A. Stevens, *The Towpath Guides, No.2., The Brecknock & Abergavenny and Monmouthshire Canals* (Cambridge, 1974), 23,63.

mountain rivers and streams with massive seasonal variations in flow with a resultant and unpredictable scouring of the foundations. The mountain rivers of south Wales are equally violent but some at least of the larger aqueducts are visibly founded on the shallow bedrock more easily accessible in those narrower valleys.

If most of the Montgomeryshire aqueducts were indeed founded on soft water-logged soils then the study of the behaviour of these varied types of earths becomes crucial. Unfortunately for early civil engineers, the study of soil mechanics did not come of age until 1925 with Terzaghi's formulation of the 'Principle of Effective Stress'. Without the use of this principle any generalizations on the behaviour of soil/water mixtures were impossible to make or use.[4]

Some comment on these problems had already been made before the 1790s—the years of the 'canal mania' when the original Montgomeryshire Canal was built. C. Vallancey in his *Treatise on Inland Navigation*, published in Dublin in 1763, commented that: *'The choice of Ground through which a Canal is to pass...is of extreme importance...the Ground should be frequently bored, where the Canal is proposed to be dug, in order to avoid, if possible, all bogs and rocks...'*

Malcolm Baldwin, an engineer who has studied this historical problem, has commented that such a contemporary statement may have been of some use but that *'unfortunately he [Vallancey] did not indicate how the borings were to be performed, nor how the results should be recorded and interpreted.'*[5]

It was often the case that the proprietors were more interested in getting their line opened than in the engineering problems. As a result, many sections of canal were built in unsuitable ground where, had a little more time been allowed the engineer, he could have suggested a more practicable route. In some instances, however, the engineer's intended line proved unacceptable to the local landowners and he was forced to deviate to avoid their property; that this could result in disastrous site conditions is well exemplified by the difficulty experienced by Telford with the Shelmore Great Bank on the Birmingham & Liverpool Junction Canal.

There is no doubt that canal proprietors would have been little concerned about the intricacies of construction. It has also been suggested that the proprietors of the Montgomeryshire Canal may have told their engineers to allow only for minimal standards of construction.[6] However the Montgomeryshire Canal has been categorised as an 'agricultural' rather than as a commercial waterway and indeed the lack of monetary motivation as a reason for building the canal was clearly illustrated in a pamphlet published in 1797: *'This Canal was not undertaken with the view of a large profit accruing from the Tolls; for there is not even a probability that any such can arise; and therefore the subscribers were the Noblemen and Gentlemen either possessed of estates in this County, or resident therein, who had for their Object the Extension of Agriculture, the Reduction of Horses...the Increase of Horned Cattle, and the preservation of the Roads; with the consequent Advantage to the Public'.*[7]

The following table clearly illustrates this: *The Shareholders of the Montgomeryshire Canal 1794-1797*[8]

Eastern branch—capital of 711-£100 shares

Peers	70 (10%)
Landed gentlemen	306 (43%)
Yeomen, graziers, tenant farmers	4 (0.006%)
Capitalists (bankers, gen.merchants & substantial rentiers)	95 (13%)
Manufacturers	—
Tradesmen	96 (14%)
Professional men	65 (9%)
Clergymen	52 (7%)
Women	23 (3%)

The landed interest, then, held some 53% of the shares and manufacturers none at all. Investors living in the rich agricultural county of Leicestershire in the east Midlands held

---

[4] M. Baldwin, unpublished M.A. thesis Imperial College, London, discussing early canal construction and soil mechanics, (extract in P.R.O. (Kew) Z. LIB 15 52/7).
[5] Ibid.
[6] J. H. Denton, *The Towpath Guides, No. 4, The Montgomeryshire Canal and the Llanymynech Branch of the Ellesmere Canal* (Birmingham, 1984), 17.
[7] C. Hadfield, *The Canals of the West Midlands* (Newtown Abbot, 2nd. edn., 1969), 190.
[8] J. R. Ward, *The Finance of Canal Building in Eighteenth-Century England* (Oxford, 1974), 53.

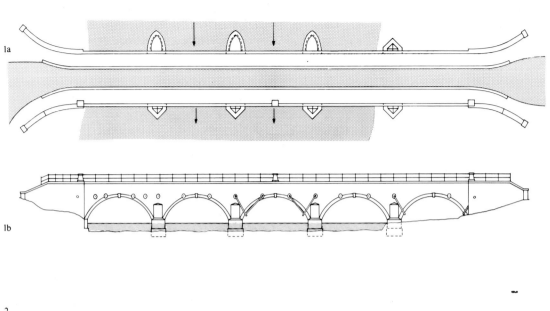

1a

1b

2

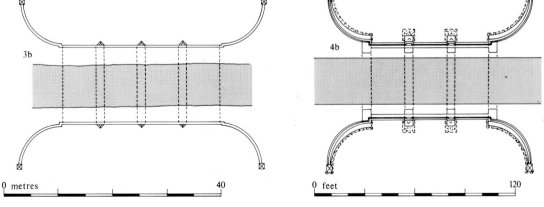

3a   4a

3b   4b

0 metres   40   0 feet   120

14

20% of the shares of the Montgomeryshire's neighbouring Ellesmere Canal and a large interest in navigation schemes all over Britain. The local Leicester paper on the 19th October 1792 gave notice of the subscription meeting of the Montgomeryshire Canal at Welshpool. However the attitude of the Montgomeryshire Canal's Committee of Management in 1811 summed up the proprietors' attitude towards outside commercial interests. The committee, in its Annual Report, congratulated the proprietors that they had built the line 'without public assistance or the intervention of strangers'. Shares had been taken in the towns on or near the line of the canal: Welshpool, Newtown and Montgomery, and in the neighbouring countryside. The average subscription was nine shares. Only about eighty shares were subscribed outside the counties of Montgomeryshire and Shropshire.[9]

Therefore the primary interest of the Montgomeryshire shareholders was clearly in establishing a dependable means of heavy transport to serve their large estates. This is shown by the fact that the Montgomeryshire Canal Act limited dividends to ten per cent. (in fact the first dividend paid on the canal in 1808 was only two and a half per cent.).[10] It is also worth considering the point that these prosperous landed gentry who funded the canal also built the most generous workers' housing in the area (see chapter four) and constructed large model farms (chapter two). They were not people who were likely to have encouraged either the skimping of costs or the use of inadequate

standards of construction. In fact the largest aqueduct on the Montgomeryshire—over the River Vyrnwy—absorbed no less than some 6% (£4,500) of the £71,000 construction costs of the original canal.[11]

It is also unlikely that the canal engineers could, or indeed would, have moved their aqueducts to more suitable sites than those actually chosen even if much larger sums of money had been at their disposal.

Could the contractors actually building the aqueducts have used poor standards of workmanship? John Simpson and William Hazeldine (of Shrewsbury) were indeed criticised by the canal committee for not following instructions exactly when fulfilling their contract to build the Vyrnwy Aqueduct. Apparently one of the arches had a 1ft (0.3m) difference in size from the five 39ft (11.9m) span arches actually specified for the aqueduct.[12] However both their concurrent and subsequent track-record in building aqueducts was superlative. The work on the Vyrnwy aqueduct would have taken place between March 1794 and 1796.[13] By the 9th September 1795 it was arranged that John Simpson was to become co-contractor of the matchless Pontcysyllte Aqueduct and he quickly became the sole contractor and then subsequently on 5th February 1800 his tender to complete the great aqueduct was accepted.[14] Of this the eminent and very experienced engineer William Jessop was to say, *'I cannot leave Pont Cysyllte without saying that the columns, without any exception, are executed in a more masterly manner than anything of the kind that I have before seen'*,— praise indeed![15] On 17th March 1802 John Hazeldine's tender for executing and erecting the cast-iron deck of the Pontcysyllte Aqueduct from his new (1799) Plas Kynaston foundry was accepted and this outstanding aqueduct was opened on the 26th

Fig. 5. Aqueducts; drawings 1a and 1b are of the aqueduct over the River Vyrnwy that caused so many problems on the Montgomeryshire Canal, as is evident by the ironwork of successive repairs. No. 2 was built by the eminent engineer William Jessop on the Cromford Canal (over the River Derwent) a few years before the Vyrnwy Aqueduct was constructed; a project on which Thomas Dadford Senior, later one of the Montgomeryshire Canal engineers, was a contractor. The early problems there are evidenced by the huge stepped buttresses flanking the large central arch and the two inner arches preventing the collapse of the flanking land arches. Such experiences on his own aqueducts prompted Jessop to say that such teething troubles were normal on the Montgomeryshire Canal. The Vyrnwy flood arches—Nos. 3a and 3b (the northern arches) and Nos. 4a and 4b (the southern)—have caused endless engineering problems throughout the life of the canal as have all the Montgomeryshire Canal aqueducts.

[9] Ibid., 53,89,92.

[10] Hadfield, *Canals of the West Midlands*, 190-93.

[11] J. R. Ward, *Finance of Canal Building*, 53 and A. Spencer, P. Horsley and J. Cooper, *About the Montgomery Canal....Towpath Guide. 2. Welshpool to Llanymynech* (Welshpool, 1981), 10.

[12] Verbal information, Graham Deamer.

[13] Hadfield, *Canals of the West Midlands*, 190.

[14] Ibid., 172-73 and C. Hadfield and A. W. Skempton, *William Jessop, Engineer* (Newton Abbot, 1979), 148, 151.

[15] Ibid., 150.

November 1805.[16] On the same day a double-track tramroad was opened from the north end of the aqueduct to Acrefair and the first traffic was coal from Hazeldine's colleries. This gives an indication of Hazeldine's wider entrepreneurial activities. In c.1790 Hazeldine had also opened a foundry at Coleham in Shrewsbury where he was responsible for casting the parts for the world's first iron-framed building constructed at Ditherington (Shrewsbury) in 1796-97. He was later an organiser of all sorts of large works around his west Midlands and mid Welsh trading empire; he even owned one of the wharves at Newtown canal basin. He was the efficient and dependable organiser of large capital engineering projects and Simpson was the unsurpassed practical mason.

Simpson and Hazeldine were both to work on another great aqueduct while that on the Vyrnwy was still under construction. This was Jessop and Telford's Chirk Aqueduct to which John Simpson, William Hazeldine and William Davies were appointed contractors. It was William Davies who built the great earthworks on the approaches to Pontcysyllte and he may have fulfilled a similar role on the Chirk Aqueduct. Again Simpson's and Hazeldine's work must have been exemplary for William Jessop examined their work and in January 1800 wrote, 'The masonry of Chirk Aqueduct is very perfect.'[17] In 1809 Hazeldine was still involved in efficiently carrying out waterway construction schemes. After the Act was passed in that year authorizing the construction of a towing-path along the River Severn from Coalbrookdale to Shrewsbury, 'William Hazeldine the ironmaster of Bridgenorth invested £500; he was appointed surveyor, and got the path and its attendant gates, bridges and culverts open on 1st December at a cost of £5,000.'[18] Hazeldine went on to cast many large iron bridges for Telford and in the 1820s was building Telford-style bridges all over the United Kingdom on his own account. Many are still standing and the bridges over the River Severn built in Montgomeryshire in the 1850s are without doubt based on these designs.[19] Such model careers on the part of the Vyrnwy Aqueduct contractors suggest that the causes of the general failure of the Montgomeryshire Canal Aqueducts lie elsewhere.

The engineer of the original Montgomery-shire Canal was John Dadford with his brother Thomas Dadford junior to advise him, the two being jointly paid. It has been suggested that the formal association of the respected and capable canal engineer Thomas Dadford junior with his younger brother John was done in order to make the latter acceptable as the engineer of the large waterway.[20] In the event the effect of any dependable advice from brother Thomas was minimal, for like other competent engineers at the time of the canal-mania he was rushed off his feet.

Work on the Montgomeryshire Canal began after the appointment of John Dadford as engineer on 18th July 1794 and lasted until August 1797. In 1791 Thomas Dadford junior, who from 1790 had been one of the contractor-engineers of the Glamorganshire Canal (with his father, Thomas Dadford senior, and the Sheasbys), was appointed engineer of the Leominster Canal.[21] Then in 1792 he was made engineer of the Monmouthshire Canal. He was to give three-quarters of his time to the work, and was not to work elsewhere except on the Leominster, and 'during the continuance of his employment he is not to have any concern in any contract for cutting'.[22] However, even the Monmouthshire Canal Company very soon diverted Thomas's time from their own very extensive construction works. On the 16th October 1792 the Monmouthshire Company themselves ordered him to survey the line of the neighbouring proposed Brecknock and Abergavenny Canal from Pontypool to Brecon. In October 1794 the Monmouthshire Company further ordered Dadford to stake out the line of the Brecknock and Abergavenny Canal. At the end of 1795, despite the Monmouthshire Canal Company's earlier strictures, Thomas Dadford junior was employed as the engineer of the Brecknock and Abergavenny Canal.[23] He built the several

[16] Ibid., 151-52, 286.
[17] Ibid., 149.
[18] Hadfield, Canals of the West Midlands, 125.
[19] For more details see R. Forsythe, 'The Iron Road Bridges of Montgomeryshire' (1984), a typescript now in the National Monuments Record for Wales, Aberystwyth.
[20] Personal communication from Charles Hadfield.
[21] C. Hadfield, The Canals of South Wales and the Border (Newton Abbot, 2nd. edn., 1967), 192.
[22] Ibid., 129.
[23] Ibid., 163.

aqueducts on that line very successfully, including the huge embankment over the aqueduct at Gilwern and the large four-arched masonry aqueduct over the Usk at Brynich near Brecon. Up until December 1796 Thomas Dadford was also engineer of the Leominster Canal.[24]

All this diversification of work soon began to show worrying results. Thomas Dadford junior was only allowed to spend a quarter of his time on the Leominster Canal and the time he could further spare for the Montgomeryshire Canal must have been negligible. In 1795 part of the Leominster Canal's as yet unused Southnet tunnel fell in and in December the eminent engineer John Rennie was asked to report on the work done. He was highly critical of Dadford's work.

In the absence of his older and more experienced brother Thomas, it must have been John Dadford who was almost totally responsible for the engineering on the Montgomeryshire Canal. His inexperience and youth may account for many of the problems that subsequently arose on the Montgomeryshire Canal. His first noted work was helping his father and elder brother John to survey the course of the proposed Neath Canal between June and September 1790. His first independent work was a 'Plan of a Canal and Rail Road for forming a junction between the Glamorganshire and Neath Canals' produced in 1792; only four years before his appointment as engineer to the Montgomeryshire Canal Company.[25] (Thomas Dadford junior, by contrast, had been appointed as engineer to the Stourbridge Canal in 1776, some nineteen years before the Montgomeryshire work).[26] John also had diversions from his Montgomeryshire work; in 1792-93 his boats were carrying goods on the Glamorganshire Canal. John helped Thomas prepare the plans of the Brecknock and Abergavenny Canal in 1792-93, and in 1792 John began that Canal Company's work by building a railway from Gelli-felen collieries to Glangrwyney Forge that was finished in August 1794. In June 1794 John began the survey for a second railway which was built but then came under immediate criticism from, amongst others, the nationally known engineer Benjamin Outram. This line, running from the Brecknock and Abergavenny Canal to the Llam-march Mines, was opened on the 15 June 1795 but by the 17th October 1811 was totally replaced by a second line.[27] John was closely associated with the works of his elder brother and this association on other projects besides the Montgomeryshire Canal unfortunately carried on after John was appointed engineer of this scheme on the 18th July 1794. John had already acted as Thomas's lieutenant in the Montgomeryshire project when he appeared before the House of Lords' Committee considering the Montgomeryshire Canal Bill on the 25th March 1794. On the 28th July 1794 he was back working on the Brecknock and Abergavenny Canal and he certified a bridge there on the 28th July 1794, and even as late as the 20th May 1795 he was being paid by that Canal Company. In addition he was also working on his brother's Monmouthshire Canal and employed to cost masons' work, etc. from the 28th April 1795.[28] In other words he was acquiring yet further commitments to his association with Thomas Dadford junior throughout the period when the detailed planning of the Montgomeryshire Canal and the founding of its large structures was taking place. John's resignation in autumn 1795 and his emigration to America suggests that he felt in some degree responsible for the failure of the heavy civil engineering works of the Montgomeryshire Canal.

As has already been suggested the partial collapses of the main Montgomeryshire aqueducts may have been due to the failure in unstable ground of the foundations supporting the colossal weight of very substantial aqueducts built to traditional designs carrying a vast weight of waterlogged puddling-clay enclosing the water-channel of the canal (Fig. 6). It may also be wondered why the Montgomeryshire aqueducts were not constructed using both the much lighter cast-iron construction and the less substantial hydraulic lime-mortar waterproofing then being pioneered on the adjoining Ellesmere Canal at Chirk and Pontcysyllte. Both William Hazledine and John

[24] Ibid., 193.
[25] Charles Hadfield's private index of canal engineers.
[26] C. Hadfield, Canals of the West Midlands, 73-75.
[27] G. Rattenbury, Tramroads of the Brecknock & Abergavenny Canal (Oakham, 1980), 82-6.
[28] Charles Hadfield's index of canal engineers.

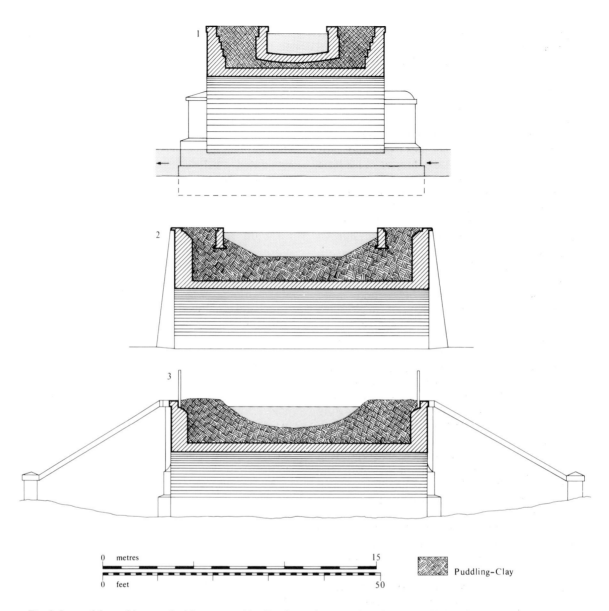

0 metres 15

0 feet 50

Puddling-Clay

Fig. 6. Some of the problems on the Montgomeryshire Canal aqueducts may have been caused by the huge bulk of waterlogged puddling-clay and masonry employed in building and waterproofing such vast structures, founded only on the soft alluvial soils of the turbulent upland rivers of the area. Drawing No. 1 shows a cross-section of the Vyrnwy River Aqueduct; No. 2 is of the southern flood-arches in the Vyrnwy Valley and No. 3 is of the northern flood-arches there. Both the latter carry canal channels of full width while the more hazardous river-crossing was achieved via a considerably reduced navigable trough.

Simpson were in fact also working as the main contractors on those innovative structures in addition to their construction of the Montgomeryshire Canal Company's Vyrnwy Aqueduct. What is not so well known is that the Dadfords were associated by aquaintance with even earlier revolutionary structures in south Wales, and what is more interesting is that the Dadfords were in a position to know of these early experimental structures as they were built.

In June 1790 Thomas Dadford junior began

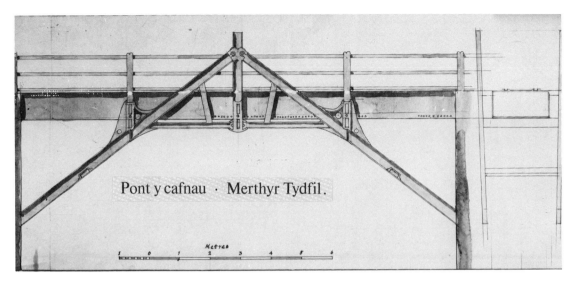

Fig. 7. Pontycafnau, Merthyr Tydfil was probably the first iron aqueduct and railway bridge built (in 1793) and would have been known to the Montgomeryshire Canal engineers. Note the dovetail, and mortice and tenon joints—both typical of woodworking practice but also found on very early iron structures. The central vertical originally supported the high-level feed aqueduct for the Æolus Water-wheel (named after the Greek god of the air because of its loftiness).

work as one of the engineer-contractors of the Glamorganshire Canal together with his father, Thomas Dadford senior, and his father's long-term associate, Thomas Sheasby senior. John Dadford must also have been involved with the Glamorganshire Canal for like his father he is mentioned as one of the first carriers on the canal in 1792-93. The work of building the Glamorganshire Canal was completed on the 10th February 1794.

The head of the Glamorganshire Canal was connected to the Gurnos Limestone Quarries via a railway sanctioned by the Glamorganshire Canal Company in April 1792. The line was built between January and June 1793 by the Cyfarthfa ironmaster William Crawshay, whose works were then becoming the largest in the world under his supervision and the guidance of Watkin George, Crawshay's local engineering genius. The line involved the construction of a cast-iron bridge 14.2 metres in span over the River Taff. This combined railway bridge and aqueduct was named the *Pontycafnau* (literally 'the bridge of troughs') and still stands intact. (Fig. 7). A second bridge cast from the same pattern stood in front of the main furnace bank at the head of the canal. In 1794 one of these bridges was drawn for William Reynolds' 'Sketchbook' and in 1795

Reynolds and Telford were working together on the Longdon-on-Tern Aqueduct with its rather similar raking struts.[29] This of course was built in the neighbouring county to the Montgomeryshire Canal. The subsequent iron constructions at Chirk and Pontcysyllte on the Ellesmere Canal (the Montgomeryshire's sole joined canal) drew on Telford's previous experience at nearby Longdon. Even more remarkable was the large iron aqueduct at the Cyfarthfa Works (Fig. 8); clues to its former existence are given by the bolt holes at the top of the central support of *Pontycafnau's* surviving structure and by its descriptive name, 'the bridge of *troughs*'. In fact the present bridge remains only house the lower of two water troughs or channels, as can be seen from the accompanying illustration. In 1802 Walter Davies had described the new structures: '*Cyfarthfa Works—Mr. Crawshay proprietor— The Aqueduct bring[in]g the Water of the Taaff to turn the Machinery here is ab[ou]t 80 feet above the bed of the river at low water, and extends ab[ou]t 606 feet in length.*'[30] In 1806 Abraham Rees brought these works to nation-

[29] D. Hague and Stephen Hughes, 'Pont-y-Cafnau: the first iron railway bridge and aqueduct?', *Association for Industrial Archaeology Bulletin* 9(4) (1982), 3-4.

Fig. 8. 'Water being conveyed...for a great distance in an iron aqueduct'...'80 feet above the bed of the river...and...606 feet in length'. This, the upper feed aqueduct for the great Æolus Water-wheel at Merthyr Tydfil was built in the period 1793-96 (it may have been finished in 1794 or -95) and would have been known to the Dadfords who constructed the large, and more conventional masonry aqueducts on the Montgomeryshire Canal (sketch after an engraving and a painting by Penry Williams).

al notice in his *Cyclopaedia*: 'At Merthyr there is a famous water-wheel, made of cast-iron, 50 feet diameter, at Mr. Crawshaw's works; the water being conveyed thereto for a great distance in an iron aqueduct.'[31] These new works must have been widely known locally, and especially to the Dadfords working on the canal, as the tail-race water from the works was the uppermost feeder of the canal, and as the two new iron aqueducts conveyed additional sources of supply from the Taf-fechan to a canal notoriously short of water. This major aqueduct structure must have been planned by January 1793 and the great water-wheel (called the *Æolus* wheel by contemporaries because of its great height) with its two levels of water feed worked for the first time on the 24 October 1796.[32].

This was not the only type of lighter aqueduct construction then being used within the Dadfords' experience. Thomas Dadford senior had worked with Thomas Sheasby senior, the Tamworth architect, since 1785 and in 1794 the latter began construction of the Swansea Canal aqueducts. Instead of using the bulky and weighty puddling-clay, until then used as the usual sealant in British aqueduct construction, he used a hydraulic (i.e. impervious) mortar mixed from a local source of hydraulic lime found under the site of the Port Talbot Docks.[33]

[30] My thanks to Peter Wakelin for drawing this reference to my attention whilst cataloguing the industrial archaeological references given in manuscript 'tours' of Wales deposited in the National Library of Wales.
[31] Reprinted as *Rees's Manufacturing Industry (1819-20)*, vol.1 (Newton Abbot, 1972) ed. Neil Cossons, 365.
[32] Gilbert Gilpin letters in the Lloyd-Jones Collection (Shropshire Record Office, 1781/6/22).

Why then, with these precedents at hand, didn't John Dadford and his brother Thomas use such lighter structures in bridging the apparently unstable soils and rivers of Montgomeryshire? Firstly it must be said that Thomas Dadford junior was already overcommitted and that his employers in South Wales, instead of restricting his allotted tasks, as had been their avowed intention, were exacerbating the situation. It is also clear that the inexperienced John Dadford, whatever his competence may have been, was largely, if not entirely, left on his own to complete the Montgomeryshire Canal, and indeed was still expected to go and assist at his elder brother's other multifarious projects. If the Montgomeryshire Canal engineers were so overcommitted and lacking in experience, it may be an interesting question to ask if the leading engineers of the day could have coped more adequately with the problems of building the Montgomeryshire Canal aqueducts? The most prominent canal and civil engineer of his day was undoubtedly William Jessop, the former assistant of the great John Smeaton. In 1792-93 both the conventional aqueduct structures then being built on his Cromford Canal also suffered partial failure. His troubles may have been directly related to the problems of containing such a huge mass of waterlogged puddling-clay in very large masonry structures.[34] Such experiences may help to explain his proposals for new lighter forms of structure to be used on the Montgomeryshire's neighbouring Ellesmere Canal. On 14th July 1795 Jessop himself made the adventurous recommendation to the Ellesmere Canal Committee that they should build high iron aqueducts at both Pontcysyllte and Chirk.[35] However this suggestion was only made after preparations were well advanced to build masonry aqueducts on those sites, and indeed after construction had also started on the Montgomeryshire Canal aqueducts. Even then Jessop and his outstanding assistant Thomas Telford were still very hesitant over the new constructional techniques to be employed on these very large structures. All the previous and relatively experimental iron aqueducts, such as Longdon (completed in 1796) and Outram's contemporary Holmes Aqueduct at Derby, were fairly small and the trough of the

high and long upper aqueduct at Cyfarthfa was only 3ft 6ins (1.07m) wide and 16ins (0.41m.) deep (i.e. much smaller than the 10ft 10ins (3.3m) wide and 4ft 4ins (3.3m) deep trough on the Vyrnwy Aqueduct). After Fulton left the construction of the Peak Forest Canal in September 1795, the idea of building a large cast-iron aqueduct at Marple on that particular waterway was also scrapped in favour of a conventional masonry aqueduct by no less a figure than Benjamin Outram himself. By 15th February 1798 William Jessop had concurred with Telford and Hazeldine that the difficulties in giving Chirk an iron trough were too great, a conventional masonry aqueduct was to be built instead.[36] It should be remembered that this was a decision taken by the two most prominent engineers of the canal-age some six months after the opening of the whole Montgomeryshire Canal. It would seem that the Dadfords could hardly be blamed for not using the new iron technology to overcome the problems of a major aqueduct like that over the Vyrnwy, although the problems of the lesser aqueducts might have been overcome in this manner then, rather than with the reconstructions that were later necessitated.

An alternative would have been to use the hydraulic mortar sealant used on the Swansea Canal from 1794. Telford and Jessop would have known of its earlier use in the structures of continental canals, and in Smeaton's famous Eddystone Lighthouse where a hydraulic lime from Aberthaw in Glamorgan was used. By 27th November 1799 it had been decided partly to utilise this method in sealing the hard-fired bricks incorporated in the side walls of the Chirk Aqueduct water-channel which was carried on a deck of cast-iron plates. Jessop said of this work: *'There is no earth or puddle made use of; the water-way is formed with a cast-iron*

[33] S. R. Hughes, 'The Industrial Archaeology of Water and of Associated Rail Transport in the Swansea Valley Area', unpublished M.Phil. thesis (University of Birmingham 1984), 149-55.

[34] R. B. Schofield, 'The design and construction of the Cromford Canal 1788-1794', in a pre-printed synopsis of a paper in the forthcoming *Transactions of the Newcomen Society* 57 (1985-86) 1, 20, 22.

[35] C. Hadfield, *Canals of the West Midlands*, 171.

[36] C. Hadfield and A. W. Skempton, *William Jessop, Engineer* (Newton Abbot, 1979), 149.

bottom, and square masonry on the sides; the spandrels of the arches are hollow. By this mode of construction, a very considerable proportion of the masonry is saved in the breadth of the Aqueduct; the risque of expansion or contraction from puddling is avoided. In case of any leakage, the water may find its way through the spandrels, without injuring the Work; and every part of the Masonry and the bottom of the water-way, may be readily examined at all times.'[37]

Even so, that aqueduct was not completed until 1801, and the earlier Swansea Canal Aqueducts in fact had no substantially lighter structure when compared to conventional structures with a sealant of puddling-clay. The iron structure of the great Pontcysyllte Aqueduct was not started until the experimentation at Chirk was completed and the work there was finished on the 26th November 1805.[38]

On the Montgomeryshire Canal one arch of the conventional masonry/puddling-clay aqueduct over the Vyrnwy collapsed, there were problems with the aqueduct at Berriew over the Rhiw and also with some minor works. In the autumn of 1796 John Dadford resigned and went to America. He was replaced on his brother Thomas's initiative by Thomas Dadford senior, 'under whom they were bred, and who has had great experience in Canal works'. However, perhaps not surprisingly, the Montgomeryshire Canal Committee were critical of their engineers and called in the eminent William Jessop to advise them. In fact it was a common contemporary practice to call in other engineers to assess the work done and the same had just happened to Jessop himself twice on the Cromford Canal during August 1793 and again in 1794.[39] Jessop soothed the Montgomeryshire Canal Committee by saying that such teething troubles were normal. His business partner, Benjamin Outram, had in fact been much more critical of Thomas Dadford junior's work on the Brecknock and Abergavenny Canal for much less reason. Jessop may have sympathised with the Dadfords' problems or even felt unable to criticise them for a variety of reasons. The two leading writers on canals have made the following comments on his own competence in this direction, '*Masonry aqueducts were not Jes-*

sop's strong suit' and '*Jessop, never very good on masonry aqueducts*'.[40] In January 1792 Jessop, as already mentioned, had reported a failure in his Amber Aqueduct on the Cromford Canal in Derbyshire and it was agreed that he should not be paid during the time taken for the construction of the rest of the canal. In August 1793 troubles occurred on the other substantial aqueduct carrying the Cromford Canal and the unfortunate Jessop's offer to pay the full cost of necessary rebuilding in this daring structure, with his own canal shares assigned as security, was accepted by the Cromford Canal Company.[41] It is fairly certain that the Dadfords would have been aware of this as Thomas Dadford (probably senior) was one of the two contractors of the Cromford Canal appointed in November 1789. Dadford and his partner were committed to a short contract period in which to construct several major civil engineering structures. The resultant problems made them give up the project on the 8th January 1791 after beginning the earthworks and structures over the whole length of the waterway.[42] Presumably John Dadford would also have been in attendance on the Cromford Canal project as was so often the case in the family schemes. The whole family now left to concentrate on their various canal schemes in Wales and the borderland, the first of which had started some six months before.

Indeed, it can be seen that Jessop and the Dadfords knew each others faults and could comprehend that all were civil engineers in the overworked infancy of their profession. They knew that there was scant understanding or sympathy from their contemporary employers whose concern was to see a return on their investment.

The consulting engineer for the later Western Branch of the Montgomeryshire Canal was William Jessop's short-lived son Josias. His designs were built by John Williams between

[37] C. Hadfield, *Canals of the West Midlands* 173.
[38] Ibid., 176.
[39] Schofield, 'Cromford Canal', 22 and 24.
[40] L. T. C. Rolt, *Navigable Waterways* (London, 1973), 64 and C. Hadfield, *The Canals of the East Midlands* (Newton Abbot, 1966), 51.
[41] Schofield, 'Cromford Canal', 20, 23-4.
[42] Ibid., 12, 15.

1815 and 1819-21 and included one fairly small three-arched (3.82m spans) aqueduct at Aberbechan. By 1859 it had been proposed that this too needed replacement but instead was repaired and then promptly partly collapsed and was rebuilt again.[43] It may be that Josias had repeated his father's probable mistake on the Derwent Aqueduct of the Cromford Canal in not building the base of the aqueduct walls thick enough to restrain the stresses imposed by the huge mass of unstable puddling-clay behind.[44] A similar problem was to occur later on the ill-fated Vyrnwy Aqueduct. The evidence of collapse and repair are still very apparent on the Aberbechan Aqueduct today. The top of the upstream face of the aqueduct is still bulging outwards and only the southernmost of the three arches retains the original stonework rather than the blue engineering brick of later rebuilding. The upstream face of the centre arch and the downstream face of all three arches have been heavily repaired in blue brick.

George W. Buck was a harbinger of the new technology of cast-iron and was appointed engineer of the Eastern Branch of the Montgomeryshire Canal in 1819 and of the Western Branch in 1832 shortly before he became one of Robert Stephenson's railway engineer assistants in December 1833. He rebuilt the Luggy Aqueduct at Brithdir with cast-iron in 1819[45] and instigated the use on the Montgomeryshire Canal of the cast-iron lock-gates already employed on the Ellesmere Canal.[46] By 1823 the Vyrnwy Aqueduct was leaking and every arch was fractured, the canal committee apparently reporting that it had been ill-built of bad materials.[47] Certainly the distorted appearance

---

[43] J. H. Denton, *The Towpath Guides, No. 4, The Montgomeryshire Canal and the Llanymynech Branch of the Ellesmere Canal* (Birmingham, 1984), 75.

[44] Schofield, 'Cromford Canal', 22-3.

[45] 'Montgomeryshire Canal Report Books', 1816-1846, entries for the 16th June 1819 and 2nd October 1820 (Public Record Office, Kew).

[46] Hadfield, *Canals of the West Midlands*, 195

[47] Ibid. and 'Monts. Canal Report Books', 27th February 1823 and 21st June 1823.

Fig. 9. A photograph showing the cast-iron beams on the Vyrnwy Aqueduct connected to wrought-iron tie-rods going both under and above the central arch in an attempt to stop the huge structure splitting apart. (Community Programme)

23

of the whole structure is clear for all to see today. The centre of each of the five arches of the aqueduct has sunk, as is clearly visible from the coursing of the masonry in the spandrels between the arches. The second arch in from the southern (hillside) end of the aqueduct has slumped particularly badly.

However, the stresses produced in the re-puddling carried out to remedy the leakages appear to have been too great for the aqueduct walls which bulged alarmingly, and Buck is said to have thrown himself on the ground and groaned in despair (surely not the only one of the Montgomeryshire Canal engineers to have done that!).[48] In fact the stonework over the central arch on the western or upstream elevation still exhibits a very significant bulge and overhang over the masonry below. Buck carried out an extensive programme of emergency reinforcement by inserting red-hot iron tie-rods through the structure of the aqueduct above all the arches in order to tie the outside faces of the structure together (the tie-rods under the central and northern arches can clearly be seen). The position of these is still clearly visible in the location of the ovaloid cast-iron facing-plates with their cross of reinforcing ribs. The gross distortion of the central walling of the aqueduct together with the splitting away of the arch face underneath called for more drastic measures and this unstable masonry was held back against the main aqueduct structure by a linked series of large 'fish-bellied' cast-iron beams—five on the collapsing upstream face of the aqueduct and four on the relatively stable downstream face. The complexities of manoeuvring these massive cast-iron beams into place over a very turbulent river can only be imagined. A clue as to how this was done is given by the existence of wrought-iron loops attached to each beam by holes made through their central reinforcing ribs. The loops still survive on the central upstream beams and on all those on the downstream elevation of the central arch. These suggest that a crane (or cranes) positioned on the upper deck of the aqueduct was used to lower the beams into place. Boats must also have been used on the river in order to manoeuvre the two large tie-rods into place under the central arch in order to prevent it cracking apart. The reinforcements at the

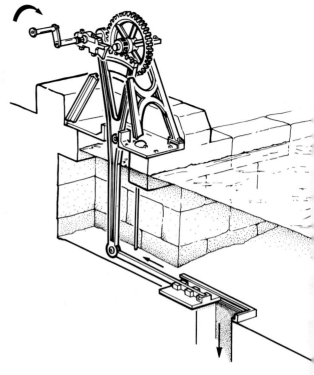

Fig. 10. G.W. Buck, Montgomeryshire Canal Eastern Branch Engineer from 1819 to 1831, was very keen on the use of the relatively new material of cast-iron. The unique lock ground-sluice controls shown here were probably introduced by him.

northern end of the aqueduct are a yet later addition that will be discussed below. The tie-rods reinforcing the northerly of the Vyrnwy flood-arch aqueducts have terminals of concentric circles unlike the 'floriated' design used in this later Shropshire Union Railways and Canal Company programme of aqueduct reconstruction and this may also indicate activity by G.W. Buck.

Originally there may have been no parapets on the aqueducts or perhaps, more likely, there had been timber fences which had rotted by the 1820s. In 1828 Buck fixed iron railings to the towing-path elevations of the Berriew and Vyrnwy Aqueducts and also to the two smaller aqueducts over the adjacent flood-plain.[49] Those on the Vyrnwy Aqueduct have three

[48] A. Spencer, P. Horsley and J. Cooper, *About the Montgomery Canal....Towpath Guide. 2. Welshpool to Llanymynech* (Welshpool, 1981), 10.

Fig. 10a. Buck's lock ground-sluice gearing was cast at Coalbrookdale—as the cast-mark shows.

intermediate stone supports of finely tooled masonry carried out in a style that resembles miniature Egyptian-style temple pylons. Thirty-six tapering columns of cast-iron support two longitudinal bars of wrought-iron with their square section carried through prominent bulbous thickenings in the intermediate cast-iron columns. The lower circular rail is a later addition. By contrast Buck's railings on the other aqueducts were replaced in the aqueduct refurbishment of the 1890s.

George Buck may also have devised in 1831 the paddle gearing that is so prominent a feature of most locks on the Eastern Branch, cast as their imprinted maker's name shows at the famous ironworks of Abraham Darby at Coalbrookdale (Fig. 10a).[50] This gearing must have been much easier to operate than the simple ratchets that had earlier raised the sluices of a lock vertically. George Buck was obviously destined for greater things, and in

1833 resigned to become Robert Stephenson's first assistant on the London to Birmingham Railway.[51] His influence was not to end here, for his successor, J. A. S. Sword, modelled his Lledan Brook (Welshpool) Aqueduct replacement in 1836 on Buck's earlier Luggy Brook Aqueduct of 1819 at Brithdir (Figs. 11-13). Both were composite iron beams consisting of three groups of cast-iron plates bolted together to form the bases and sides of the aqueducts (although the later Lledan Aqueduct had additional reinforcement).

This form of aqueduct was hardly new. The 14.2 metre span of the Pontycafnau Aqueduct of 1793 was a continuous casting but then again this only had to carry a shallow non-navigable trough. The earlier large aqueducts of iron all had panels based on the somewhat irrelevant artisan training of their designers: the Longdon-on-Tern Aqueduct of 1795 and the Pontcysyllte Aqueduct deck of 1802-05 both have spans composed of cast-iron panels cast in the form of arch-stones or 'voussoirs', as befitted the work of Thomas Telford, the mastermason, whilst the large *Æolus* Aqueduct had trough spans seemingly composed of two longitudinal panels cast in a form approximating to timber strakes, as might have been expected in the work of Watkin George, the former carpenter.

The design of some smaller contemporary structures show features that gradually came to terms with the specific characteristics of the new material of cast-iron. A beam deflecting under load will be stretched on its underside (i.e. put under tensile stress) and compressed along its upper surface. Cast-iron, like stone, is strong in compression but weak under tension. Benjamin Outram's first cast-iron canal aqueduct at the Holmes in Derby, built in 1794, had undergone structural failure by 1802.[52] It was composed of simple 4cm-thick

[49] Monts. Canal Report Bks., 24th October 1828. All references to this source are from the work of Philip Horsley.

[50] H. Arnold, 'The Montgomeryshire Canal, Part 1 of a profile of the canals to Newtown', *Waterways World* June-July 1976, 32-5, 42-4, 33.

[51] Ibid.

[52] R. B. Schofield, 'The Construction of the Huddersfield Narrow Canal', *Transactions of the Newcomen Society* 53 (1981-82).

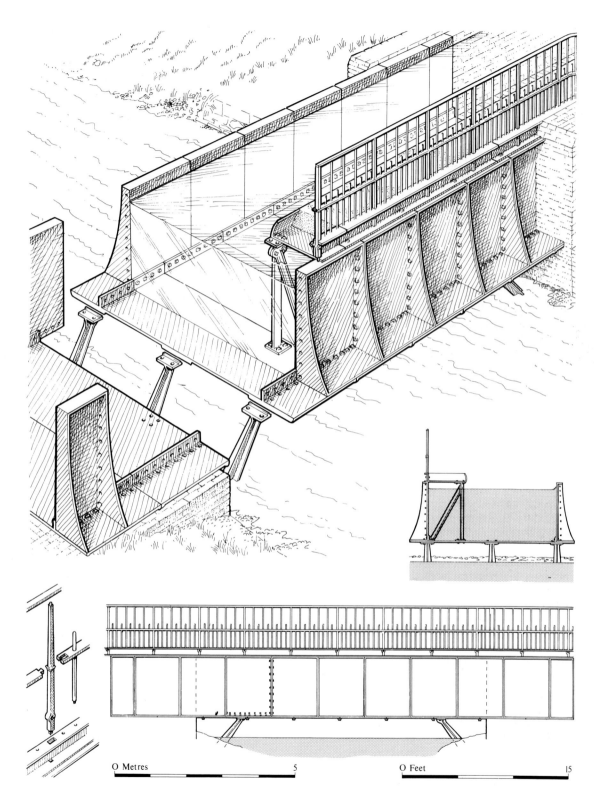

O Metres   5   O Feet   15

Fig. 12. Brithdir Aqueduct, an iron-trough built by G.W. Buck in 1819.

iron plates of various sizes bolted together along scarfed joints. The evidence of the remains of that structure suggests that the wall-plates failed in compression along the upper flanges and this in turn led to an exaggerated tensile loading or stretching along the base of the aqueduct causing a longitudinal crack to open along the floor plates.

Outram's second cast-iron aqueduct over the River Tame at Stalybridge on the Huddersfield Narrow Canal was built in 1800-01[53], and the cast-iron aqueducts on the Montgomeryshire Canal bear a close structural resemblance to this earlier structure in Yorkshire. It seems that Outram had realised that his first aqueduct was grossly under-designed but it has been concluded that a full appreciation of the structural behaviour of cast-iron constructions

was still absent.[54] Both side-plates and floor-plates were in fact given considerable flanged reinforcements yet the vulnerable compression or top flange was not thickened as might have been expected, as Professor Schofield notes in his analysis of the structure. However, there is apparently no fracturing or buckling of these structures, and therefore the top-plates of these aqueducts were probably of sufficient design strength to prevent collapse. Conversely the bolted joints linking these side-plates were probably of insufficient strength to prevent longitudinal stretching of these composite structures. The 'rust joints' between these plates on the Huddersfield Canal, and probably on the Montgomeryshire, were composed of a mixture of iron turnings and borax made into a paste with boiling water. It can clearly be seen that the Brithdir Aqueduct trough has subsided under the colossal weight of the water-filled structure so that the joints between

---

Fig. 11. G.W.Buck rebuilt the Luggy Brook Aqueduct at Brithdir in 1819. The side plates of his long cast-iron trough gradually slumped under the huge weight of the water contained and the span of the trough was reduced by heavy masonry abutments in c. 1890.

---

[53] Ibid., 29.
[54] Ibid., 31.

Fig. 13. Brithdir Aqueduct.

the side-plates have completely closed on their upper section but widened to some 2cms at their base. By 1875 this problem was obviously so bad on the Stalybridge Aqueduct that the middle of the 17m trough was supported by wrought-iron suspension rods both from the abutments and from the masonry arch carrying the towing-path alongside. The Brithdir Aqueduct of 1819 had its smaller 12.93m trough length reduced to a clear span of 8.1m during the 1890 aqueduct rebuilding programme by the expedient of adding clasping masonry abutments to either end of the trough. This type of unsupported composite trough composed of rectangular cast-iron plates had a design life of 71-74 years before leakages and the threat of collapse finally obliged canal operators to reinforce their structures. The system of flanges on the side-plates and bed-plates of the Stalybridge Aqueduct seems more

elaborate than that found on the later Brithdir structure, but this lack of elaboration seems to have produced no ill effects on the Montgomeryshire structure. It seems quite likely that Buck would have seen the Stalybridge structure on one of his perambulations examining transport practice in the north of England and may have based his Brithdir design on it.

The Montgomeryshire Canal aqueducts were still following a course of gradual collapse when J. A. S. Sword took over as Buck's successor as engineer of the Eastern Branch of the Montgomeryshire Canal. In 1836 he replaced the Lledan Brook Aqueduct in Welshpool with an iron-trough flanked by paths carried on masonry arches (Fig. 14). The modules that made up the trough sides were similar (but not exactly the same) as those found on Buck's earlier structure at Brithdir. A significant difference is that strong cast-iron beams reinforced the point of tension at the base of the aqueduct sides so that these have not slumped and required attention, as did the earlier examples after some 71-74 years. The modern-style 'I'-section of the beams belies the needs of cast-iron as a building material (see below) but nevertheless these have served their required purpose for 150 years. The fine ornamental cast-iron railings on the towing-path side of the aqueduct are said to be of an identical pattern to those on the Congleton (1826-31, Macclesfield Canal, engineered by William Crosley, planned by Thomas Telford), Stretton (1832, Birmingham and Liverpool Junction Canal, engineered by Thomas Telford) and Nantwich (1835, Birmingham and Liverpool Junction Canal, engineered by Thomas Telford) Aqueducts which suggests a common origin.[55] Perhaps all were cast at the Plas Kynaston Foundry adjoining the Ellesmere Canal at Pontcysyllte.

In 1859 there were also proposals for Aberbechan to be rebuilt as an iron-trough aqueduct after a life of only forty years but instead it was rebuilt as a conventional masonry aqueduct reusing most of the original ashlar facing-stone.

In the late 1880s and early 1890s there followed a further wholesale campaign of

[55] M. J. T. Lewis, 'Cast-iron Aqueducts', *Journal of the Railway and Canal Historical Society* XXII(1) (March 1976), 33-5.

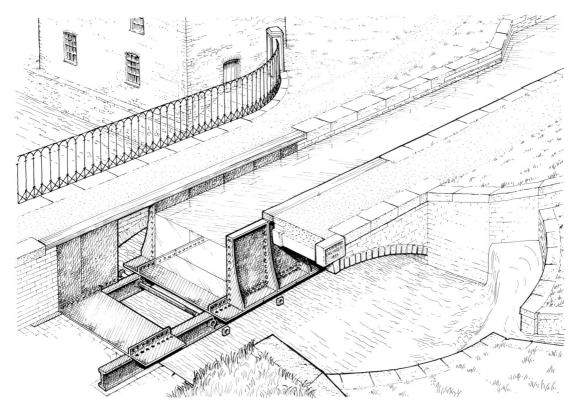

Fig. 14. The Lledan Brook Aqueduct at Welshpool. Buck's use of cast-iron clearly influenced his successor J. A. S. Sword. In 1836 Sword rebuilt this structure with an iron trough but with supporting beams of cast-iron that produced a more stable structure than Buck's earlier Brithdir Aqueduct. The adjoining weir was to divert water to the earlier Domen Mill.

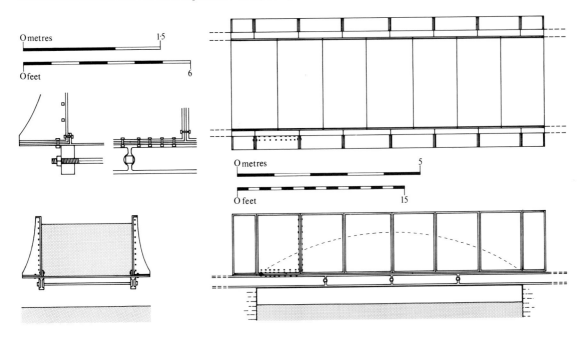

29

Fig. 15. Welshpool (Lledan Brook) Aqueduct, a reinforced cast-iron trough with flanking arches constructed by J. A. S. Sword in 1836.

aqueduct strengthening and refurbishment by the Shropshire Union Railways and Canal Company. The extensive use of blue engineering brick combined with the evidence of circular floriated terminals (showing that wrought-iron tie-bars are holding the original core of the structure together) can be seen on all the Montgomeryshire Canal aqueducts.

The four northern arches over the Vyrnwy flood-plain (Fig. 5) may retain their original stone facing and internal arches of red-brick set on stone piers but in the early nineteenth century had tie-rods inserted with circular terminals of concentric circles. In about 1890 the facing of the arches for a depth of some 2m was replaced by four courses of engineering brick.

The three southern flood arches were totally refaced in blue brick, as is recorded by the words 'RESTORED 1890' written on a stone plaque set over the western face of the centre arch. The central core of red-brick arches set on stone abutments remains held together by tie-rods having the usual floriated terminals of c.1890. The northern arch is still leaking water.

The Vyrnwy River Aqueduct once again received extensive treatment in 1892. The upstream face of the northerly arch was probably splitting away from the main aqueduct

structure under the pressure of the unstable mass of waterlogged puddling-clay behind. Buck's tie-bars were therefore replaced with a more substantial support of fish-bellied cast-iron girders held by tie-bars passing under the aqueduct arch in a similar fashion to that earlier used by Buck on the central arch. The additional technical sophistication of a 'Hodge-kinson girder' in which the ends of a cast-iron beam are narrower than the middle (see below) was not applied to the seven girders fastened to the face of the Vyrnwy Aqueduct in 1892, and the use of beams with parallel sides may have been to maximize the area of the aqueduct face physically restrained by the additional tie-bars. However, more plausibly, perhaps Buck and his successors could not be bothered to undertake fine calculations for the execution of relatively minor bridges and aqueduct repairs (see below). The northern abutment of the Vyrnwy Aqueduct also has the floriated circular tie-bars of additional reinforcements.

Large trees floating down the turbulent waters of the River Vyrnwy still catch on the upstream face of the Vyrnwy Aqueduct every year. To resist the impact of such large objects the upstream buttresses of the Twrch Aqueduct on the Swansea Canal were completely encased in a substantial reinforcement. Here on the Vyrnwy there was a complete replacement of the earlier triangular buttresses on the upstream elevation in the river by more protuberant buttresses with eliptical sides and bull-nosed dome-like caps. Buttresses of this design executed in finely hammer-dressed masonry can be seen on the Vyrnwy, Berriew and Aberbechan Aqueducts. The hammer-dressed work is similar to that on the stone supports for Buck's railings on the Vyrnwy Aqueduct but the design was certainly followed in 1889 when such buttresses seem to have been repaired in smooth-faced masonry at the Berriew Aqueduct.

The aqueduct at Berriew over the Rhiw was very heavily rebuilt in 1889 when the earlier masonry core was completely encased in blue engineering brick. A stone plaque on the centre of the downstream face bears the inscription 'RESTORED 1889' and the iron railings on each side of the aqueduct deck date from this time.

The aqueduct at Brithdir also seems to have received attention in about this period. New abutments executed in blue engineering brick reduced the span of the sagging iron-trough and were held together by very substantial cast-iron plates restrained by tie-bars. The timber deck and iron railings on the off-side of the canal were probably added at this time.

Further attention may well have been given to the Aberbechan Aqueduct as is suggested by the very heavy patching in blue engineering brick.

In very recent years further extensive works have taken place on the Berriew and Vyrnwy Aqueducts, and further leaks and bulging walls on the Montgomeryshire Canal aqueducts suggest that the need for substantial maintenance and intermittent rebuilding will carry on for as long as people are interested in the navigation and archaeology of the canal.

C Locks and Bridges.

The locks and bridges of the Montgomeryshire Canal were fairly orthodox in design and construction except for the cast-iron trappings later added by George Buck. A pair of cast-iron gates from Welshpool Lock (and Buck's name carved in stone—Fig. 18) are preserved in the Waterways Museum at Stoke Bruerne near Northampton. Two sets of bridges on the canal which are not of the orthodox arched kind may nevertheless have a fairly early origin. Buck is likely to have been the originator of one of these types. Some of the earlier bridges on the canal have been replaced by flat-decked structures supported on cast-iron beams with an easily recognisable curved upperside (Fig. 19) These are totally unlike modern 'I'-section steel beams and with good reason.

Figs. 16. Cast-iron lock-gates from Welshpool Town Lock with the words 'G. W. BUCK ENGINEER', cut into the lock sill. Now at the Stoke Bruerne British Waterways Museum, Northamptonshire. (Community Programme)

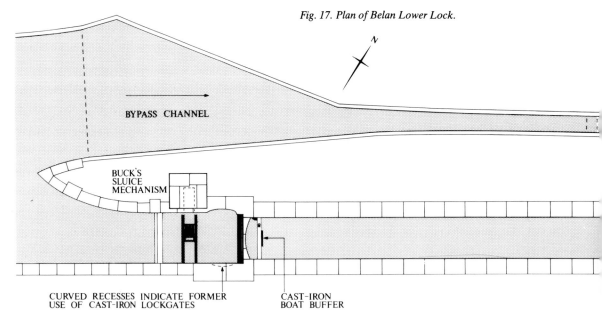

Fig. 17. Plan of Belan Lower Lock.

N

BYPASS CHANNEL

BUCK'S
SLUICE
MECHANISM

CURVED RECESSES INDICATE FORMER
USE OF CAST-IRON LOCKGATES

CAST-IRON
BOAT BUFFER

By the second decade of the nineteenth century similar forms of beam most extensively used for structural purposes were of an inverted 'T'-section—a type largely evolved so that intermediate brick arches could be supported on the bottom 'shelves' of the beam.

Fig. 18. 'G. W. BUCK ENGINEER'
(Community Programme)

Largely by accident this type of beam roughly coincided with the structural needs of cast-iron as a building material. However, despite this, these characteristics of the material were completely misunderstood and in the 1820s Tredgold proposed a modern-type 'I'-section as ideal for the cast-iron beam but which, in fact, would have been totally unsuitable.

Unlike later wrought-iron or steel beams, cast-iron is weak in tension despite being as strong in compression as these other materials. Hence it cannot resist strain by bending but will snap under heavy loading. A consistent strength to a beam can be achieved by having both a maximum depth of beam and a greatest width of the *lower* flange (the base of a loaded beam is stretched whilst the top is compressed) in the middle of the beam. Parabolic curves reducing these two dimensions towards the extremities of the beam (where the effects of heavy loading would be greatly reduced) would be an ideal form. This was first worked out scientifically by the Manchester physicist Eaton Hodgkinson in the 1820s, and perhaps first realized in George Stephenson's Water Street Bridge built at Manchester on the Liverpool and Manchester Railway in 1830.[56]

[56] R. S. Fitzgerald, *Liverpool Road Station, Manchester. An Historical and Architectural survey* (Manchester, 1980), 22-4.

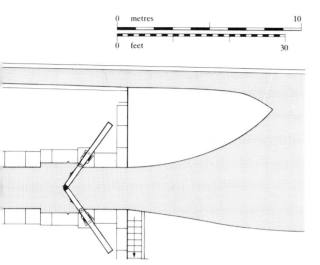

0 metres 10

0 feet 30

The construction of the Montgomeryshire Canal beam-bridges does not use this scientifically refined rationale, i.e. there is no curve to the plan-form of the lower beam-flange.

However, like many structures from the first two decades of the nineteenth century, they do have an increased depth in the centre of each beam (a 'fish-belly') and a wide lower flange but without any variation in form of the flange itself. It seems likely that these were introduced on both branches of the Montgomeryshire canal by 'iron-mad' George Buck before his departure for the London and Birmingham Railway in 1833. Some of these bridges on the Eastern Branch may date from soon after Buck's appointment in 1819—the successive use of stone and then brick abutments for these structures suggests that they were being built over a considerable period (the first iron girder bridge(s) known to have been built in the modern period was built by Watkin George at Merthyr Tydfil in the 1790s (an example from the Glamorganshire Canal at Rhyd-y-car is preserved at Merthyr)). The apparent absence of such bridges on the old Ellesmere Canal suggests that the Montgomeryshire iron bridges were built prior to the amalgamation of the two branches of the Montgomeryshire Canal with the Ellesmere in 1847 and 1850. All three bridges (nos. 96 to 98) flanking the

Fig. 19. Pentreheylin Bridge, one of six surviving 'fish-bellied' cast-iron beam bridges which may date from 1819-33.

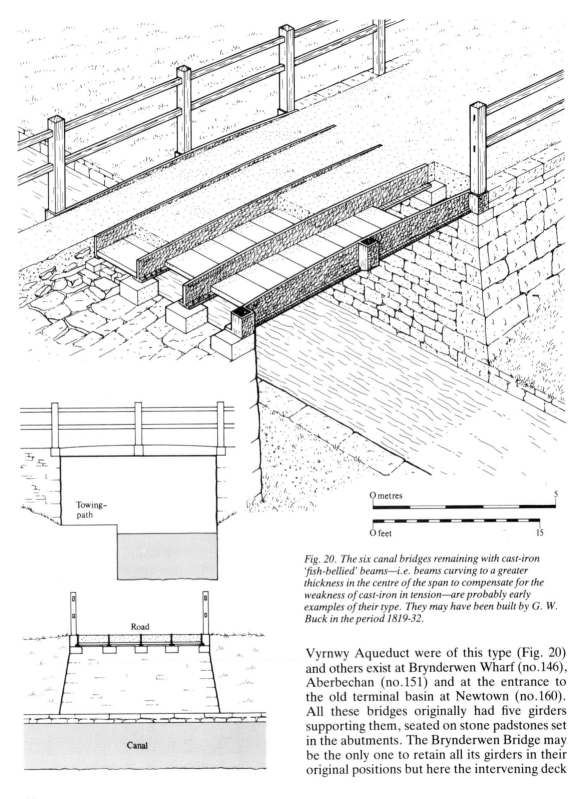

Towing-
path

Road

Canal

O metres 5

O feet 15

Fig. 20. The six canal bridges remaining with cast-iron 'fish-bellied' beams—i.e. beams curving to a greater thickness in the centre of the span to compensate for the weakness of cast-iron in tension—are probably early examples of their type. They may have been built by G. W. Buck in the period 1819-32.

Vyrnwy Aqueduct were of this type (Fig. 20) and others exist at Brynderwen Wharf (no.146), Aberbechan (no.151) and at the entrance to the old terminal basin at Newtown (no.160). All these bridges originally had five girders supporting them, seated on stone padstones set in the abutments. The Brynderwen Bridge may be the only one to retain all its girders in their original positions but here the intervening deck is supported by plywood! Originally the deck may have been laid on slate as at Bridge 98 (Pentreheylin Hall) although the original length of the intervening spans here has been altered with the insertion of three extra beams from the adjoining Bridge 97. These early iron bridges are of great interest and if they have to be removed then the beams should be retained and reused (as at Aberbechan) and not destroyed as happened recently at Williams' Bridge (no.96). Bridge 160 seems particularly vulnerable. Later cast-iron beam-bridges of more orthodox section were added during local road and bridge improvements.

Two of the first were built in the 1840s and 1850s by Thomas Penson, the Montgomeryshire County Surveyor. Penson was also an avid user of cast-iron and built elegant 'Telford-style' cast-iron arched bridges over the River Severn at Llandinam (27.5m span, 1846) and then at Abermule (33.5m span, 1853). The members of the latter arch proudly proclaims that Penson had built the second (and by implication the first) iron bridge in Montgomeryshire. This obviously ignores Buck's earlier iron aqueducts and bridges as insignificant achievements. However, despite the fact that some of the iron structures on the Montgomeryshire Canal may have been early examples of their type, they are not among the first iron bridges built. The Chinese were, in fact, building cast-iron girder bridges by about A.D. 1000 and a 22 metre-long iron bridge had been built in Britain in 1769, a full ten years before the famous *Ironbridge* in Shropshire.[57]

Penson himself built a fairly modest iron beam-bridge over the canal at Aberbechan in 1852 (bridge 152) to carry his improved road from Newtown to Llanfair Caereinion. It carries a dated legend showing it was cast at the Brymbo Ironworks in Denbighshire (where substantial relics remain of the early nineteenth-century works). By contrast, Buck probably had all his structural ironwork cast at Coalbrookdale in Shropshire (the remains of the works there are now part of the Ironbridge Museum; the iron castings were probably brought up river by barge and transferred to the canal at Pool Quay) as the paddle-gear of the Eastern Branch shows by its cast-marks. In the succeeding year Penson also built an approach to his new river bridge at Abermule,

Fig. 21. Lifting-bridge on the Montgomeryshire Canal just to the north of Welshpool. Two bridges of this type remain on the canal. (Community Programme)

also carried over the canal on a Brymbo-made iron girder bridge (no. 147). These slightly arched girder bridges are of a more conventional section. The more ornate approach bridge to Glanhafren House (no. 143) is carried on completely flat iron beams cast in 1889.

The present drawbridges on the canal along-

---

[57] The first European iron bridge known to have been constructed was built at Kirklees Hall near Brighouse, in west Yorkshire in 1769 (ten years before the Ironbridge in Shropshire) and was 72ft (22m) in span (D. Nortcliffe, 'The First Iron Bridge', *Industrial Past* 7(1) (Spring 1980), 14-7). The Chinese bridge at *Ch'en tu* built in c.1000 A.D., consisted of three iron beams, each about 5-6ft. (1.5m-1.8m) long, 1ft. (0.3m) wide, and four inches (0.1m) thick. (J. Needham, *Science and Civilisation in China*, Volume 4, Physics and Physical Technology, Part III 'Civil Engineering and Nautics'; *Journal of the North-China Branch of the Royal Asiatic Society* 53, 37-59, 43)

Fig. 22. An early twentieth-century photograph of one of the two turn- or swing-bridges still to be seen to the south of Garthmyl. (Community Programme)

side the Oswestry road north of Pool Quay are steel replacements of earlier timber bridges (Fig. 21). These, the Abbey Bridge (No. 112) and the Moors Farm Bridge (No. 114), existed as drawbridges as early as 1818.[58] Similar bridges on the Western Branch near Brynderwyn were replaced by iron girder swing-bridges in the late nineteenth century (Nos. 142 and 144). These rather elegant turn-bridges almost certainly date from after the amalgamation of the Montgomeryshire with the Ellesmere Canal management after the purchase of the Western Branch of the former canal in 1850 by the Shropshire Union Railways and Canal Company for examples of this type of bridge can be found on both canals. The two near Brynderwyn can be seen from the main Welshpool to Newtown road.

It is difficult to know why drawbridges should have been built in preference to the more common stone-arched bridges. However, they are situated on little-used farm tracks in situations where the canal is level with or slightly above the surrounding land. Presumably the infrequency of road use and the cost of a raised bridge did not justify the building of more expensive masonry bridges.

Perhaps George William Buck's period in office should be seen as the only time in the history of the Montgomeryshire Canal when an attempt was made to experiment and at least keep pace with the latest developments in engineering. He was clerk and engineer to the Eastern Branch of the Montgomeryshire Canal from 1819 until December 1833 and also of the Western Branch from December 1832 to December 1833. In 1828 he was given fourteen days leave to inspect the new Stockton and Darlington Railway and was present at the Rainhill Locomotive Trials in the following year[59] and then in 1833 left for a career in building locomotive lines. The new developments in civil engineering were to take place on the new railways but at least Buck left the Montgomeryshire Canal with a formation that could more nearly reach the reliability more generally found on contemporary waterways.

[58] Monts. Canal Report Bks., 20th May 1818.
[59] H. Arnold, 'The Montgomeryshire Canal', *Waterways World*.

2

The Water Economy

Canals built in the rural and undeveloped valleys of mid and south Wales in the 1790s were the earliest large consumers of water in their respective localities and thus had a surplus that could be used to power industrial installations placed alongside without the owners of pre-existing works complaining. This was the case on the Eastern Branch of the Montgomeryshire Canal but the later Western Branch of the waterway was built in an area where a concentration of large-scale industry already existed. Therefore, the original plans to provide an ample gravity supply to the head of the canal from the tail-water of an existing textile mill (Fig. 23) were doomed to failure as this would have depleted the power available in the two large textile mills downstream of the centre of Newtown; buildings which still remain prominently sited on the banks of the Severn. This situation coincides exactly with that on the head of the Glamorganshire Canal at the Welsh iron metropolis of Merthyr Tydfil. At the Welsh textile centre of Newtown a water-wheel driven pump was built downstream of the textile mills and augmented by a steam-engine driven installation as at Merthyr (Fig. 26).

The water economy of the canal was controlled by six types of features: feeders, locks, by-pass weirs, overflow weirs, outlet sluices and mills. The initial supply of water to the canal was brought from adjacent rivers or streams by feeders which operated with either pumps or more commonly by simple gravity.

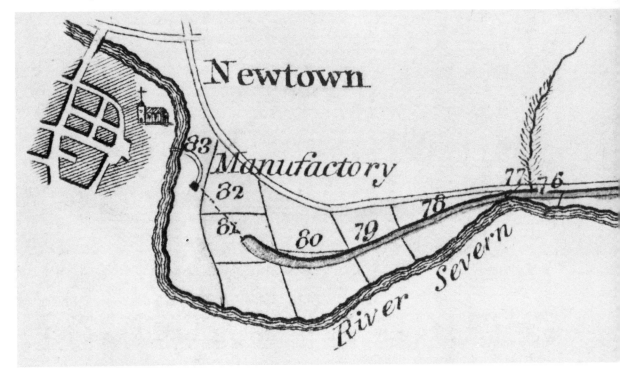

Fig. 23. Plan (1814) showing the originally proposed water supply to the head of the Western Branch of the Montgomeryshire Canal from the tail-race of a woollen manufactory. What it does not show are the two woollen-mills downstream whose water needs prevented this simple gravity feed from being executed. (National Library of Wales)

Table illustrating the Montgomeryshire Canal Water-economy (from Newtown to Carreghofa)

Feeder source	Type of feeder	Date feeder first used by canal	Date of disuse of feeder	Name of locks (Bradshaw's)	Depth of locks	Mills using water from the navigation channel	Date of use of mills	Eastern (E.B.) or Western Branch (W.B.)	Locks dropping from East or West
Severn (Old Mill Leat)	Gravity (Not built)	Planned	—					W.B.	
Severn	Pump	1821	c.1949					W.B.	
				Rock	2.54m			W.B.	West
				Dolfor	2.48m			W.B.	West
				Freestone	2.68m			W.B.	West
Bechan (Old Mill Leat)	Gravity	1818	?					W.B.	
				Newhouse	2.37m			W.B.	West
				Byles	2.2m			W.B.	West
				Brynderwen	2.59m			W.B.	West
Llifior	Gravity	1805	1947					W.B.	
Severn	Gravity	1805	1818					E.B.	
Rhiw (Old Mill Leat)	Gravity	1797	1818					E.B.	
				Berriew	2.58m			E.B.	West
				Brithdir	2.78m			E.B.	West
				Belan Upper	2.13m			E.B.	West
				Belan Lower	1.52m			E.B.	West
						Powis Castle Estate Bone-mill	c.1830– c.1890	E.B.	
						Powis Castle Estate Sawmill	c.1830– c.1948	E.B.	
						Welshpool Town Lock Corn-mill	before 1838 —?		
				Welshpool Town	1.78m			E.B.	West
Lledan (Old Mill Leat)	Gravity (occasional use)	1797	?					E.B.	
				Pool Quay	2.72m			E.B.	West
				Crowther Hall	2.79m			E.B.	West
				Cabin	2.68m			E.B.	West
				Bank	8.5m			E.B.	West
						Wern Cornmill	after 1850– after 1900	E.B.	
				Burgedin Bottom	2.58m			E.B.	East
				Burgedin Top	2.46m			E.B.	East
				Carreghofa Lower	2.41m			E.B.	East
Tanat (Old Mill Leat)	Gravity	1797	1822					E.B.	
Tanat	Gravity	1822		Carreghofa Upper	2.36m			E.B.	East
Dee	Gravity							Ellesmere	

A Feeders

The table above gives some idea of the number of gravity feeders required to supply the Montgomeryshire Canal with water.[1] All water fed to the Western Branch of the Montgomeryshire Canal would have been released into the Eastern Branch with the traffic passing between the two canals. This explains why the Severn feeder, built as an after-thought in 1805 to the Eastern Branch at Garthmyl, could be dispensed with when the Western Branch was built. Perhaps it was not so surprising that the innovative George Buck, then engineer of the Eastern Branch, was to design and build the

[1] The names and falls of locks are taken from J. H. Denton, *The Towpath Guides, No.4, The Montgomeryshire Canal and the Llanymynech Branch of the Ellesmere Canal* (Birmingham, 1984).

Fig. 24. The double-weir of the canal feeder at Penarth on the River Severn. The canal intake and a salmon ladder are visible on the far bank.

water-wheel powered pump that was to supply water to the uppermost pound of the Western Branch from 1821. One presumes that it was the necessity of building this pump that delayed the full opening of the new section of canal from 1819 until 1821. The accompanying map (Fig. 23) shows what the original gravity scheme of water feed had been until the worried Newtown textile-mill owners took steps to safeguard their supply of water.

Such 'water-engines' were not a new concept, they had long been used in mines. In 1787 one had been built on the Arun Canal, another existed on the Glamorganshire Canal before 1805 (its successor still survives), and in 1813 the Claverton Pump on the Kennet and Avon Canal was completed with the delivery of pipes from the Neath Abbey Ironworks; the last water-powered canal-pump built in the British Isles may have been that erected on the Carlisle Canal in 1835.[2]

The engine built at Newtown by Buck in 1821 cost £1,812 6s. The 22ft (6.7m) diameter water-wheel was of wood and iron construction. The shaft of this undershot wheel extended beyond the wheel in order to drive a two-throw crankshaft and beam mechanism which operated two bucket pumps lifting the equivalent of eighty lockfuls of water, the 2.7m

[2] Most of the information in this section on the canal-pumps at Newtown and elsewhere comes from C. P. Weaver, 'Claverton Pumping Station', *Journal of the Railway and Canal Historical Society* XXV(4) (November 1979), 141-53.

Fig. 25. The remaining 1860 pump-house at Newtown; the canal formerly ran along the foreground, and to the rear of the buildings are the remains of the water-wheel pit, leat and weir.

difference in level between the River Severn and the Montgomeryshire Canal, every twenty-four hours.

The remains still exist of the wheel-pit and of a timber weir that consisted of wrought-iron rods supporting a vertical wall of heavy timber planks. Provision was made at both Western Branch weirs to accommodate the needs of the much-prized salmon migrating up-river and the Newtown weir was given a second short fall some 0.9m lower than the feeder supply weir. This curving timber wall led the feeder water obliquely into the wheel-pit whilst the pump intakes were sited just upstream of the wheel. The 1860 engine-house of stone that still survives presumably housed the earlier of the standby steam-engines which was subsequently replaced by a horizontal single-cylinder textile-mill engine driving a submerged impeller pump through bevel gearing, steam being supplied by a single Cornish boiler. This later plant must have been housed in the very utilitarian brick engine-house and coal-store with attached chimney (Fig. 26) that was demolished in October 1972.

The water-wheel continued in general use for over a hundred years and only ceased working in 1924. A diesel pump was then installed on the river bank at the rear of the later engine-house and fed water into the supply pipe previously used by the steam-engine. Both the water- and steam-engines were finally scrapped and removed in the early years of World War Two. The timber weirs

40

Fig. 26. The Newtown pump-houses and pump-keeper's house as they stood in the 1960s. The late nineteenth-century steam-pump-house and its attendant chimney have now been demolished. (Gordon Rattenbury)

were seriously damaged in a great flood in 1929 and the collapse of these structures was complete by the mid-1930s.

The use of the pumped water continued after the abandonment of the canal for navigational purposes in 1944. To meet this need two portable diesel-driven pumps made by Ruston and Sykes were installed in 1944 and 1947 respectively. Pumping ceased soon after nationalisation in 1948 by which time only a creamery remained as a customer using the water.

B Locks and By-pass Weirs

Every time a lock was used some 136,400 litres (30,000 gallons) of water might be released to the pound below. An imbalance of water supply within a flight of locks might be caused by boats terminating their journeys at wharves only part of the way up. Considerable variations in water needs along the canal were also caused by the disparity in the amount of water needed to fill locks of varying sizes. Crowther

Hall Lock for example has a fall of 9ft 2ins (2.79m) while the lower lock at Belan only drops some 5ft (1.52m), the nineteen locks on the Montgomeryshire Canal having a mean fall of 8ft (2.4m). In order to overcome such problems, and to ensure that all intervening pounds of water between locks were kept topped up, it was necessary to install a weir immediately above each lock and a water 'by-pass' running alongside the lock chamber to the pound below. A continuous flow could then be maintained along the waterway.

C Overflow Weirs and Outlet Sluices

In times of flood, frequent in hilly country like that of Montgomeryshire, it was necessary to have waste-weirs so that water surplus to the needs of navigation could be harmlessly released into nearby streams and rivers. Shallow sluice-gates ('flood paddles') were also often placed in these overflow weirs to lower the level of the canal in times of flood. Often placed alongside these weirs are deeper outlets or 'ground-sluices' to drain the canal for the periodic cleaning of silt. At narrowings of the waterway at bridges, or where the water-channel crosses an aqueduct bridge, slots can be seen in the bank to take 'stop-planks', so enabling individual sections of water-channel to be isolated in case of damage and/or the need to repair a specific section of canal.

D Mills

On canals where there were not severe contraints on the use of water surplus to the needs of navigation it was possible to present industrialists with a ready-made leat (i.e. the canal itself) on which to build their water-powered manufactories. As this latter category is an unusual aspect of canal construction it is worth concentrating on this aspect of the water economy of the Montgomeryshire Canal. The topography and relatively undeveloped state of late eighteenth-century Wales made the canals ripe for such exploitation of readily available water resources.[3] In south Wales the construction of the valley canals with their resultant stimulation of huge industrial growth ensured the eventual obliteration of the remains of

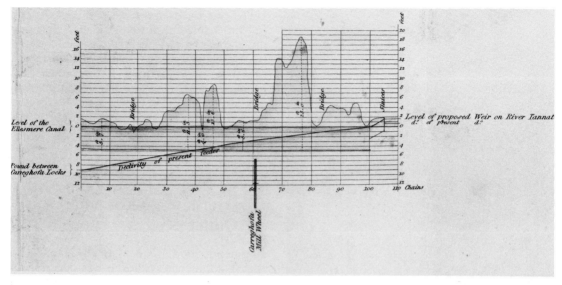

Fig. 27. A drawing made in 1820 to illustrate the realignment and levelling of the Tanat Feeder to Carreghofa Locks. Note the position of the Carreghofa Mill wheel. (National Library of Wales)

nearly all such early installations. In rural mid Wales, however, the fewer installations have all left archaeological remains, most of which are quite substantial.

It is probable that eight water-mills used canal or canal-feeder water:

   Aberbechan Fulling-mill* (SO 1425 9357: 4 kilometres from Newtown);
   Berriew Corn-mill* (SJ 1868 0083: 14 kilometres from Newtown);
   Powis Estate Bone-mill (SJ 2216 0585: 20 kilometres from Newtown);
   Powis Estate Sawmill (SJ 2217 0586: 20 kilometres from Newtown);
   Welshpool Town Lock Corn-mill (SJ 2260 0731: 21 kilometres from Newtown);
   Domen Corn-mill* (SJ 2295 0735: 21 kilometres from Newtown);
   Wern Corn-mill (SJ 2517 1412: 30 kilometres from Newtown);
   Carreghofa Corn-mill* (SJ 2491 2101: 38 kilometres from Newtown) which had two water-wheels.

   Four of these mills (those marked with an asterisk above) pre-dated the canal. On first consideration it may seem odd that three of the four mills built on the canal after its construction[4] used the same 'pound' or level of water: that above Welshpool Lock. This pound was far from being the longest on the Canal, but it did lie immediately above Welshpool where much of the trade of the Montgomeryshire Canal's Eastern Branch terminated. Consequently there had to be a constant flow through the by-passes of the locks above this point to maintain water needed for the purposes of navigation. The Welshpool Town Lock Corn-mill was sited on the by-pass of the lock at the end of this pound to take advantage of this supply without interfering with the trade lower down, as well as being sited at the largest intermediate town (and hence market for its grain) on the canal.

   The siting of the Powis Estate Mills and Timber-yard on this pound was decided by the necessity of their being near the main road down from the principal woodlands of the estate as well as near its administration centre.

---

   [3] See S. R. Hughes, 'The Swansea Canal: Navigation and Power Supplier', *Industrial Archaeology Review* 4(1) (Winter 1979-80), 51-69.
   [4] All three mills near Welshpool probably dated from the early nineteenth century: the two Powis Estate mills date from between 1817 (British Library, Ordnance Survey Drawings, Sheet 198, Bill dated to 1817) and 1840 (National Library of Wales, tithe map of 'Poole Parish', Upper Division, dated to 1840). The mill at Welshpool Town Lock seems to have first been mentioned in 1838 (Monts. Canal Report Bks., 8 January 1838).

Fig. 28. The Wern Overflow at the sump level on the canal. All surplus water (and two locksful for every boat traversing the waterway) tumbled over this weir until it was realised what a wasted asset this large fall of water was. The wall and sluice on the left were then built to divert the water to drive a corn-mill situated on the channel to the right.

The earl's family were the principal share-holders of the canal and so had substantial choice over the siting of their mills. The earls were anxious to expand the industrial base of their estates which already included quarries at Llanymynech and Porth-y-waen and the mills at Pool Quay: all served by the canal. The stream to the south of the castle was already depleted through feeding the park lakes via a large dam and reservoir and extensive leat or watercourse, and it was obviously desired to place the estate timber-mills alongside their intended transport outlet. If this stream alone had been adequate to drive the mills, it would have been advantageous to place the mill on the canal's north bank both from the point of view of its situation in relation to the feeder stream and for achieving the best access to the adjoining canal (there was no intervening towing-path on the north bank of the canal). There was already a waste-weir on this pound of the canal to release surplus water to the River Severn and a new waste-weir alongside the mill augmented the mill-pond whose prim-ary source was probably the stream which reached this point via an inverted syphon under the canal. A deep and long cutting had to be made to house the water-wheel and achieve a reasonable fall of water here; a feature that could have been avoided if the stream above the canal had been adequate to drive the canalside mills. This finely kept estate yard with its still-operating sawmill is one of the most impressive and fascinating sites on the canal.

In most treatises on canal construction one is

Fig. 29. The deep draught-tube of the Wern corn-mill turbine, situated at the end of a water-feed channel from the Montgomeryshire Canal.

offered a dual classification of canals: the simple lateral type running alongside a river which usually feeds it by means of a weir or weirs at its upper end, or the more advanced 'summit-level' type which scales the water-sheds between adjacent valleys with attendant problems of summit water supply. The 56 kilometre line now known as the 'Montgomery Canal' in fact functioned as a 'sump canal', the reverse of the second type. Almost in the middle of water-flows and flights of locks descending from either direction is the bottom or sump level at Wern. The Wern Mill was in the prime position for a water-power installation attached to the canal and the only surprising factor is the length of time it took for enterprising individuals to realise what a great resource was going to waste. The boats passing through this lowest pound of the canal (and the great majority of boats on the Montgomery-shire Canal would do so) released one or two locksful (between 30,000 and 60,000 gallons / 136,380—272,760 litres) of water over the waste-weir at Wern. In addition to these advantages, this bottom level was carried on a considerable embankment which made the provision of a larger vertical fall of water a simple proposition.

The remoteness of the site from the nearest industrial centre at Welshpool must have been

the main factor delaying its use until the later part of the nineteenth century. The potential of a somewhat similar situation on the Swansea Canal was very quickly noted by a particularly gifted canal engineer and entrepreneur, Edward Martin.[5]

A reference to the abstraction of canal-water to power Aberbechan Corn-mill almost certainly refers to the use of water from the Bechan Brook upstream of the mill and not to a fifth water-power installation using water from the canal itself.[6] Early and mid nineteenth-century maps do show both Upper and Lower Mills at Aberbechan, but they are above the canal and none of the buildings on the valley side of the waterway was ever noted as a water-mill.[7]

The most interesting archaeological remains connected with the water economy of the canal are undoubtedly those of the Powis Castle Estate Sawmill at Whitehouse Bridge, some 1.6 kilometres south of Welshpool on the Newtown Road.

[5] At *Felin Ynys Dawe*, see Hughes, *Swansea Canal*.
[6] J. H. Denton, *The Towpath Guides, No.4, The Montgomeryshire Canal and the Llanymynech Branch of the Ellesmere Canal* (Birmingham, 1984), 74-5.
[7] 'Shropshire Union Rly. and Canal Plans, 1845 and 1859'.

The Powis Castle Estate Mills

The early nineteenth-century Powis Estate Sawmill ('2' on the adjoining plan) stands in the midst of a still-functional and very busy estate timber-yard. A host of various ancillary buildings of widely disparate dates surround the yard and their complex and interesting history will be described in chapter four. This present section will deal solely with the water supply and water-power engineering and machinery relating to the mills and the Montgomeryshire Canal.

The first Ordnance Survey drawings of the mill site in 1817 show a stream running under the canal and through an open field.[8] This stream is now taken under the canal in an inverted syphon (Fig. 33); a feature also used under the canal in Welshpool in order to maintain the head of water of the Domen Mill-leat. The inverted syphon was a well-tried device. It was an expedient much used by the Greeks and Romans in order to carry water channels across declivities without the need for expensive masonry aqueducts and without any significant loss of the height of water in the water channel. The device had been used in that marvel of early-modern canal engineering, the seventeenth-century *Canal du Midi,* and so was hardly an innovation when used at the Powis Yard.

The mill was sited (it was probably built in the 1820s or 1830s) so as to be able to take water from both the stream and from the

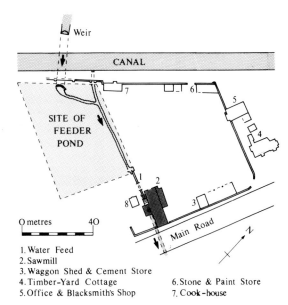

Fig. 30. Plan of the Powis Castle Estate Timber-yard.

1. Water Feed
2. Sawmill
3. Waggon Shed & Cement Store
4. Timber-Yard Cottage
5. Office & Blacksmith's Shop
6. Stone & Paint Store
7. Cook-house

Montgomeryshire Canal itself. Where a mill took surplus water from a navigable canal it normally did so at an already existing waste-water weir so as not to deplete the water needed for the purposes of navigation. However, the water supply to the Powis Castle Estate sawmill pond is controlled by a sluice-gate sunk below the water level of the adjacent canal (Fig. 33) and therefore directly removing the top level of water in the navigation even when surplus water was lacking. Lord Clive of Powis Castle was an influential man as chairman of the Montgomeryshire Canal (Eastern Branch) and of the adjoining Ellesmere Canal and his mills may have been given advantages unavailable to other mills. There is an interesting analogy here with the Duc d'Orléans' Paper Manufactory at Langlée near Montargis. This was built in the eighteenth century on the Montargis Canal in France as a result of the Duc's influential position in respect to the canal company. It so depleted the water on the navigation that extended litigation followed.[9]

Fig. 31. Casting of a dog on the iron water-feed channel at the Powis Castle Estate sawmill. (Sue Isaac)

[8] Ordnance Survey Drawings, Sheet 198, Bill dated to 1817 (British Library).

[9] H. Pinsseau, *Histoire de la Construction de l'administration et de l'exploitation du Canal D'Orléans de 1676 à 1954* (Paris, 1963), 174-76 and D. Diderot, 'Papeterie', *Dictionnaire des Sciences, Planches, Tom 5* (Paris, 1751-77).

0 ⟷ 250cm

0 ⟷ 9ft

Fig. 32. Isometric drawing of the overflow sluice and controls on the cast-iron water-feed to the Powis Castle Estate Sawmill. These were made at Ruabon in 1844 and were presumably transported by canal.

There is no evidence of similar problems arising on the Montgomeryshire Canal. However, the Powis mills must have been heavily dependent on the water supply from the canal for it was the silting of the canal that prompted the switching of the sawmill to electrical power in *c* 1948.[10]

The sawmill and the estate timber-yard benefitted from the gradual and piecemeal policy of improvement that was the hallmark of the Powis Castle Estate throughout the nineteenth century.[11] Thus it is possible to see that the timber-yard had been considerably improved by 1840 with the head forester's office being built with its front wall resting on the earlier timber-yard wall ('5' on the plan). On its lower storey were a blacksmith's smithy and nearby two houses for workers at the yard.

Between 1840 and 1845 the originally small mill-pond near the canal was replaced by a very large rectangular pool stretching nearly all the way from the canal to the sawmill building.[12]

Many of the large canalside mill-ponds on the Swansea Canal doubled as loading docks but this expedient does not seem to have occurred to the builders of the lesser number of mills on the Montgomeryshire Canal.

---

[10] Verbal information, Powis Castle Estate workers.
[11] Powis Castle Estate drawings collection (Powis Castle Estate Timber-yard).
[12] Tithe map of 'Poole Parish', Upper Division, 1840 and 'Shropshire Union Rly. and Canal Plan, 1845.'

Fig. 33. Section through the water-feed supplies to the Powis Castle Estate Sawmill. The water level in the stream was often inadequate to power the mill by itself and the sluice from the Montgomeryshire Canal had to be opened. When the canal eventually became disused and then silted up, the mill had to be converted to electric power which it still uses. On the drawing the distance from the inner lip of the inverted syphon (under the canal) to the overflow shaft, which originally had miniature ornamental figures at its corners, has been foreshortened from 118m.

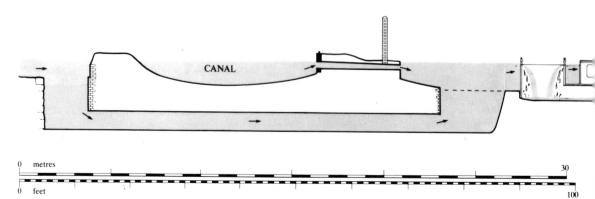

CANAL

0 metres ⟷ 30

0 feet ⟷ 100

In fact the enlarged pond almost certainly dates from 1844 when the fine cast-iron feed trough from the mill pool to the water-wheel was installed. A dated decorative panel of the trough has unfortunately been removed and stands outside the entrance to the blacksmith's shop ('5') and bears the date of casting and maker's name—'R. & W. JONES RUABON 1844'. The iron panels would almost certainly have been delivered by canal-boat. (This named panel at present supports a rubbish-cum-bonfire heap and ought to be moved elsewhere for safe-keeping.)

The cast-iron trough is very finely ornamented with a series of figures of horses, dogs, fat men and other devices! These seem to have been made from a fairly small stock of patterns that were used on a few of the panels that might have been seen by such visitors to the mill as the earl himself. A very similar form of decoration can be seen on the cast-iron casing of a small enclosed water-wheel made in the 1840s in order to rotate the churns of the dairy at Donnington Hall in Leicestershire. (This was cast at Moira Foundry and is now in the Moira Furnace Museum.) Another example of the 'polite' fittings that enhanced the yard were four small cast-iron figures standing at the corners of the cast-iron overflow shaft from the mill-pool. Unfortunately only the feet of these figures now remain; they have been 'restored' in the accompanying drawing of the mill-feed.

Fig. 34. Casting of a horse and rider on the iron water-feed channel at the Powis Castle Estate sawmill. (Sue Isaac)

The mill-pool itself was filled in for use as a tree-nursery after the cessation of the use of water-power in *c.* 1948. The dual feeds to the pond from the canal and the inverted syphon can still be seen although they are sometimes heavily overgrown. The cast-iron water-wheel feed and the water-wheel itself are still in place, although at present several of the wooden spokes of the wheel are broken.

By 1840 a second mill-building stood to the south of the water-wheel and may have been driven off this or by a second wheel.[13] This

Continued on page 50

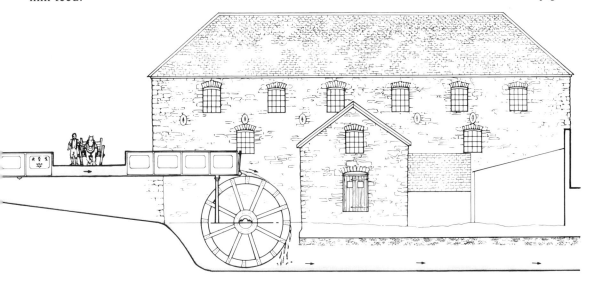

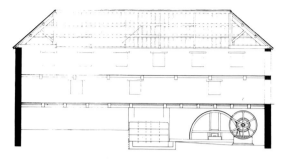

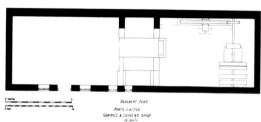

Fig. 35. *Drawings prepared in the 1890s during the re-equipment of the Powis Castle Estate Sawmill. In the basement of the mill the great pit-wheel, on the same shaft as the external water-wheel, conveyed a higher speed drive to a line-shaft. From this five pulleys transferred power to machinery on the upper floors of the mill. The large stone blocks in the centre of the mill provided a firm foundation for the large horizontal saw on the ground floor of the mill (Fig. 53) by the use of six large iron holding-down bolts piercing the blocks—the expedient usually used for securing large machinery in industrial structures. (Powis Castle Estate drawings collection 31)*

Powis Estate Sawmill, Welshpool

Fig. 37. *The Powis Castle Estate Sawmill showing the transmission of power from the water-wheel to the main horizontal saw. The water-wheel depended on water from the Montgomeryshire Canal.*

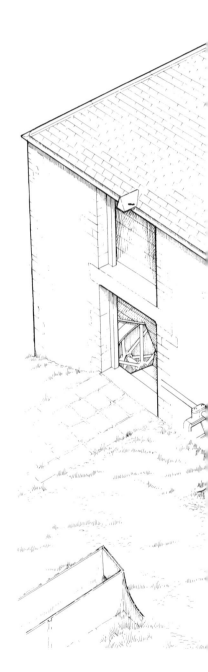

Fig. 36. *Casting of a wolf on the iron water-feed channel at the Powis Castle Estate Sawmill. (Sue Isaac)*

48

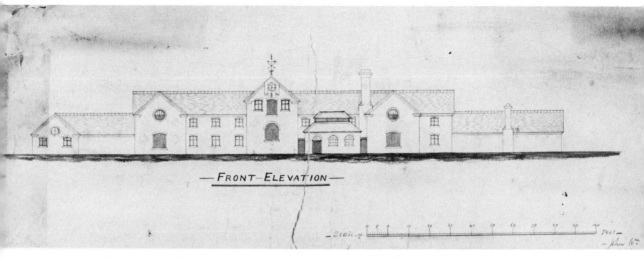

Fig. 38. Front elevation of 'The Earl of Powis's Model Farm' (Coed-y-dinas) which still remains and is visible from the course of the Montgomeryshire Canal. (Powis Castle Estate drawings collection 207)

ground bones into bone-meal as fertiliser for the Powis Castle Estate (the neighbouring Leighton Estate also had a bone-mill).

The advertising catalogue issued by Robinson's, the sawmill outfitters, in the period 1890-1902 (Fig. 53) gives us a date for the re-equipping of the sawmill with its present sawing equipment. The two adjoining estate plans of the sawmill (Fig. 35) also show the mill before the present wing on the south side was added in order to house the new horizontal saw-frame obtained from Robinson's in this period. In the open lean-to shed against the timber-yard wall near this point are two very large composite millstones. The dressing on these are unlike those of a corn-mill and it has been suggested that these are the old face-runner-stones of the bone-mill—such mills more usually used edge-runner-stones. (The earl's geological collection survives in the same building.)[14]

The axle of the present water-wheel extends into the sawmill basement and is transferred onto the main belt-drive-shaft by two great toothed wheels and a chain which rather resembles a giant bicycle chain (Fig. 111). The marks of a previous, and more conventional, pit-wheel-drive can still be seen and this is what is shown on the surviving late nineteenth-century basement plan (Fig. 35).[15] The belt-drives originally drove a variety of machinery positioned on the upper floors of the mill.

The rails and trolleys of a narrow-gauge line for moving heavy timber survive on the ground floor of the sawmill; the former under a later circular saw-bench (also supplied by Robinson's of Rochdale) which presumably was originally driven from the main drive-shaft in the basement.

E Other Uses For Canal Water

There were many other uses for water that was surplus to navigational needs. An agreement survives from 1929 granting the use of canal-water to Mr. H.M. Green of Bank Farm, Pool Quay. In return for £5.15s. he had the right to water:

a) for driving an hydraulic ram (not to exceed 72,000 gallons (327,000 litres) daily);

b) for milk cooling (not to exceed 700 gallons (3,180 litres) daily);

c) for washing the dairy floor and milk utensils (not to exceed 100 gallons (455 litres) daily);

d) for drinking-water for cattle (not to exceed 1,000 gallons (4,555 litres) daily).

Most of the surviving water (leasing) agreements from the Montgomeryshire Canal date from the 1920s and '30s, but there is some evidence to suggest that these were renewals of

---

[13] Tithe map of Poole Parish.
[14] Verbal information, Owen Ward.
[15] Powis Castle Estate drawings collection.

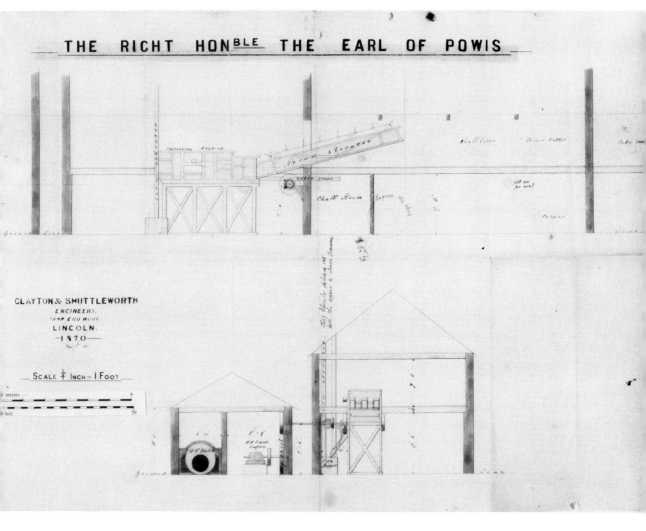

THE RICHT HONᴮᴸᴱ THE EARL OF POWIS

CLAYTON & SHUTTLEWORTH
ENGINEERS,
THP END WORK
LINCOLN.
—1870—

SCALE 4 INCH = I FOOT

Fig. 39. Agricultural improvement alongside the Montgomeryshire Canal did not just include the liming of land. At 'The Earl of Powis's Model Farm' (Coed-y-dinas) a ten-h.p. steam-engine was supplied with condensing and boiler-feed water from the Montgomeryshire Canal via the Powis Castle Estate sawmill-pond. The engine then drove a 'thrashing' (threshing) machine, a chaff-cutter, a straw-cutter, a pulper and a cake-breaker. The engine-house and line-shafting brackets can still be seen. (Powis Castle Estate drawings collection 208)

earlier agreements.[16] There were many who used canal-water for domestic purposes, such as Mr. M.E. Matthews who also leased the 'Bunkers Hill Wharf' at Fron to the south-west of Garthmyl.

Thus it can be seen that a lateral waterway in a relatively undeveloped part of Britain could supply water for a multitude of uses beyond that of navigation.

Coed-y-dinas Model Farm

Various canals in the coal-mining districts of south Wales, and in the Black Country area of the west Midlands of England, supplied water to the boilers and condensers of a multitude of colliery steam-engines.

By contrast it was agriculture that was the

---

[16] 'London and North Western Railway, Extracts from Agreements, Welshpool District No. 2., 1922-34' (British Waterways Board, Montgomeryshire Canal Office), entries transcribed by Graham Deamer.

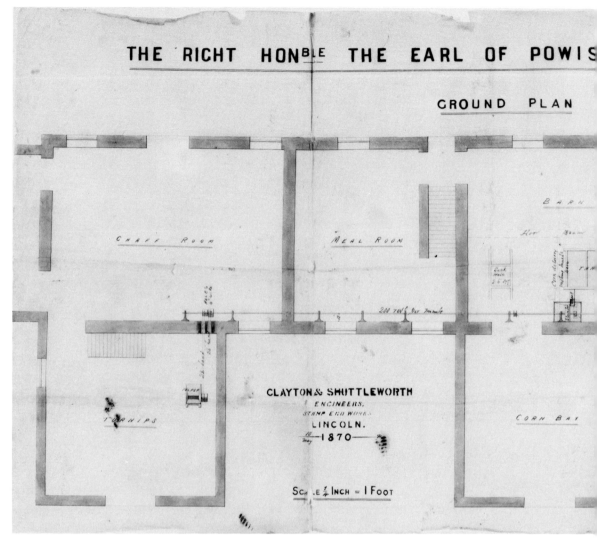

Fig. 40. Detail of a plan of Coed-y-dinas showing the transmission of power from the steam-engine to the agricultural machinery. (Powis Castle Estate drawings collection 208)

main industry of the great estates that lay alongside the Montgomeryshire Canal and they were supplied with lime by the canal. From the 1840s onwards the principles of high Victorian mechanised farming were applied to the nearby Leighton Estate on a scale rarely seen elsewhere. Numerous water-turbines and steam-engines were part of a grand plan to work the estate on the most modern principles.[17] The Earls of Powis were continually improving their estate on a more piecemeal plan than their *nouveaux riches*

neighbours. The Powis Estate home-farm at Coed-y-dinas was renamed 'The Earl of Powis's Model Farm' on grandiose plans for rebuilding in 1862 and 1870.[18] Both these schemes envisaged a steam-engine driving a whole array of Victorian farming machinery. Part of the scheme, including the steam-engine,

---

[17] 'Leighton Park Estate, Report of Student Surveys, 1986 and 1987', *The Ironbridge Institute Research Papers, Nos. 20 and 23.*

[18] Powis Castle Estate drawings collection 207.

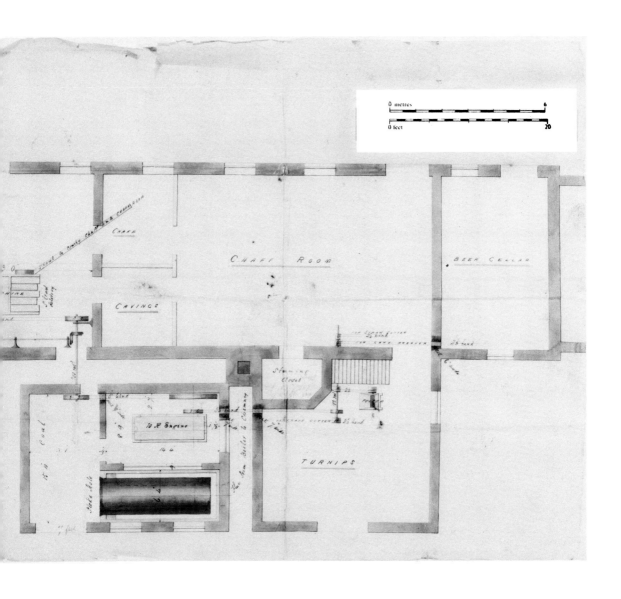

was actually completed in 1872 and the complexity and ambition of the scheme is obvious from the accompanying drawings.

The buildings of the farm (SJ 2239 0557) are still extant and the engine-house and some of the line-shafting remain in place, but the engine and machines have now gone. The large front range (Fig. 38) even has a wrought-iron plate-girder in its structure of a type more usually associated with railway terminals and a small internal railway was designed to run around the 'model' buildings as on the neighbouring Leighton Estate.

The water available to the farm animals in great slate tanks was gravity-fed from the mill-pool at the Powis Castle Estate Sawmill and the condensing and boiler water for the steam-engine was controlled from a gate also fitted to the pool.[19]

Once again it is possible to see that the canal was part of, and indeed helped to create, the economic system of a whole section of the Severn Valley.

---

[19] Verbal information, the farmers at Coed-y-dinas.

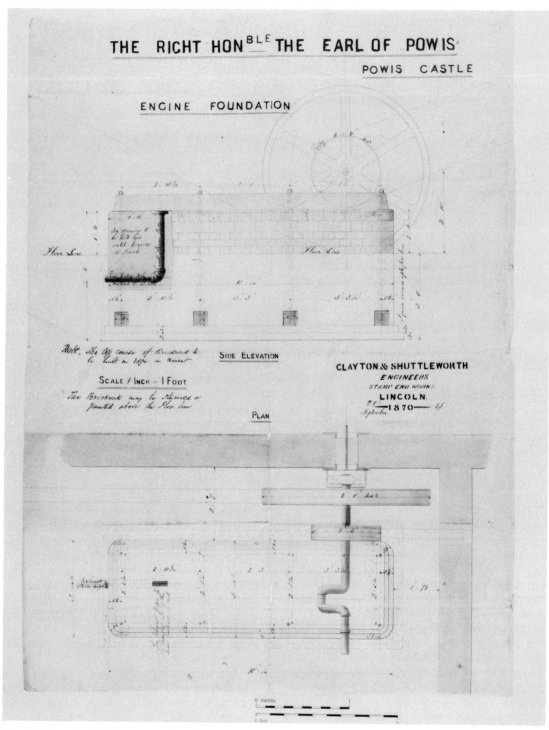

Fig. 41. The trade of the Montgomeryshire Canal was largely based on the intensive agricultural development of the surrounding area. Sometimes that crucial interdependence went further; here at Coed-y-dinas canal water provided the steam to drive farm machinery.

3

Trade Installations

This branch may most peculiarly be styled the Agricultural Canal,
the chief articles of its import into the county being limestone and coal; and of its export,
timber, grain, and the produce of the dairy.[1]

The nature of the traffic generated by a waterway determines the types of features built to service that trade. Perhaps the main features common to all waterways were the intermittent public wharves, the docks for loading and unloading and the dry-docks for repairing boats; all other accretions are determined by the local topography and geology. On the Swansea Canal, for instance, the trade consisted almost entirely of coal and required over 225 kilometres of railways of various types to carry the bulky produce of the multitude of shallow coal-pits and adits to the canal wharves in the valley below. The Montgomeryshire Canal, by contrast, had only one substantial railway, from a stone quarry at Welshpool. Moreover, the major trade of the Montgomeryshire Canal was in limestone and that was conveyed to the canal-line of the adjoining Ellesmere Canal via a few short railways (Fig. 117) from the large limestone quarries at Llanymynech and Porth-y-waen.

A The Lime Trade

The distribution of limekilns

What the local farmers alongside the Montgomeryshire Canal required on their land was the degradable fertilising slaked-lime or calcium hydroxide (Ca $(OH)_2$) and obviously not the large blocks of indissoluble limestone ($CaCO_3$) cut from the quarry face. Here lay a problem for the lime produced from kilns is an exceedingly volatile cargo to carry, especially in an inevitably leaking canal boat where any water contact will slake the lime in a volatile process making a caustic product. However, for every three tonnes of lime produced in a kiln six tonnes of limestone and one tonne of coal were required.[2] There were obviously considerably increased transport costs in conveying these materials to limekilns situated near the point of use of the lime rather than

near the limestone quarries and collieries producing the anthracite coal or culm used to fuel the kilns. As a result there were experiments in transporting lime on early nineteenth-century railways, but only when special precautions were taken, and even then the transported lime could only be disposed of at a selling price considerably below that of lime actually produced in kilns sited at the points of sale along the transport line.[3] On the Stockton and Darlington Railway special iron waggons had to be used in order to convey lime,[4] and on the Brecon Forest Tramroad the lime was carried in barrels to a special lime storage shed at the terminus with two overline sheds *en route* to protect the cargo whilst in transit.[5] At least one attempt was made to make the even more hazardous transport of lime by water; ships were used to convey quicklime from the kilns at the coastal limestone quarries at Mumbles in Swansea Bay. However, the continued use of limekilns situated around the coasts of Wales and the west of England illustrates how unsuccessful and dangerous such ventures were.

Consequently lime had to be produced in limekilns built into the canal formation at sites along the entire length of the Montgomeryshire Canal. These kiln-banks are the major features relating to the trade of the Mont-

---

[1] Rev. Walter Davies, 'General View of the Agricultural and Domestic Economy of North Wales', Quoted in A. Howell, 'Roads, Bridges, Canals and Railways in Montgomeryshire' III, *The Montgomeryshire Collections* XIV (1881), 89-106.
[2] M. Palmer and P. Neaverson, 'The Ticknall Lime Industry and its Transport System', *Leicestershire Industrial History Society Bulletin* 10 (1987), 5-21,18.
[3] P. R. Reynolds, *The Brecon Forest Tramroad* (Swansea, 1979), 91.
[4] Von Oeynhausen and H. Von Dechen, *Railways in England, 1826 and 1827* (Cambridge, 1971), 32.
[5] S. R. Hughes, *The Archaeology of an Early Railway Network: The Brecon Forest Tramroads* (forthcoming), Chapter 3, Section VI.

gomeryshire Canal and have some claim to be considered as inseparable a part of the canal system as public wharves or warehouses. The materials processed on these three types of sites came or went via the waterway. The kilns themselves are also only found built into the canal formation. By contrast other canal-generated industries, such as the maltings or foundries mentioned in chapter five, were often located at a distance from the line of waterway.

The largest limekiln-bank, at Newtown, had twenty-two kilns. Only two of the Newtown kilns remain, and these have a bungalow sitting on top of them (SO 1141 9174). The two most impressive and accessible of the remaining kiln-banks are those at Belan (SJ 2176 0535: 19 kilometres from Newtown) and Buttington (SJ 2411 0891: 24 kilometres from Newtown); both are now picnic sites.

The high costs of road transport had completely ruled out the building of any kilns remote from the Llanymynech, Porth-y-waen or Crickheath Limestone Quarries prior to the construction of the canal. However, despite the hazards of transporting quicklime, teams of horses and waggons had conveyed lime to estates situated along the future line of the canal. This activity must have been curtailed abruptly upon the completion of the canal, as the document of comparative costings between the old and new forms of transport vividly illustrates (Fig. 42). From 1797 lime was available from the canal terminus at Garthmyl at a cost of 13d a bushel in contrast to the 18d it had cost previously using road transport to that point.[6]

These savings in cost, safety and quality of received product must have resulted in a large programme of kiln-building undertaken concurrently with the completion of the canal. However, it is very obvious from the archaeological remains that the kiln-banks were greatly enlarged in extent during the working-life of the canal, as will be discussed with reference to the kiln-banks at Belan and Buttington.

The Montgomeryshire Canal and many other contemporary transport schemes were conceived at a time when the demand for lime for agricultural purposes was considerably stimulated by the high grain prices caused by the Napoleonic Wars. Much has been made by historians of the large quantities of lime needed to improve the poor hill properties enclosed by landowners at this time. This was indeed true of some areas such as the vast upland Great Forest of Brecon (or Fforest Fawr) and its attendant tramroad scheme. However, the lush lowlands on the great estates situated in and around the Severn Valley between Welshpool and Newtown were already some of the richest farmland in Wales. In fact, most of the lime consumed along the Canal, both during and after the Napoleonic Wars, would have gone to long-established major farms such as the Earl of Powis's home farm of Coed-y-dinas (Fig. 38). Contemporaries noted in 1809 that farms were consuming forty times more lime for land-dressing than had been the custom fifty years previously.[7] In fact the stone-built draw-kiln with its potentiality for continuous and large-scale production only came into widespread use for agricultural purposes about the middle of the eighteenth century.[8] The accelerated pace of the agrarian revolution under the twin stimuli of high grain prices and cheap water transport is very evident when it is considered that the amount of lime burnt along the Montgomeryshire Canal doubled (and also presumably the number of kilns) between 1806 and 1814.[9] Cheaper coal with which to burn the lime also became available with the opening of direct access to the large Ruabon Coalfield in 1805.

Secondary kilns at both the Belan and Buttington banks could well date from this period. In 1814, 45,307 tonnes of limestone and 11,745 tonnes of slack with which to burn it were carried along the canal; this constituted three-quarters of the total tonnage for the

---

[6] The comparative costings illustrated were discovered by Graham Deamer in the Glansevern Collection of Manuscripts (National Library of Wales, Aberystwyth) and approximate to other comparative figures of 18d and 12d a bushel of lime transported by road and canal transport to Garthmyl in 1797 (information from Peter Wakelin quoting Walter Davies, 'Notebook including a tour of Wales in 1797', National Library of Wales Manuscript 1695B).

[7] Palmer and Neavison, 'The Ticknall Lime Industry', 5.

[8] B. C. Skinner, 'The Archaeology of the Lime Industry in Scotland,' *Post-Medieval Archaeology* 9 (1975), 225-30.

[9] Hadfield, *Canals of the West Midlands*, 193.

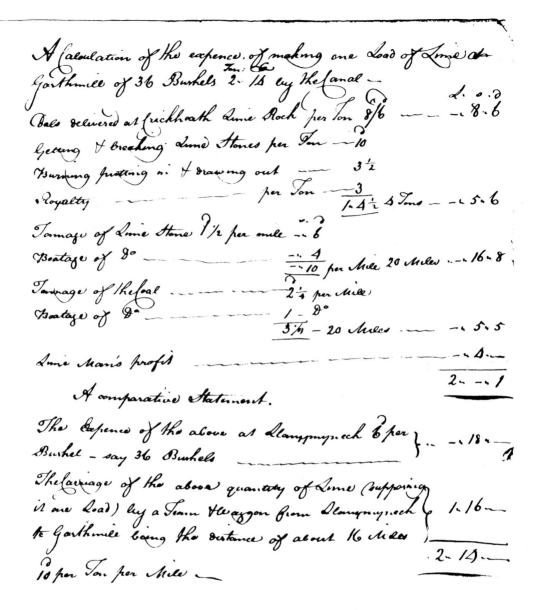

Fig. 42. Table of costs produced by the Glansevern Estate at the opening of the Montgomeryshire Canal showing how the cost of lime at Garthmyl had been reduced from 18d to 13d a bushel by the building of the canal. (Glansevern Estate Collection, 13683, National Library of Wales)

year. When peace was declared, however, the bubble burst and limestone traffic was reduced to 23,839 tonnes by 1817.[10] By 1840-41 the tonnage carried had gradually risen again to a peak of 57,407 tonnes of limestone per annum, with just over a third going to the newer kilns on the Western Branch of the canal.[11] There were now ninety-two kilns on the Mont-

gomeryshire Canal: thirty-four kilns were on the 12 kilometres of the Western Branch and fifty-eight were on the 29½ kilometres of the Eastern Branch; a density of of 2.8 and 1.97 kilns per kilometre respectively. The great

---

[10] Ibid.
[11] Ibid., 195-96.

concentration of kilns at Newtown served the upper reaches of the Severn Valley as the earlier terminus of Garthmyl had done previously. These great centres of lime-burning need to be excluded from the figures required for working out the true frequency of kilns throughout the canal line. Without these large totals the kilns throughout the Western Branch numbered eleven and on the Eastern Branch forty-five kilns. Kiln densities throughout their lines were 0.94 kilns per kilometre for the less prosperous farmland of the Western Branch and 1.5 kilns per kilometre for the Eastern Branch. The even less rich Swansea Valley had an average of only 0.8 kilns per kilometre.[12] As we might expect there is a good correlation between the extent of rich valley floor land adjoining the various waterways and the respective density of kilns.

The mix of the number of kiln-banks and the density of kilns varied from canal to canal. For example the average kiln-bank on the Montgomeryshire Canal had three kilns and was sited at a distance of 2.9 kilometres (Western Branch) or 2.3 kilometres (Eastern Branch) from its nearest neighbour; the mean distance between kiln sites on the Swansea Canal was only 1.3km, but there were only single kilns in each bank on that particular canal. Significantly, these single kilns on the Swansea Canal were attached to small, relatively poor farms with a varying degree of external sale of lime. By contrast, the larger kiln-banks on the Montgomeryshire Canal were usually operated by specialised lime- and coal-merchants. Consequently the annual consumption by Swansea Canal kilns might vary from 506 to as little as 21 tonnes of limestone.[13] The average annual supply for all thirteen of the northerly Swansea Canal kilns was thus as small as 149 tonnes in 1821-22. By contrast the average intake for each of the Buttington kilns on the Montgomeryshire Canal in 1828 was as large as 839 tonnes.[14]

The Buttington limekilns are a fairly typical three-kiln bank surviving in an excellent state of preservation on a public picnic site (SJ 2411 0891: 1.6 kilometres north of Welshpool opposite the Shrewsbury turn from the Welshpool-Oswestry road). The three kilns are built below the level of the canal on the hillside, as were nearly all such kilns. The three circular charg-ing-holes are thus at canal level, their three mouths clearly visible as rings of yellow firebricks which have fused with the heat. Successive layers of Porth-y-waen or Llanymynech limestone and Ruabon, Chirk or Morda coal were poured into them and burnt in order to produce a continuous supply of lime at the bottom. The two kilns nearest the canal overbridge are obviously built as a unit with a low-arched passage connecting their two respective drawing tunnels; they were, perhaps, designed to house rakes, shovels and barrows for use in drawing burnt lime from the kiln bottom and loading it on waiting carts. Filled sacks of lime would almost certainly have been stored in these dry alcoves. A change in the character of the rubble masonry north of the entrance arches of these two kilns suggests that the third kiln is of a different date; its recessed position indicates a date of building prior to that of the adjacent kilns. It is of similar dimensions and type to them, however, and the two later kilns may well date from the 'lime-boom' years of the Napoleonic Wars. In 1828 2,518 tonnes of limestone and 557 tonnes of coal were delivered here; in 1832, 1,968 tonnes of limestone and 650 tonnes of coal.[15] The different ratios of coal and limestone burnt can be explained partly by the fact that the limeburner, David Jones, was also a coal-merchant. It is likely that many limeburners also doubled as coal-merchants since the canal company's records note wildly varying figures in the ratio of coal and limestone delivered at limekiln wharves. A few metres north of the Buttington kilns is a small stone platform projecting from canal level with a path of blue bricks leading from the towing-path to the platform's edge. This is probably where coal was deposited onto carts waiting at the lower level. The early nineteenth-century house next to the wharf (with a modern extension at the back) was occupied by the man in charge of the kilns and wharf.[16] A one-way system was

[12] Based on an examination of the surviving traffic returns for limestone carriage on the uppermost 15.3km of the Swansea Canal ('Cheque Book', Boat Check Book 1812-22 of the Upper Swansea Canal, National Library of Wales, Aberystwyth, MS 14098D).
[13] Ibid.
[14] Monts. Canal Report Bks., 23 June 1828 (P.R.O.).
[15] Ibid. and 23 June 1832.
[16] 'Shropshire Union Rly, and Canal Plan, 1845'.

Fig. 43. The charging-hole of kiln no. 2 at the Buttington Kiln-bank showing how most of the tops of the Montgomeryshire kilns are at, or about, canal level to facilitate the use of canal-borne limestone and coal.

operated whereby the present drive of this house continued to the canal bank, curved round in front of the platform and kilns and headed back towards the nearby main road, joining the adjacent side road as it did so.[17]

Since it is known that a limeburner at Garthmyl had two boats to supply his six kilns,[18] one boat would probably have been adequate to supply the bank at Buttington. On the far side of the canal the early nineteenth-century 'Canal Cottages' consisted of two stables and two houses with gardens running down to the canal.[19] It is tempting to suppose that the occupants of these cottages operated boats but in fact the census returns indicate

that this was not the case. In 1841 a boatman did live up the lane at the scattered cottages at 'Rhallt' whilst the entries for 'canal cottages' that appear in the 1871 and 1881 censuses record a number of railway-workers living in these houses.

The Buttington kilns are one of the very few groups of limekilns which have left any details of production. The 'Buttington Kiln Day-Book' records all sales of lime for the years 1830 and 1831.[20] In those years the owner was David Jones of Dolanog House in Welshpool

17 Shown on same plan.
18 Monts. Canal Report Bks., 18 November 1844, and Tithe Map of Berriew, 1840 (National Library of Wales).
19 'Shropshire Union Rly. and Canal Plan, 1845'.
20 'Buttington Kiln Day-Book', 1830-31 (Powysland Club Library, Powsland Museum, Welshpool).

(this stood near the opposite side of the canal from the main canal wharf there).

The day-book allows us to learn much about the production of lime and its distribution from a fairly typical Montgomeryshire Canal kiln-bank, as is illustrated by the accompanying graph and map. The graph (Fig. 45) shows how very seasonal lime-burning was. Prior to the introduction of powered road transport, liming was always undertaken in the summer as the appalling condition of the muddy local roads in the winter made it difficult to carry heavy loads along them. More importantly, perhaps, summer and early autumn was also the appropriate time in the agricultural calendar to carry out liming; as is evident from the graph, all

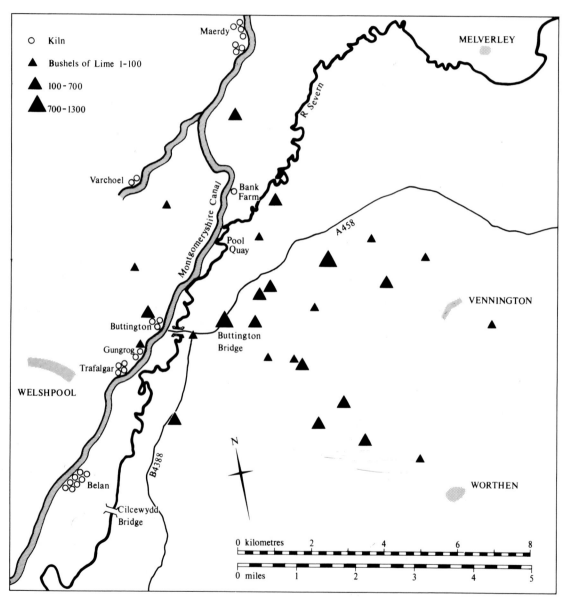

Fig. 44. Map showing the very localised distribution of burnt-lime from a Montgomeryshire Canal limekiln-bank. At Buttington in 1830 virtually the whole output of the kilns was transported over Buttington Bridge (across the River Severn) to nearby farms.

60

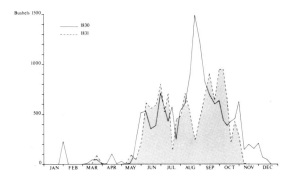

Fig. 45. This graph of lime sales at the Buttington Limekilns (Fig. 43) shows how very seasonal lime-burning was. Liming of the fields took place between the harrowing of early summer and that of the Autumn.

significant lime production at Buttington kilns took place between the beginning of June and the end of October. The wheat fields, often full of stubble, were ploughed in the spring and then harrowed to kill any weeds that appeared in the early summer. Then the lime was applied at the rate of about three tons of lump-lime to the acre (seven and a half tonnes per hectare), carefully slaked and ploughed in immediately. Then in the early autumn late weeds were harrowed, manure ploughed in and autumn wheat planted.[21] Sometimes the lime was harrowed in with grain or turnip seed.[22]

The amount of lime-mortar used for building purposes seems to have been minimal in these rural surroundings. One or two bushels of lime, for instance, were delivered during 1830 to Thomas Nicholas who was working on the Buttington Churchyard wall.

The map of the distribution of lime from Buttington limekilns (Fig. 44) shows just how localised the market was from one of the kiln-banks alongside the canal. Buttington kilns were sited near one of the two bridges crossing the River Severn in the Welshpool area and most of the output of the kilns was fed across the bridge to the relatively rich farms around the edges of the Long Mountain and Breidden Hill. The furthest extent of this marketing area reached some 13 kilometres from the canal to the far edge of the Welsh uplands intruding into Shropshire.

[21] D. Lewis, 'History of the parish of Cray, 1851-1951, Part 1; II. Farming', *Brycheiniog* IX (1963), 120-21.
[22] Palmer and Neavison, 'The Ticknall Lime Industry', 5.

The dating and construction of limekilns

The largest bank of kilns, apart from the great concentration of kilns at the canal termini at Garthmyl and Newtown, was that at Belan (SJ 2176 0585: 1.6 kilometres south of Welshpool) which is now a picnic site. The eight kilns at Belan form an excellent introduction to the diversity of kiln types alongside the Montgomeryshire Canal. The accompanying table of the dimensions and capacities of kilns alongside the canal clearly illustrates how the various surviving kiln-banks fit into the picture that emerges. Information on twenty-eight of the ninety-two kilns that stood alongside the canal is available; an indication of the high rate of survival of these structures up to the present period, although substantial economic development in the area will inevitably accompany the re-opening of the canal. The situation in the narrow industrial 'corridors' of south Wales is quite different, only one of the sixty limekilns that once stood along the Swansea Canal remains substantially complete. The numbering of the kilns in each kiln-bank indicates the original, and not the modern, sequence of kilns in each group running from south to north so that kilns '3' and '4' of the Garthmyl southern limekiln-bank appear on the table even though only two of the original five kilns in that bank still survive.

From the table it can be seen that the main dating criteria for the kilns on the canal is not generally the diameter of the mouth of a kiln, or the capacity of the burning-cone, but is rather related to the materials used in the construction of the arches spanning the access to the drawing-holes of the kilns and to the dimensions of these arches. Indeed this might be expected to be the case when there is clear indication that every burning-cone has been relined and renewed many times in a working life that might have lasted for about one hundred and twenty years of being subjected to a heat of 900-1,000°C. The burning-cone of Kiln 1 at Belan shows every indication of having had its size altered and position moved so that the drawing-hole in the second arch of the bank has been blocked, and the central iron beam of the reconstructed kiln appears to the side of the second earlier access to the kiln bottom (Fig. 47).

Table of the dimensions and capacities of the limekilns alongside the Montgomeryshire Canal

Name	Date	Kiln Height	Diameter of Kiln Mouth	Width of Kiln Front Per Kiln	Number of Drawing Holes Per Kiln	Estimated Cubic Capacity	Span of Drawing Arch at Springing	Span of Drawing Arch at Ground	Walling Material	Vaulting Material	Grid Reference
Garthmyl Southern Limekiln Bank											
Kiln 3	c.1820-40	e6.4m	e2.6m	6m	1	25.5m³	4.2m	4.2m	Stone	Brick	SO 1941 9926
Kiln 4	c.1820-40	6.4m	2.6m	6m	1	25.5m³	4.2m	4.2m	Stone	Brick	SO 1941 9927
Garthmyl Middle Limekiln Bank											
Kiln 1	c.1810	e5m	2.9m	6.8m	1	24.8m³	1.76m	1.9m	Stone	Brick	SO 1933 9938
Kiln 2	c.1810	5m	3m	6.8m	1	26.5m³	1.76m	1.9m	Stone	Brick	SO 1933 9938
Kiln 3	c.1810	e5m	2.9m	6.8m	1	24.8m³	1.76m	1.9m	Stone	Brick	SO 1932 9939
Berriew Southern Limekiln Bank											
Kiln 1	c.1790s	3.95m	—	—	1	—	1.7m	—	Stone	Stone	SJ 1897 0182
Kiln 2	c.1790s	4.1m	2.6m	—	1	16.3m³	—	—	Stone	Stone	SJ 1897 0183
Kiln 3	c.1800	4m	—	—	1	—	2.35m	2.35m	Stone	Stone	SJ 1898 0184
Brithdir Limekiln Bank											
Kiln 1	c.1820-30	5m	2.73m	—	1	21.95m³	3.93m	3.93m	Stone	Brick	SJ 1995 0228
Kiln 2	c.1790s	e5m	—	—	1	—	1.65m	—	Stone	Stone	SJ 1995 0230
Kiln 3	c.1800	e5m	2.5m	—	1	18.4m³	1.85m	—	Stone	Stone	SJ 1996 0230
Belan Limekiln Bank											
Kiln 1	c.1815	e5.36m	e2.32m	—	2	17m³	2.26m	2.26m	Stone	Brick	SJ 2172 0531
Kiln 2	c.1815	5.36m	2.32m	5.3m	1	17m³	2.25m	2.25m	Stone	Brick	SJ 2173 0531
Kiln 3	c.1840s	6.08m	3.12m	10m	1	34.8m³	5.35m	5.25m	Stone	Brick	SJ 2173 0532
Kiln 4	c.1840s	e6.08m	e3.12m	6.8m	1	34.8m³	5.4m	e5.3m	Stone	Brick	SJ 2174 0532
Kiln 5	1790s	e5.55m	—	6.8m	1	—	1.56m	1.98m	Stone	Stone	SJ 2175 0534
Kiln 6	1790s	e5.55m	—	7.1m	1	—	1.56m	1.98m	Stone	Stone	SJ 2176 0535
Kiln 7	c.1800	—	—	6.2m	1	—	2.11m	2.11m	Stone	Stone	SJ 2176 0536
Kiln 8	c.1800	—	—	4.9m	1	—	2.08m	1.99m	Stone	Stone	SJ 2177 0536
Buttington Limekiln Bank											
Kiln 1	c.1790s	e5.15m	2.7m	—	1	22.1m³	1.59m	1.8m	Stone	Stone	SJ 2412 0891
Kiln 2	c.1790s	5.15m	2.7m	—	1	22.1m³	1.6m	1.8m	Stone	Stone	SJ 2413 0891
Kiln 3	c.1797	e5.15m	3.27m	—	1	32.4m³	1.46m	1.9m	Stone	Stone	SJ 2413 0892
Maerdy Northern Limekiln Bank											
Kiln 1	c.1815	e6.1m	e2.8m	—	1	28.17m³	2.17m	2.17m	Stone	Brick	SJ 2639 1695
Kiln 2	c.1815	e6.1m	e2.8m	6.5m	1	28.17m³	2.03m	2.03m	Stone	Brick	SJ 2639 1696
Kiln 3	c.1815	e6.1m	2.8m	4.5m	1	28.17m³	2.03m	2.03m	Stone	Brick	SJ 2639 1697
Kiln 4	c.1815	e5.5m	e2.8m	6.5m	1	25.4m³	2.03m	2.03m	Stone	Brick	SJ 2639 1697

Table of Montgomeryshire Kilns

We might expect that the earliest kilns would be those constructed entirely of stone and with the smallest and most primitive access archways. In fact the smallest kiln access portals have no true archway spanning them but rather have a corbelled opening; the sidewalls of the narrow entrance passage lean inwards as much as 21-22 cm. (Buttington Kiln 3 and Belan Kilns 5 and 6), while the roof-slopes join at a peak rather than as a true semicircular or eliptical arch. The entrance passages are all narrow varying between 1.46m and 1.6m at the springing of the vault and between 1.8m and 1.98m at ground level.

The front retaining walls of these early kilns, as seen on Kilns 5 and 6 at Belan (Fig. 47), are of a distinctive type seen on late eighteenth- and early nineteenth-century civil engineering works. The front of the wall does not rake back at a very marked angle, as on the mid-nineteenth-century Kilns 3 and 4 at Belan, but is thickened towards the base by a series of steps about 10cm in width. The first of these is some 220cm from the ground, the second 86cm above that, the third another 113 cm, and the fourth and last 122cm again. In between these steps the face of the wall slopes back some 6cm. All the kilns of this type were probably built for or shortly after the opening of the original Montgomeryshire Canal in 1797. The three kilns at Buttington are all of this type but constructed in two building phases: the front wall of Kiln 1 and 2 curves back to butt against the earlier Kiln 3.

There is a second type of completely stone-built kiln which has been added to kilns of the first type on the kiln-banks at both Belan (Kilns 7 and 8—Fig. 47) and at the southern

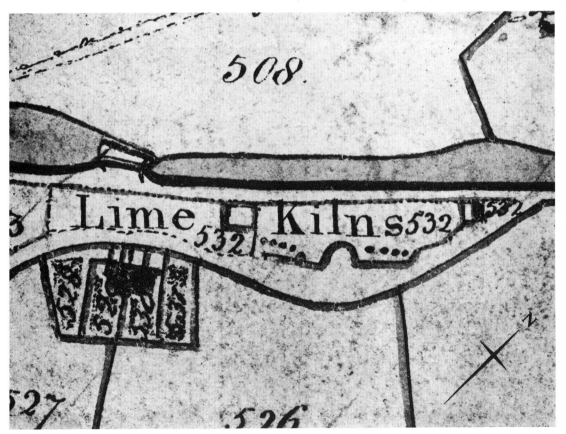

Fig. 46. The schematised plan of the Belan Limekilns (the charging-holes are shown as large dots) shown on the 'Poole' Parish (Upper Division) tithe map of 1840. The census returns show that the early lock-keepers at Belan and/or the limekiln lessees lived in the canalside house labelled '532' on the right and at least some of the men working the kilns lived in the four houses labelled 529-30.

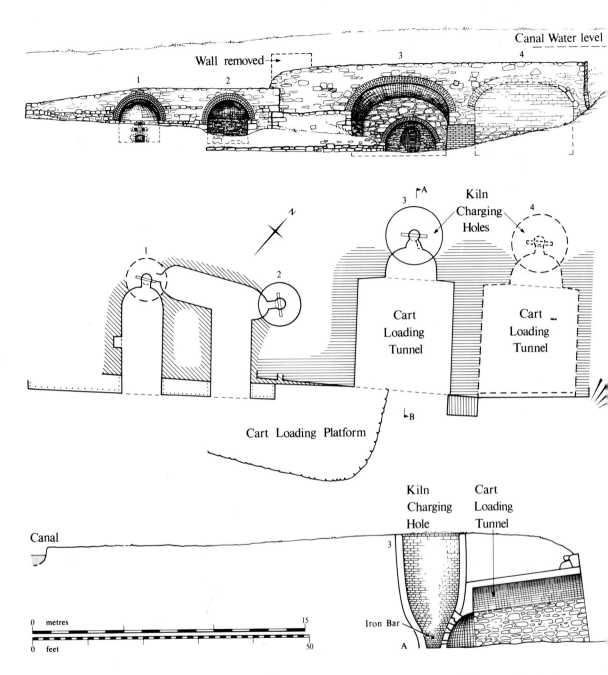

Canal Water level

Wall removed

Kiln Charging Holes

Cart Loading Tunnel

Cart Loading Tunnel

Cart Loading Platform

Kiln Charging Hole

Cart Loading Tunnel

Canal

Iron Bar

0 metres   15

0 feet   50

kiln-bank at Berriew (Kiln 3). This type had a slightly wider access to the kiln drawing-holes (between 2.08m and 2.35m wide at the springing of the vault) roofed by a segmental arched vault. The sides of the kiln access vaults on these kilns are generally vertical, although Kiln 7 at Belan has chamber walls that actually lean

outwards. The front retaining walls of these kilns are raked back from bottom to top a distance of about 30cm at Belan and do not have the stepped profile of the earlier kilns.

Possibly contemporary with the above type, but more likely slightly later, are limekilns with a narrow vault and corbelled side walls similar

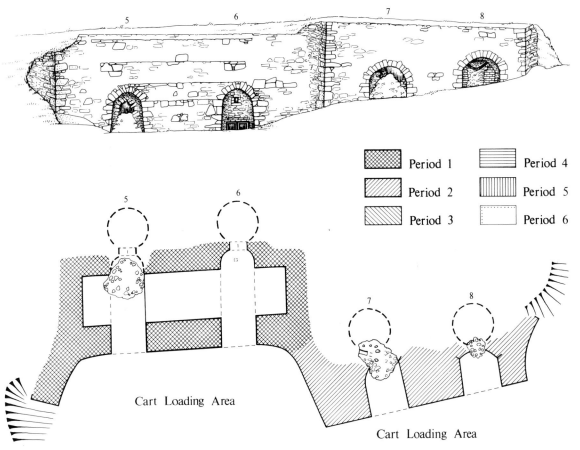

Fig. 47. The limekiln-bank at Belan (now a picnic site) was the largest single group of kilns on the Montgomeryshire Canal, apart from the Newtown terminus group. Kilns nos. 5 and 6 may have been built at the opening of the canal in the 1790s and nos. 7 and 8 soon afterwards. Kilns nos. 1 and 2 have brick drawing-hole vaults of small span and were probably built in the opening years of the nineteenth century whilst kilns nos. 3 and 4 have later huge vaults or tunnels that probably accommodated carts and waggons while the volatile quick-lime was loaded.

to the first type of kiln but with the access passage roofed in brick. The use of brick in building came early to the area surrounding the Montgomeryshire Canal. Llanllwchaearn Church near Newtown was rebuilt in 1815 using bricks conveyed free of toll down the Montgomeryshire Canal[23], and in 1824 the Canal Company (Eastern Branch) realised they could make their own bricks from their clay-pit at the Wern and built a kiln there.[24] Thus the second type of stone kiln has provisionally been ascribed a date of c.1800 and the most primitive type of brick-built kiln (Montgomeryshire Canal limekiln Type 3) a date of c. 1810.

A fourth type of limekiln with a wider

entrance passage roofed by a properly formed semicircular arched brick vault can be seen at Belan Kilns 1 and 2, Maerdy Kilns, and the four visible entrance passages to the northern limekiln-bank at Garthmyl. The passages are between 2.03m and 2.26m in width. A possible dating of c. 1815 has been attributed to these kilns.

The Montgomeryshire Canal was extended to Newtown and opened in the period 1819-21. Some twenty-two kilns were built here by 1833

---

[23] Ex inf. Lawrence Butler.
[24] A. Spencer, P. Hurley and J. Cooper, *About the Montgomeryshire Canal....Towpath Guide. 2, Welshpool to Llanymynech* (Welshpool, 1981), 5.

Fig. 48. The vast drawing-hole vault of kiln no. 3 at the Belan Kiln-bank. The base of the burning-cone and an iron bar to support the combustible contents are visible through the collapsed hole at the rear of the vault.

and the drawing-holes and passages of two survive. They have large semicircular brick vaults some 3.81m wide which could well have accommodated carts for loading the volatile lime under cover. The similar large brick arches in the southern limekiln-bank at Garthmyl (Fig. 89) and on Kiln 1 at Brithdir probably date these latter kilns to a similar period (c. 1820-30).

Altogether larger are the great brick vaults of Kilns 3 and 4 at Belan (Fig. 47). The spans of these huge arches are some 5.35-5.4m and they well date from the years of maximum lime traffic in the 1840s. The Earl of Powis's Model Farm at Coed-y-dinas (Fig. 38) would have received lime from this kiln-bank, and the earl's rival agrarian improver John Naylor began his vast improvements on his adjoining lands at Leighton in the 1840s. It is likely that Naylor took very large quantities of lime from Belan kilns.

It is worth seeing how this development on the Montgomeryshire Canal compares with the development of other limekilns in early and mid nineteenth-century Wales.

Prior to the mid-eighteenth century turf-built clamp-kilns had been in common use for perhaps only a season at a time. Coal, peat or timber were used to burn the local limestone in turf-kilns some 12m long, 6m wide and, when filled and covered, some 2.3m high. The process was slow and uneconomic, for after the kiln had burnt itself out, taking up to ten days, it had to be largely destroyed in order to extract the contents.[25]

The remains of a concentration of 171 limekilns recorded in about one square kilometre of upland Breconshire by the Royal Commission on Ancient Monuments in Wales illustrate the type of kiln likely to have been built by local farmers on the limestone outcrop between the mid eighteenth century and the enclosure of the Great Forest of Brecon in 1819 (Fig. 50).[26] Most of these kilns on Carnau Gwynion are very primitive in structure consisting of circular or 'D'-shaped dry-stone towers crudely constructed from the local

---

[25] Skinner, 'Archaeology of the Lime Industry in Scotland', 225-30.

Table of dimensions and capacities of limekilns in early and mid-nineteenth century Wales.

Name	Date	Builder	Kiln Height	Diameter of Kiln Mouth	Width of Kiln Front Per Kiln	Number of Drawing Holes Per Kiln	Estimated Cubic Capacity	Grid Reference
A. THE GREAT FOREST OF BRECON—COMMONERS' AGRICULTURAL KILNS								
Carnau Gwynion; Plas-y-gors Farm	1820s	John Christie	4.5m	2.5m	7.4m	1	16.6m^3	SN 9200 1494
Carnau Gwynion; Kiln 39/11	Late 19C?	——	4.7m	1.7m	4.8m	1	8m^3	SN 9210 1463
Carnau Gwynion; Kiln 40/16	Mid 19C?	A local farmer?	3m	e2.5m	7.0m	1	11m^3	SN 9185 1456
B. WEST WALES COASTAL LIMEKILNS								
Morfa Bychan Limekiln	Early to Mid 19C	——	3.1m	2.5m	7.0m	3	11.4m^3	SN 5670 7776
Wallog Limekiln	Early to Mid 19C	——	4m	2.35m	7.2m	3	13m^3	SN 5899 8570
C. LIMEKILNS ALONGSIDE CANALS IN SOUTH WALES								
Swansea Canal; Hafod Copperworks	By 1876	Vivian & Co.	7m	e2.1m	5.8m	1	18.2m^3	SN 6609 9499
Neath Canal; Maes-gwyn Farm	Early 19C?	A local farmer?	5.5m	a3.0m	5.5m	1	28.9m^3	SN 8588 0517
Glamorganshire Canal; Ynysygored Farm	Early 19C?	A local farmer?	4.5m	2.3m	6.1m	2	14m^3	SN 0707 0085
D. LIMEKILNS ALONGSIDE THE BRECON FOREST TRAMROAD								
Penwyllt; Twyn-y-ffald	c.1825	John Christie	8.2m	e2.7m	7.4m	1	35.2m^3	SN 8528 1591
Penwyllt; Twyn-y-ffald	c.1827	John Christie	8.2m	e2.8m	7.9m	1	37.8m^3	SN 8527 1590
Sennybridge; Castell-du	c.1834	The Brecon Forest Tramroad Company	4.7m	e1.8m	4m	1	9m^3	SN 9167 2832
Ynysgedwyn Incline Head	poss. 1834	Joseph Claypon	6.3m	e2.7m	6m	1	27.1m^3	SN 8006 0939
Penwyllt; Twyn Disgwlfa	c.1836	Joseph Claypon	8m	e3.2m	7m	1	48.3m^3	SN 8554 1612
Penwyllt; Twyn Disgwlfa	by 1842	Joseph Claypon	8m	e4.4m	9.8m	1	91.2m^3	SN 8557 1613

The cubic capacity of a kiln is estimated using the formula: volume = $0.75\pi d^2 h \div 4$; d = the diameter of the kiln-mouth and h = the kiln height. Many kiln-mouths have been filled in but the diameter was about 0.35 of the front width of the kiln on free-standing kilns and 0.45 of the front of a single kiln standing in a bank. The abbreviations a = approximate and e = estimated. Such figures only, of course, give a rough approximation of the possible capacity of a kiln.

Table of kilns throughout Wales

limestone and mostly without any lining of fire-bricks. Of the 166 kilns where it was possible to estimate an original height some 2% were about 1.5m in height, 19% some 2m in height, 60% some 3m in height, one kiln was about 4m high, and only two approached the usual 5m height of the Montgomeryshire kilns—and one of these was built in the 1820s by a wealthy London merchant and farmer, John Christie. The largest of the farmers' kilns had a capacity of only about 10m^3. The farmer's single kiln at Ynysygored on the Glamorganshire Canal similarly had a capacity of only about 14m^3. The small mid-nineteenth-century limekilns at the Sennybridge Depot of the Brecon Forest Tramroad fired only some 8m^3 of material because of the great expense of transporting limestone and coal a very con-

siderable distance by rail on adverse gradients. Similar high transport costs may have accounted for the small size of the single kilns found all along the west coast of Wales.

The capacity of three of the Montgomeryshire kilns (Belan nos. 1 and 2 and Berriew no. 2) may indicate that these, at 16-17m^3, originally had a capacity only marginally greater than those of the west Wales coast. In time,

---

[26] Seventy-nine of the 171 kilns at Carnau Gwynion lie outside the area reserved for limestone extraction in 1819—the boundary wall overlies the remains of several kilns and the majority of kilns within the enclosure area are of a similar primative type to those built outside the enclosure (information from D. Leighton, D. Percival and B. Malaws working on a National Archaeological Survey, Wales, project).

Fig. 49. *The firing-cone or bowl of the large kiln no. 3 at the Belan Kiln-bank. The iron-rail above the base was to stop the burning mass of limestone and coal becoming so compacted that easy raking of the lime produced became impossible.*

however, most of the Montgomeryshire kilns were given a capacity of about 25m^3, similar to that of the Neath Canal kiln at Maes-gwyn. The relatively standard size of the kilns was determined largely by the height of the Montgomeryshire Canal above any fairly easily drained piece of adjoining valley land, and that was usually about 5m. The kiln-bowl mouth was usually about 2.5-2.9m in diameter and any enlargement of capacity was arrived at by increasing the number and not the size of the kilns. It was only sensible for ease of loading to keep the mouths of the kilns as level with the canal as possible. Limekilns built along an early horse-worked railway could be made considerably taller and still charged relatively easily by the expedient of building large ramps to the top or bottom of the kilns. Thus the large banks of kilns at the Penwyllt Limestone Quarries on the Brecon Forest Tramroad had heights of 8m and capacities up to 91.2m^3 by the 1840s. The contemporary Kilns 3 and 4 at Belan on the Montgomeryshire Canal also show an enlargement of capacity over earlier kilns—to 34.8m^3—by the expedient of increasing the bowl diameter to 3.12cm and the height of the kilns to 6.08m. The floor of these kilns are now prone to waterlogging and originally there must have been large drains to convey the ground-water to the Severn flood-plain.

The great majority of the Montgomeryshire Canal kilns had only a single drawing-hole for each kiln but these kilns stood in a relatively sheltered valley with long (4.1m in Kilns 1 and 2 at Belan; 5.7m in Kilns 3 and 4 and the remaining kilns at Newtown) and fairly large entrance tunnels. As far as can be assessed, 55% of the primitive Carnau Gwynion kilns had double drawing-holes and 2% had triple drawing-holes; all the coastal kilns on the Ceredigion coast have triple drawing-holes. However, both these groups of kilns stood in very exposed mountain top and coastal positions. Lack of capital with the former kilns and the non-availability of good building-stone or brick in the latter case meant that deep and spacious chambers over the drawing-holes were out of the question. These kilns, therefore, had to be provided with alternative drawing-holes that could be used to avoid the worst effects of the prevailing wind.

Fig. 50. *Map showing the 171 small limekilns existing in and around a single walled enclosure on a mountain top in the Brecon Beacons. The widespread use of a vast numbers of such crudely constructed structures was largely superseded by the construction of many canalside kilns in the late eighteenth and early nineteenth centuries. The wind-swept sites of the earlier kilns on the limestone outcrop demanded the provision of many lime drawing-holes, a feature not found along the sheltered banks of the Montgomeryshire Canal.*

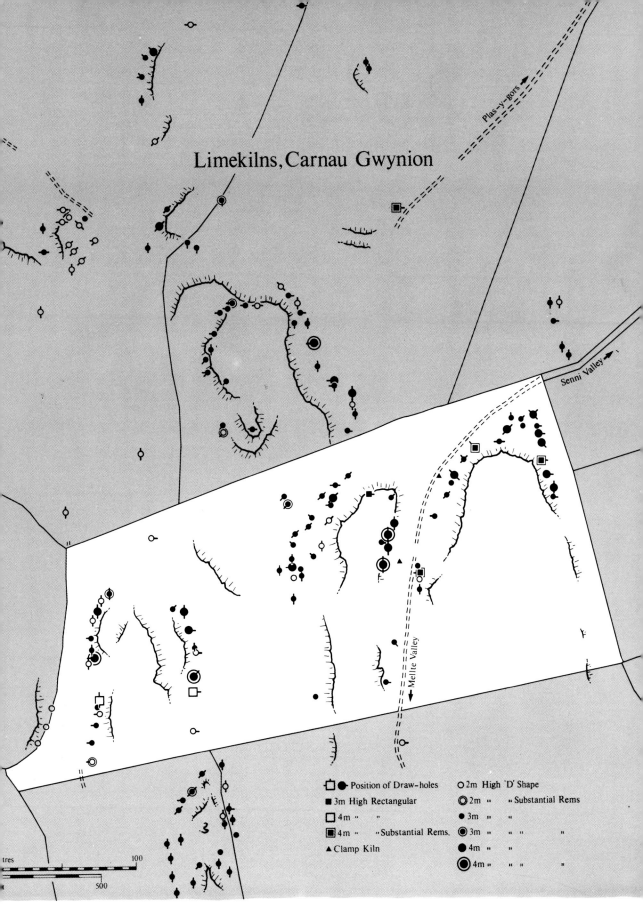

Limekilns, Carnau Gwynion

Plas–y–gors

Senni Valley

Mellte Valley

		Position of Draw-holes		○ 2m High 'D' Shape
■		3m High Rectangular	◎	2m " " Substantial Rems
□		4m " "	●	3m " "
▣		4m " " Substantial Rems.	◉	3m " " " "
▲		Clamp Kiln	●	4m " " " "
			◉	4m " " " " "

tres   100

500

B The Coal Trade.

Trading along the Montgomeryshire Canal in three commodities was pre-eminently noticeable to contempories; a traveller between Newtown and Welshpool in 1801 remarked that '... *roads are so torn up and destroyed by the wagons loaded with stones* [i.e. probably burnt lime] *and coal to which may be added immense trees for ship timber that are in constant motion to and from the .... Canal, that they are almost impassable*'.[27] The second of these items mentioned, coal, was brought into this area on its own account in substantial quantities rather than just as an ancillary material for lime-burning. In 1844 household coal made up one-fifth of the total traffic of the Western Branch.[28] Much coal, and particularly slack, would have been sold by lime-merchants as a sideline. In addition, there were seventeen specialist coal-wharves sited throughout the length of the Montgomeryshire Canal: eight on the Western Branch and nine on the Eastern Branch.[29] The higher density of limekiln-banks along the length of the latter canal probably accounts for the lower density of specialist coal-wharves along its length: there were at least 0.7 coal-wharves per km on the Western

[27] Hadfield, *Canals of the West Midlands*, 192, quoting T. Martyn, 'An Account of a Tour of Wales', (1801), N.L.W. MS 1340C.
[28] From figures given in Hadfield, 195.

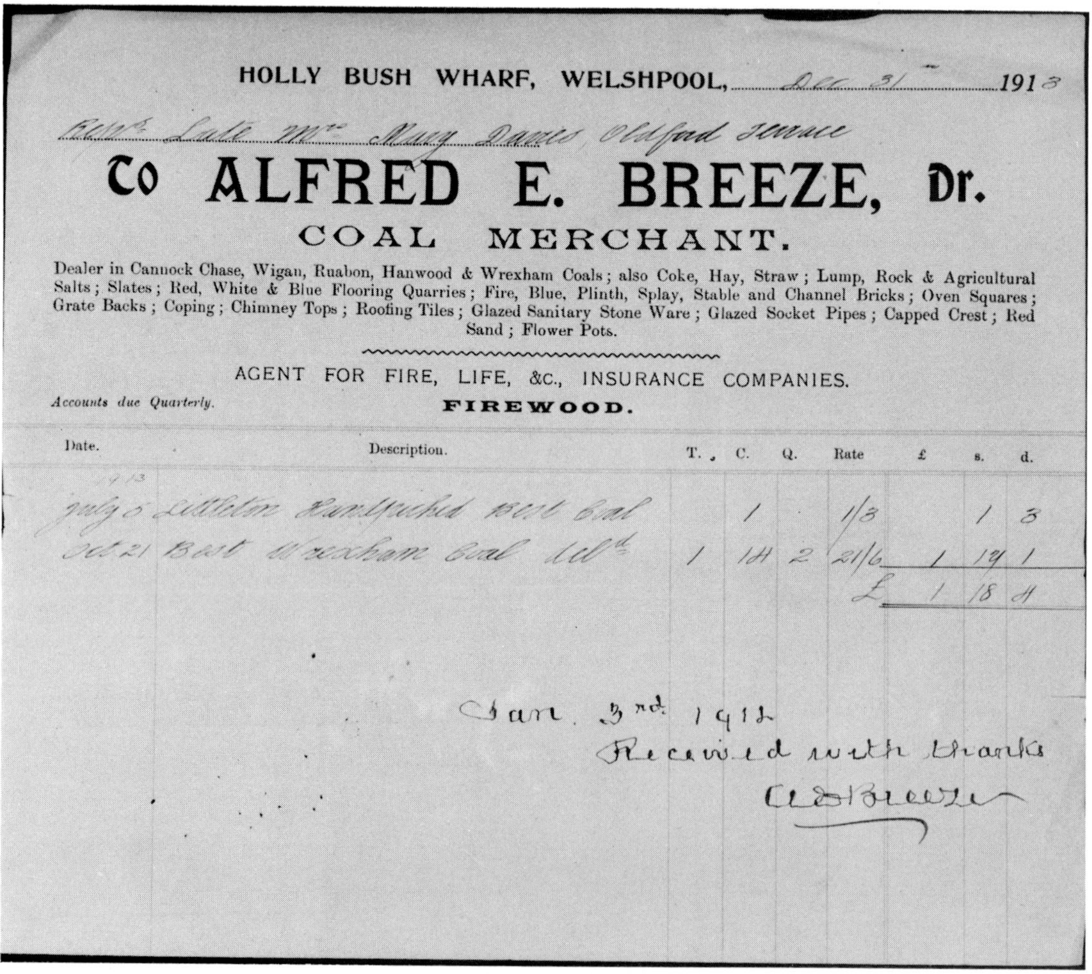
HOLLY BUSH WHARF, WELSHPOOL, Dec 31 1918

Exors Late Mrs Mary Davies Oldford Terrace

To ALFRED E. BREEZE, Dr.

COAL MERCHANT.

Dealer in Cannock Chase, Wigan, Ruabon, Hanwood & Wrexham Coals; also Coke, Hay, Straw; Lump, Rock & Agricultural Salts; Slates; Red, White & Blue Flooring Quarries; Fire, Blue, Plinth, Splay, Stable and Channel Bricks; Oven Squares; Grate Backs; Coping; Chimney Tops; Roofing Tiles; Glazed Sanitary Stone Ware; Glazed Socket Pipes; Capped Crest; Red Sand; Flower Pots.

AGENT FOR FIRE, LIFE, &c., INSURANCE COMPANIES.

Accounts due Quarterly.

FIREWOOD.

Date.	Description.	T.	C.	Q.	Rate	£	s.	d.
1918 July 5	Littleton Handpicked Best Coal		1		1/3		1	3
Oct 21	Best Wrexham Coal dd	1	14	2	21/6	1	19	1
					£	1	18	4

Jan. 3rd 1918
Received with thanks
A E Breeze

Fig. 51. A goods receipt issued in 1918 showing the range of goods stocked at the canalside Holly Bush Wharf in Welshpool. (Powysland Museum Collection)

Branch and 0.3 coal-wharves per km on the Eastern Branch. In view of the 7,790 tonnes of household coal carried up the Western Branch in 1844[30] the one coal-wharf shown on contemporary maps (at Newtown) would have been somewhat inadequate. It seems certain that some, if not all, of the fifteen other 'wharves' at the Newtown terminus of the Western Branch must have accommodated this trade. The same would also have been true of the thirty-two 'wharves' of unspecified purpose sited at intervals alongside the Montgomeryshire Canal: nineteen on the Western Branch and thirteen on the Eastern Branch.

The best preserved of the old coal yards is probably that at Hollybush Wharf (Fig. 51), on the opposite canal bank from the towing-path above Welshpool Lock. A double red-brick stable block of the mid nineteenth century survives next to the old lock-house, 'Glascoed'. On the west (left) of this are the ruins of a stone-built lean-to. Across the yard and fronting the Newtown-Welshpool road are an early nineteenth-century house and cartshed cum warehouse, both executed in green-sandstone rubble. The yard frontage of the house is of red brick and both properties are now tenanted by 'Tyre-services of Great Britain'.

C The Timber Trade.

Of all the traffic on the Western Branch only one-fortieth consisted of produce being 'exported', and almost three-quarters of this was timber.[31] In the 1840s three specialist wharves were noted on the Western Branch and ten on the Eastern Branch; that is a density of 0.25 timber-wharves per kilometre on the former and 0.34 on the latter. The accompanying poster[32] (Fig. 52) shows how a predominant factor in determining the value of timber was its proximity to the canal or to the River Severn at Pool Quay from whence the timber was floated down on large rafts on its way to the Naval Dockyards. It is worth noting that the pillar on the top of Breidden Hill near Welshpool was erected to commemorate the victory of Admiral Lord Rodney over the French Fleet in 1792, and well it might: the local estates benefitted mightily from Rodney's and Nelson's lauding of Montgomeryshire Oak as the material for building their large fleets of huge wooden fighting ships.

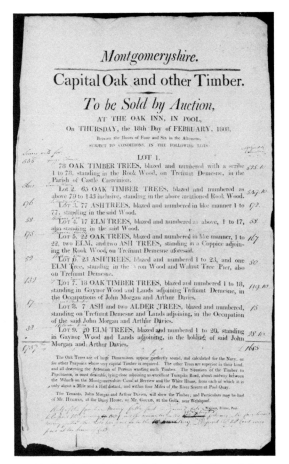

Fig. 52. Powis Castle Estate timber advertised for sale in 1808 as 'calculated for the Navy' and within easy access of water transport along the Montgomeryshire Canal and/or the River Severn from Pool Quay. (Powysland Museum Collection)

The Powis Castle Estate Timber-yard

The poster illustrated (Fig. 52) advertises timber situated on the Powis Castle Estate and much of this was processed in the Powis Estate Timber-yard. The sawmill (about 1.6km south

[29] The statistics given throughout this book on the number and distributions of features throughout the canal are based on the relevant tithe maps of 1840-46, the 'Shropshire Union Railway....Plan' of 1845 and the 'Shropshire Union Railways and Canal and London & North Western Railway, Plans and Sections of the Railway from Buttington to Welshpool and Newtown, November 1859', and on all their attached schedules of owners, lessees and occupiers. The two railway plans were proposals for railways to be laid on top of the existing canal formation. It can be assumed that even these three large-scale sets of plans ignore some details.

[30] Hadfield, *Canals of the West Midlands*, 195.

[31] Ibid.

[32] Powysland Museum Collection, Welshpool.

YY

HORIZONTAL SINGLE-BLADED SAW FRAME.

This Machine is specially suitable for sawing-up round and irregular shaped timber into boards and scantlings. It is also most useful for sawing costly woods, such as mahogany, for not only can it be worked with a very thin saw, but the log can be examined after each board is cut, and the sawing regulated accordingly.

The construction of the table with its screw dogs for holding the timber, makes it specially useful for crooked timber, such as Ash, and other kinds of English hard wood.

The Machine works with one saw, which cuts during both the forward and the backward stroke and the feed motion is continuous. The saw frame is raised or lowered to any height above the table for determining the position of the saw cut.

In the larger sized machines the crankshaft bearings are mounted on slides, so that the crankshaft can be **raised or lowered** for cutting large or small timber.

By the addition of extension arms to the saw frame, this machine is capable of sawing through the middle of a log and quartering. These extension arms are only supplied when specially ordered.

This Machine can also be constructed to drive with independent **Steam Engine** if required.

The following sizes are made :—

No.	Maximum size of Log.	Diam. of pulleys on Crankshaft.	Revs. per minute.	Approximate Weight.	Nominal Power.	Code Word.
1	48in. diam. by 24ft. long	3ft. 0in. by 4½in.	200	9 tons 7 cwt.	4-horse	Beauteous.
2	42in. ,, 24ft. ,,	3ft. 0in. ,, 4½in.	210	9 ,, 2 ,,	4 ,,	Bedaub.
3	36in. ,, 24ft. ,,	2ft. 6in. ,, 4½in.	240	8 ,, 8 ,,	3 ,,	Bedmate.
4	30in. ,, 24ft. ,,	2ft. 6in. ,, 4½in.	250	8 ,, 5 ,,	3 ,,	Befitting.
5	24in. ,, 24ft. ,,	2ft. 3in. ,, 3 in.	280	6 ,, 3 ,,	2 ,,	Begotten.

If to drive with Steam Engine direct, prefix "Ex" to the above Codes.

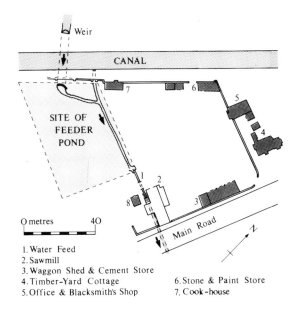

1. Water Feed
2. Sawmill
3. Waggon Shed & Cement Store
4. Timber-Yard Cottage
5. Office & Blacksmith's Shop
6. Stone & Paint Store
7. Cook-house

Fig. 54. Plan of the Powis Castle Estate Timber-yard.

of Welshpool on the Newtown Road) dates from *c*.1820-30 and has already been described in chapter two. The extensive yard wall of thin coursed stone probably dates from the same period. Wide gates lead through the wall onto both the main road and the canal towing-path. A crane for loading timber onto narrow-boats stood against the outer face of the yard wall.

It is obvious from their various styles of masonry that the buildings around the yard have been built, added to or replaced piecemeal throughout the 160 years that the yard has served the timber industry. From the sawmill (Fig. 54,'2') and proceedings anti-clockwise round the yard the buildings are as follows.

Against the north face of the mill is a corrugated-iron lean-to ('2' on the plan) added in the early twentieth century and housing ancillary machinery powered by a continuation of the main line-shaft from the mill interior. Belt-drives from this shaft drove an external

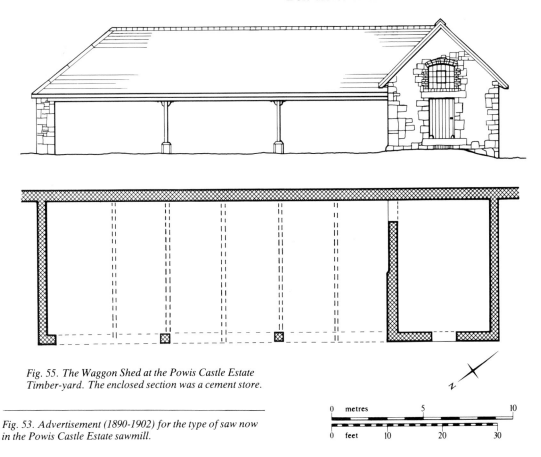

Fig. 55. The Waggon Shed at the Powis Castle Estate Timber-yard. The enclosed section was a cement store.

Fig. 53. Advertisement (1890-1902) for the type of saw now in the Powis Castle Estate sawmill.

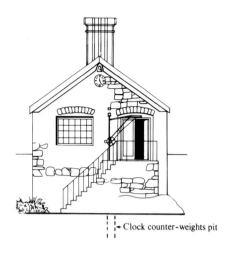

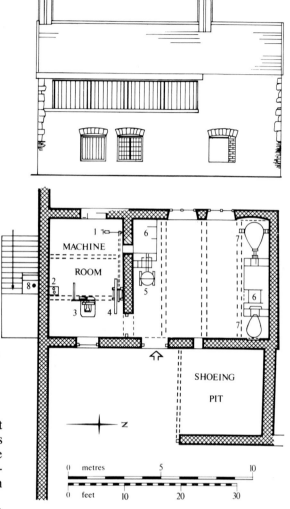

Fig. 56. This canalside building housed the Powis Castle Estate Forester's Office (first floor, to the left of the steps), the timber-yard stores (with a bench behind the long range of windows) and a smithy on the ground floor. No. 1 was a lathe (now in the sawmill extension); No. 2 is the shaft for the clock counter-weights; No. 3 is a heavy-cutter; No. 4 was a large wheel (now set against a wall) for manually turning the lathe; No. 5 is a hearth bellows; Nos. 6 are the smithy hearths; Nos. 7 are two bellows for the large smithy hearth, and No. 8 is a hand-crane for hoisting stores to the first floor.

grindstone (that still survives) and an extant lathe in the body of the building, as well as machines that have now disappeared. The lathe was originally housed in the machine-shop of the smithy ('5' on the plan) and driven by hand.[33]

To the east of this are lean-to sheds against the yard wall which in 1904 consisted of four bays—the first housed cord-wood, the second chopped wood, and the third and fourth was a general store-shed.

The green-sandstone enclosed building next to this ('3' on the plan) was built as a cement store in 1904 and adjoining this on the east is an open range of contemporary date with a roof supported by cast-iron columns.[34] This open range housed the estate timber-waggons and the waggoners lived in the fine range of estate houses built one kilometre down the road at Sarn-y-bryn-caled (see chapter four, Fig. 69). A line of sheds already stood on this site by 1840.[35]

Next to be considered is the flight of steps which leads over the old yard wall to the Head Forester's office and beyond this to the store ('5' on the plan); the smithy is on the ground floor of this building with an access from outside the yard and will be discussed separately at the end of this section. This building had

[33] Verbal information, Angus Eickhoff, the present blacksmith.
[34] Powis Castle Estate Drawings Collection (Powis Estate Timber-yard, Welshpool).
[35] Tithe map of Poole Parish, Upper Division, 1840 (National Library of Wales).

Fig. 57. The interior of the blacksmith's shop at the Powis Castle Estate Timber-yard. (Ironbridge)

already been added to the yard by 1840.[36] The front of the building houses the face, mechanism, counter-weights and the bell of a clock reputedly taken from the three-storey water-powered textile-mill that stood at Pool Quay.[37] This seems quite likely as the clock counter-weights have to be housed in an internal shaft sunk some 2m into the ground and must have been designed to fit a considerably higher building.

The estate yard store beyond the office retains its timber fittings. A large range of windows gives light from the canal elevation onto a long work-bench; in the racks behind were discovered the estate drawings collection (whilst the survey of the yard was being undertaken).

In 1899 a plan was produced to rebuild many of the estate timber-yard buildings in brick alongside the canal boundary wall of the yard.[38] Only the three-bay paint and stone store was completed at the north-west corner of the yard ('6' on the plan).

Beyond and to the south of the canal wharf gates is a wooden shed built against the yard wall. A long line of sheds on this side of the yard already existed in 1840.[39] The existing shed at this point originally housed the wheelwright's shop where the wheels of the timber-waggons were made and maintained (separate

---

[36] Ibid.

[37] Verbal information, Brian Barker, Head Forester of the Powis Castle Estate.

[38] Powis Castle Estate Drawings Collection, P.C. 47.

[39] Tithe Map of Poole Parish, Upper Division, 1840 (N.L.W.).

carpentry workshops exist in the upper floor of the sawmill). Pieces of wheel and wheel-patterns can still be found around the building.

The building at the end of this range ('7' on the plan) is, and always has been, the work-men's cook-house. It is a timber shed built against the stone boundary walls of the yard and with a cooking-hearth added laterally to the wall. A proposed rebuilding of the structure in brick in 1899 was never carried into effect.

On the south side of the main sawmill building is a creosoting tank which is being demolished. On this side of the water-wheel (and perhaps using a second water-wheel) was the Powis Estate bone-mill. In the lean-to shed against the main road are two large composite millstones. The dressing of these suggests that they are not corn-milling stones but may have been used in the bone-mill prior to its demolition in the late nineteenth century.[40]

D The General Trade

Warehouses

A class of survivals also very much in evidence along the line of the canal are the warehouses. In the 1840s and 1850s thirty warehouses were noted along the line of the canal; two were canal company warehouses at Welshpool. The Western Branch also had three storehouses (one including a 'shop'— probably a work-shop) along its length and the Eastern Branch another, and there were also three granaries alongside the canal. Canalside wharves also contained twenty-six 'sheds' (offices, stables and weighbridge houses were often noted separately) and wharfside houses often had 'outbuildings'; twenty-four buildings of this category existed. At least two of the ware-houses are reputed to have served the salt trade. It is difficult to know which of the warehouses held general merchandise rather than specialist goods; it is probable that most did. These stores are of great social significance. The 26 kilometres of the Swansea Canal contained only one known warehouse, and the same sparsity is true of the other canals of Glamorgan. A large and reasonably wealthy yeoman class lived on the rich fertile lands of Montgomeryshire and could afford the luxuries obtainable along the canal. The poor peasant

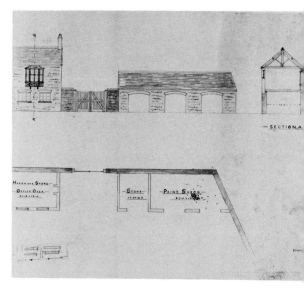

Fig. 58. In 1899 it was proposed to rebuild many of the Powis Estate timber-yard buildings in brick as this drawing shows. Only the stone and paint store were completed alongside the double-doors that lead onto the estate timber-wharf (sited on the canal towing-path). (Powis Castle Estate drawings collection 47.2)

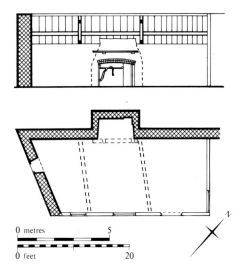

Fig. 59. The Workmen's Cook-house at the Powis Castle Estate Timber-yard. Its chimney intrudes on the canal towing-path.

farmers or 'werin' of the uplands, and the industrial workers of the valleys that closely bordered the canals of South Wales were not in position to afford such luxuries. The polite architecture that is much in evidence in the

76

Fig. 60. The former warehouse at Garthmyl being surveyed by students from the Ironbridge Institute. The low brick-built extension to the right was the warehouse-man's tiny dwelling whilst underneath was a weighbridge office. The top of the stone wall supporting the warehouse and cottage indicates the level of the canal wharf at the rear of the buildings.

surviving buildings and warehouses of the Montgomeryshire Canal contrasts sharply with the utilitarian nature of the great majority of Glamorgan canal buildings for much the same reasons. An indigenous tradition of handsome buildings is still much in evidence around Montgomeryshire whereas the poor lands of upland Glamorgan have failed to produce such a long-established tradition of good building or indeed the widespread wealth necessary for such a tradition to develop..

A substantial recorded stone-built warehouse still stands at Garthmyl (Fig. 60) and is now in use as a house. The canal terminated at Garthmyl between 1797 and the completion of the extension of the canal to Newtown in 1821, and the warehouse almost certainly dates from this period. The ground floor was supported on cast-iron columns as was, and is still, the case in the early nineteenth-century warehouse at Pentreheylin and in the late nineteenth-century maltings at Garthmyl and the Welshpool Canal Yard Warehouse. The Garthmyl Warehouse was constructed on top of a northwards extension of the stone wall that revetted several hundred metres of raised wharves alongside the terminal basin of the Montgomeryshire

[40] Personal communication, Owen Ward of the University of Bath.

Canal. This considerably eased the transfer of goods onto carts waiting at a lower level than the canal on the adjoining Newtown to Welshpool Road. A house was added to the warehouse in the early nineteenth century[41] and a weighbridge office was housed at road-level and under an extension of the house. There was also a weighbridge attached to the early nineteenth-century warehouse in the Welshpool Canal yard.

The Pentreheylin Warehouse at the southern end of the Vyrnwy Aqueduct (Fig. 63) may have been built by John Goolden of Maesbury Marsh in June 1824 or, possibly, by John James Turner of neighbouring Pentreheylin Hall in May 1831 or soon after.[42] The great similarity in style between this fairly ornate structure and Turner's adjoining Pentreheylin Hall and stables suggests that it was part of Turner's known plans to realise the commercial potential of his new estates. It was sited near a strategic centre of communications at the junction of the main Llanymynech-Welshpool road with the Vyrnwy Valley road up to Llansantffraid. The warehouse is locally reported to have housed Cheshire salt (and presumably some general merchandise), probably for the provisioning of the yeomen and gentry of the Vyrnwy Valley. In 1830 John Turner had bought Pentreheylin Hall and immediately began to sell off the oak trees on the land for use in the building of the Navy.[43] In May 1831 the field around the present warehouse was formally recognised by the canal company as a timber-wharf.[44]

The warehouse itself is a handsome two-storeyed building of lime rubble-stone with rusticated quoins and elaborate dressings to its several windows and doors. The corners of the warehouse have ornate projecting dripstones with an 'ogee' lower moulding. The two-storeyed symmetrical elevation towards the canal included a heated office on its lower floor. The barred upper two windows gave

---

[41] 'Shropshire Union Railways Plan, 1859'.
[42] Monts. Canal Report Bks., June 1824 & 23 May 1831.
[43] A. Spencer, P. Horsley and J. Cooper, *About the Montgomeryshire Canal.... Towpath Guide. 2. Welshpool to Llanymynech.* (Welshpool, 1981), 9.
[44] Monts. Canal Report Bks., 23 May 1831.

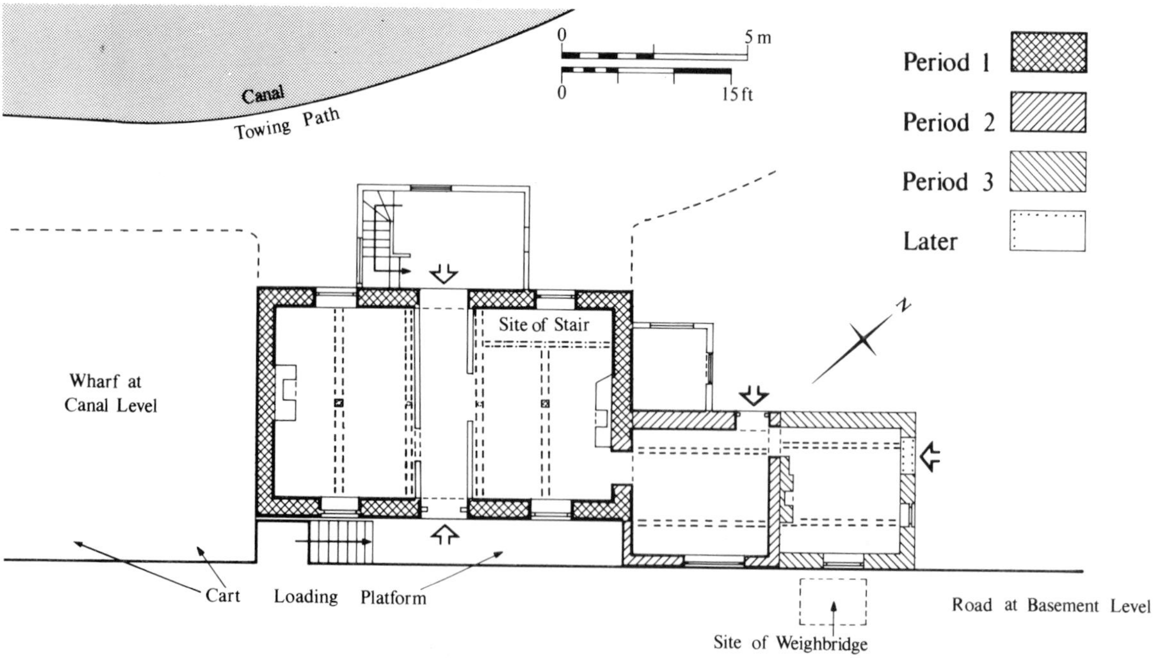

Fig. 61. The ground-floor plan of the Garthmyl Warehouse showing its strategic siting between the original terminus of the Montgomeryshire Canal and the Newtown to Welshpool Road at a lower level. A tiny warehouse-man's dwelling was later added to its north-eastern side.

Fig. 62. The Pentreheylin Warehouse (c. 1831) showing both the gable-end doors for receiving canal-borne goods and the landward first-floor door for transferring items to carts and waggons.

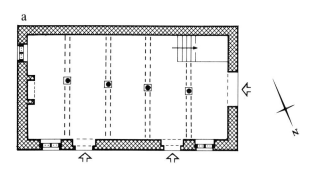

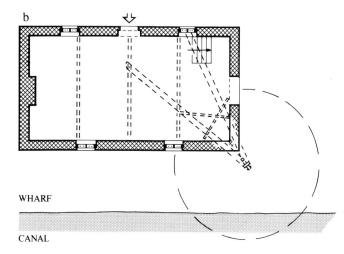

WHARF

CANAL

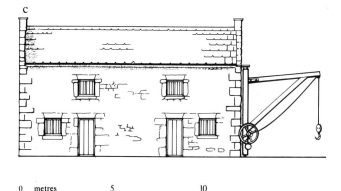

0   metres   5   10

0   feet   10   20   30

Fig. 63. The Pentreheylin Salt Warehouse, a handsome early nineteenth-century structure. 'a' shows the hearth and cast-iron columns on the ground-floor (some have now been moved out of position); 'b' shows the braced support for an external wall-crane, and 'c' shows the canalside elevation with barred windows and the crane restored.

onto a store for salt and possibly general merchandise. The planning of the warehouse takes advantage of the upward slope of the ground away from the canal to provide a central unloading door in the landward elevation that could facilitate the loading of carts parked immediately below its door sill. A large unloading door on the first-floor level is also a feature of the landward elevation of the late nineteenth-century canal company warehouse in the Welshpool Canal Yard (Fig. 64). The Pentreheylin Warehouse is the best of the early warehouses alongside the canal and forms a fine group with the adjoining aqueducts and early cast-iron bridges. It ought to be rescued from its present parlous condition as soon as practically possible.

Most, if not all, of the Montgomeryshire Canal warehouses had an integral crane. These were generally tied into the roof structure of the building in a somewhat similar fashion to foundry-cranes. The structures supporting these cranes can be seen in the drawings and photographs illustrating this section. The early nineteenth-century cranes were built of wood but the photographs of the Welshpool Aqueduct Warehouse (Figs. 1, 65) show how these were replaced by wrought-iron and steel structures in the later nineteenth century. The crane on the late nineteenth-century Canal Company Warehouse at Welshpool Yard could lift one ton.[45]

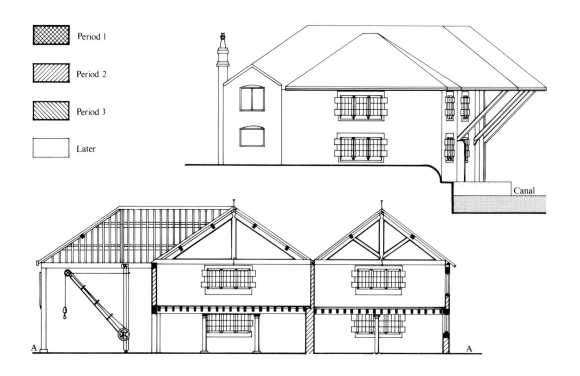

Period 1

Period 2

Period 3

Later

Canal

A   A

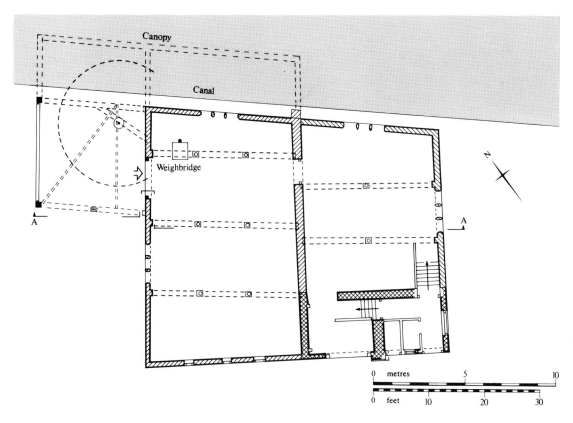

Canopy

Canal

Weighbridge

A

A

| 0 | metres | | 5 | | 10 |

| 0 | feet | 10 | 20 | 30 |

80

Fig. 65. The original wooden crane of the early nineteenth-century Welshpool Aqueduct Warehouse (Fig. 1) had been replaced by a more modern wrought-iron model by the beginning of the twentieth century when this photograph was taken.

Most of the Welshpool Yard Warehouse was built by the Canal Company in *c*.1880 as the marks on the interior woodwork show[46] and there is no evidence, as has been suggested, that it was built to serve the specific needs of the model Leighton Estate, even though built in the grand manner complete with mullioned windows. It was added to the early nineteenth-century warehouse in the canal yard at a time when the canal company was seeking to encourage the agricultural and general trade throughout its system by building stores and warehouses, such as that illustrated at Brynderwen (Fig. 109). By 1934, for instance, the Brynderwen warehouse and wharfside crane were leased by the London, Midland and Scottish Railway to Thomas Edwards Lewis of 'Goitre', Kerry—a 'Cattle Foods Agent'—for the sum of £8.10s.0d. per annum.[47] However, the earlier warehouses on the canal had certainly been concentrated in urban centres, for no less than twenty-four of the thirty warehouses known to have existed on the canal in the 1840s and 1850s were sited at the three inland ports of Welshpool, Garthmyl and Newtown.

However none of these warehouses is of a particularly large size compared to those of the larger urban centres located on some of the English waterways or to the huge dock warehouses found throughout the United Kingdom. The surviving Pease Warehouse in Hull (built in 1742), for example, is six storeys high[48], and the Goree Warehouses built in 1793 at Liverpool comprised seventeen separate properties, many of them thirteen storeys in height.[49] Cast-iron beams were not particularly well suited to the concentrated floor loadings of warehouses and timber beams continued in general use in the early nineteenth century on the Montgomeryshire Canal as elsewhere.

Fig. 64. The warehouse on the Town Wharf yard at Welshpool is the largest of those on the canal. The ground-floor plan shows the former reach of the now vanished one-ton capacity crane and the recently placed small weighbridge inside the loading doors which is similar to that sited here originally.

[45] Canal Agreements Book. Lease of Severn Street wharf and yard (Ellesmere).

[46] Personal communication, Graham Deamer.

[47] 'London and North Western Railway. Extracts from Agreements. Welshpool District No. 2., 1922-34' (British Waterways Board, Montgomeryshire Canal Office), entries transcribed by Graham Deamer.

[48] R. S. Fitzgerald, *Liverpool Road Station, Manchester. An historical and architectural survey* (Manchester, 1980), 31-2.

[49] N. Ritchie-Noakes, *Liverpool's Historic Waterfront. The world's first mercantile dock system* (London, 1984), 27-8.

Cast-iron columns of cruciform cross-section were used in the South Quay Warehouses at London Dock in 1810. In London, this, the earliest form of cast-iron column used in building, remained popular throughout the nineteenth century. Outside London, as in the Montgomeryshire Canal warehouses, it was supplanted by the hollow cylindrical cross-section with its higher resistance to any distortion under loading. Many of the large waterways warehouses of the north of England had structurally mature slender columns of cast-iron, such as those used alongside the Irwell Navigation at the New Botany Bay Warehouse at Manchester (built in 1824) and in warehouses built on the Calder Navigation at Wakefield and Sowerby Bridge.[50]. By 1906 the thickness of metal in the shaft of a hollow cast-iron column was usually one-tenth of its diameter.[51]. By contrast the rather dumpy cast-iron columns used in the building of the more modest structures alongside the Montgomeryshire Canal show no sign of any aspirations on the part of local founders or builders to equal these principles of more sophisticated construction.

Ancillary buildings and features

All trade of whatever type required boats to carry the goods, yards to build boats, dry-docks to maintain them and horses to provide motive power. The horses themselves required stables, hay stores, barns and smithies. All wharves usually required offices, weighbridges, cartsheds, and landing-quays or docks in addition to those facilities already mentioned. Of the four dry-docks known to have existed along the Montgomeryshire Canal no obvious traces remain. Forty-four stables were noted along the canal in the 1840s and 1850s but, as with all the statistics noted in this book, this should only be taken as a minimum number. Stables were not usually noted at the frequent lock-houses, yet in 1843, the lock-keeper at Carreghofa was sacked and part of the punishment enforced for his misdemeanours was that no compensation was to be paid for the stable block he had built.[52] At Burgedin locks a stable block complete with two stalls survives behind the lock-house. An interesting stable and two cartsheds with a hay store over them survived until recently alongside the site of

Newtown Basin and a barn survives in the Clafton Bridge Wharves complex.

There were at least four smithies alongside the canal, of which the most interesting today is that still operating adjacent to the Powis Estate Yard (Fig. 57). In the 1840s and 1850s there were at least eleven private offices, six weighing-machines and thirteen to fourteen docks along the canal. The likelihood of there being a multitude of weighbridges or 'weighing-machines' is clear from the first really accurate large-scale map, the 1st edition 1/2,500 Ordnance Survey of the early 1880s, which shows even small lime-wharves, such as one of those at Berriew, possessing two weighbridges to serve the trade generated by three limekilns. Nine of the docks on the canal were on the Western Branch and eight of these were at Newtown. Two or three of those on the Eastern Branch were converted from other features. This is in stark contrast with the canals of south Wales where much heavier traffic necessitated the main canal-lines being cleared of nearly all loading and unloading boats by the provision of frequent docks.

Feeder railways

The only early nineteenth-century horse-operated railway feeding traffic to the Montgomeryshire Canal was at Welshpool. This seems to have ceased functioning by the late nineteenth century when there were also narrow-gauge lines serving the canal company's Wern clay-pits and maintenance yard at Welshpool. A proposal to give the initially isolated Llanidloes to Newtown Railway of the later 1850s an outside link by extending the line through the centre of Newtown (over the Severn on a large masonry viaduct, through the site of a still extant wharf house at Newtown) and so connecting with the Montgomeryshire Canal Basin was never executed.[53] The 1861 through-railway link from Welshpool and Oswestry made the proposed continued use of the canal for these purposes unnecessary.

[50] R. S. Fitzgerald, *Liverpool Road Station*, 32-3.
[51] P. N. Hasluck, *Iron, Steel and Fireproof Construction* (London, 1906), 25.
[52] Monts. Canal Report Bks., 10 April 1843.
[53] 'Shropshire Union Railways Plans' of 1859.

4

The Canal Workforce
and their Housing

The low bulk-transport costs introduced into a previously relatively isolated rural area by the building of an arterial transport system, like the Montgomeryshire Canal, introduced an additional stratum of economic activity into the local hinterland of that new transport feature. This was serviced by an emergent class of non-agrarian workers whose homes were centred on the various wharves and dependent works built alongside the canal. Therefore, the housing considered in this chapter includes more than just a discussion of those dwellings built by the Montgomeryshire Canal Companies for their employees. The houses of that directly-employed labour force will be the first to be considered.

A The Canal Company.

On any canal the engineer/agent and the lock-keepers or lengthsmen were often housed in accommodation provided by the canal company, and this was the situation on the Montgomeryshire Canal.

All six locks on the Western Branch of the Montgomeryshire Canal had attached lock-keepers' houses. The earlier Eastern Branch had thirteen locks on ten sites. Five of these sites were served by resident lock-keepers from c.1819 and during the later nineteenth century two more were added; one of the additions of c. 1819 was to augment the Carreghofa toll-keeper's house (where the agile resident had had to previously fulfill two jobs) with a separate house for a new lock-keeper.[1] By the 1840s and 1850s only two of the six locks of the Western Branch had 'lock-offices' and the ten lock-sites of the Eastern Branch had seven lock-offices between them. In addition to the latter it is probable that the Carreghofa lock-keeper shared the extant toll-collector's hut of 1825[2] and the name 'Cabin Lock' seems to hint that an office may also have existed there. Other canal company houses were a pump-keeper's house at Newtown, a toll-collector's house at Carreghofa and an agent's house at Welshpool. Nearly all these attractive canal company houses are still lived in and only a couple are in ruins. Houses such as those at Burgedin and Carreghofa took advantage of changes in ground level to incorporate externally accessible storage basements. Both houses also still have pigsties visible in their lock-side gardens.

This density of lock-side residences contrasts sharply with the few canalside houses of the Swansea Canal in south Wales. Only a few lengthsmen and the canal engineer lived alongside the canal on that contemporary canal; the employees who staffed the lock-side huts there may have been drawn from the indigenous smallholding population of part-time farmers seeking to supplement their poor incomes. By contrast on the Dadfords' Glamorganshire Canal of 1790-94 many locks had two lock-houses apiece to ease the rigours of intense 24 hour working. However the solitary lock-keepers of the Montgomeryshire Canal reluctantly agreed to keep the locks open at night from 1 May 1837 for an extra *2s.6d!*[3]

The great majority of all workers on the Montgomeryshire Canal came from within Montgomeryshire and this applied to the lock-keepers as well. The 1841 census clearly shows this and gives some indication of the size and form of the households inhabiting these lock-keepers' houses.

B The Canal Traders

Some eighty-five houses and cottages were situated on the largely privately-owned wharves constructed alongside the Montgomeryshire Canal.[4] Sixty of these wharf-houses were situated in the waterway settlements that will be discussed more fully in chapter six. Most of these houses still survive.

---

[1] Monts. Canal Report Bks., 5 July 1819.
[2] Ibid., 26 February 1825.
[3] Ibid., 20 February 1837 and 1st May 1837.

Occupants of lock-keepers' houses in 1841:

Name	Occupants .... Age	Occupation	Place of birth
Dolfor Lock	George Lewis.....................29	'Lock Keeper'	Montgomeryshire
'Stone' Lock	Thomas Griffith 65	'Lock Keeper'	,,
(Rock Lock?)	Mary Griffith 55		,,
	Sussanah Griffith 80	'Independent'	,,
	Thomas Griffith 20	'Tailor'	,,
	William Morris 11	'Servant'	,,
Brithdir Lock	Thomas Jones 55	'Lock Keeper'	,,
	Mary Jones 55		,,

However not all lock-keepers lived in lock-keepers' houses:

'Dolfor'	James Thomas..................45 *and family*	'Lock Keeper'	*

Conversely not all houses at locks were lived in by lock-keepers as the 1841 census also illustrates.

'Freestone Lock'	William Evans 60	'Labourer'	Montgomeryshire
	Ann Evans 50		,,
	Mariah Evans................... 5		,,
	William Rubbothar ....4 months		,,

* *born outside Montgomeryshire.*

Newtown

By far the largest waterway settlement was at Newtown. It is difficult to define the exact size and distribution of the population of this settlement because the various sources of information give differing estimates of its extent. The 1845 map shows some forty-five houses built on the terminal wharves at Newtown whilst both the 1841 and 1881 census returns give the 'Canal Basin' as the address of no less than seventy-nine households. It may be that the census material includes more of the dwellings built on the wharves stretching out towards the Newtown Pump-house and also multi-occupation dwellings. Some of these multi-occupation dwellings were in the terrace of double-decker or 'stacked' houses of c. 1840 situated in four-storey buildings alongside the Llanllwchaearn Road. The lower cottages of two storeys originally opened onto the former canal level and the two storeys above them give onto the Llanllwchaearn Road. Such a multi-use of extremely precipitious sites for workers' housing is quite commonly found in south Wales and the West Riding of Yorkshire. However the rear elevations of these four-storey dwellings at Newtown have been com-pletely rebuilt so that any structural evidence for this former multiple occupation has dis-appeared.

The settlement at Newtown is worth some detailed consideration here because the range of canal-dependent jobs carried out by its occupants gives a good sample of the range of work fulfilled by those living on all the wharves alongside the Montgomeryshire Canal. However, the picture that emerges is compli-cated by the alternative employment available around the canal wharves. Even if the head of the household worked on a canal-wharf, it is

[4] All information in this chapter dated to sources in 1845, 1859, 1841, 1851, 1861, 1871 or 1881 are taken from the following: 1845- 'Shropshire Union Railway and Canal, Plan and Section of a proposed railway from Newtown in the County of Montgomery to the Grand Junction Railway at Crewe in the County Palatine of Chester with Branches, 1845' with Book of Reference (National Library of Wales); 1859- 'Shropshire Union Railways & Canal and London & North Western Railways, Plans and Sections of the Railway from Buttington to Welshpool and Newtown, November 1859', with Book of Reference (N.L.W.); 1841,1851,1861,1871,1881 refer to the census records of the area concerned available on microfilm at the Public Record Office (Portchester House) London; the National Library of Wales, Aberystwyth and Powys County Librar-ies, Newtown.

likely that his wife, sons (from the beginning of their teens), and daughters (from the middle of their teenage years) worked elsewhere.

This becomes quite a significant factor when it is considered that nineteenth-century households were often larger than modern households. The average household size in a dwelling built on the Montgomeryshire Canal Wharves at Newtown was some 3.5 persons in 1841 and 4.4 persons by 1881. When the canal basin was built, a small water-powered woollen-mill already existed alongside the site. The canal itself attracted a second woollen-factory, this time steam-driven and fed with coal brought along the adjacent canal. Also built alongside the canal at Newtown was an iron foundry which would have had its iron and coke supplies brought in along the canal. The workers in these canal-dependent works have not been included in the following lists of canal workers. The number of workers employed in the woollen industry increased dramatically throughout the later nineteenth century at the same time as railway competition resulted in a decline in the number of canal workers. In 1841 there were 280 people living at the 'Canal Basin'; of these about l09 may have been heads of households or their dependents reliant on income derived from work at the canal wharves. In 1881 the population living on the canal wharves had reached 346 but the number of those dependent on the canal had gone down to only some 59—some 15% of the people living at the canal basin.

At the time of the 1841 census there were thirty-one canal-trade workers living around the terminal canal basin. All but four were born locally or in neighbouring parts of Montgomeryshire; two of the six coal merchants and the one boat-builder and one rope-maker were born elsewhere. The most numerous class of canal employee consisted of the nine boatmen (at least three more lived in the adjoining area called the 'Ruins' in Llanllwchaearn). There were also six coal-merchants, three carpenters, two clerks, two boat-builders (one an apprentice), two 'lime men' (one also a farmer), one lime and coal agent, one 'labourer at lime' and one lime-burner, one 'clerk per lime', one timber merchant, one 'carrier by canal' and one rope-maker. Several of the twenty-four labourers listed would also have worked on the canal wharves. In fact the 1851 census is more explicit on this point. There were then twelve labourers living at the canal basin and for a few pages of the census returns the enumerator detailed their occupations more precisely so that five of the twelve labourers were described as 'labourers at lime works'. The place of employment of the one engineer living at the basin is more obscure.

The contrasts between the number and type of canal workers recorded in the 1881 census (twelve) and the 1841 census (thirty-one) vividly illustrates the great decline in the fortunes of trade on the Montgomeryshire Canal. The only apparent exception is in the number of 'timber fillers' living at the Newtown Basin; there were three living there in 1881 whereas none had been recorded in 1841. Perhaps the trade in the export of Montgomeryshire oak was still growing. However 'timber fillers' are very likely to have been recorded as 'labourers' in the other censuses. The number of boatmen had definitely declined markedly from the nine recorded living at the basin in 1841: there were only four recorded in 1881, and the relatively recent nature of the general decline in trade is perhaps indicated by the two *late* boatmen living at the basin. The most surprising apparent absence in 1881 is the lack of anyone involved in the operation of the twenty-two limekilns built around the basin. In 1841 there had been five workers specifically mentioned as working in the lime trade and there is no doubt that some of the large number of twenty-three 'labourers' living at the canal basin in 1841 were also employed on the huge number of kilns. However, in 1881 there were only some nine general labourers at the wharves who might also have done some work at the limekilns.

A new category of worker not mentioned in 1841 was the one 'canal wharehouseman' noted in 1881; the 'warehouse woman' and 'warehouse girl' noted in the 1881 census are quite likely to have been employed in one of the textile mills bordering the canal basin. The number of coal-merchants living near the canal had diminished by half from the six who had been living at the canal basin in 1841. The Shropshire Union Canal Company had an 'agent' living at the basin in 1881, but the two 'commercial clerks' probably served the woollen trade then burgeoning alongside the basin at Newtown. What had started off as a new and distinct suburb of Newtown, brought into existence by the employment opportunities provided by the canal, had by the end of the nineteenth century become one of several areas of Newtown providing labour for the centre of the woollen industry in Wales.

However, it would be a mistake to suppose that all canal-trade workers lived alongside the waterway or that all canalside cottages were occupied by people involved in the trade of the canal even in the early nineteenth century. The canal was only one component in a closely inter-linked and interdependent nineteenth-century landscape.

Even in the hey-day of the Newtown Canal Settlement, some of the canal-workers and merchants lived at a distance. In 1841 one of the coal-merchants on the canal lived in the main woollen-workers suburb at Penygloddfa and at least one of the boatmen lived in the more rural Hen-didley area. Seventy-nine year old 'Civil Engineer' John Williams, who had finished supervising the construction of the Montgomeryshire Canal to Newtown twenty years before, was then living at Caepant, and at least one timber-merchant lived elsewhere in the town. There was a close correlation between innkeepers and the operators of wharves at Newtown, and in 1851 Samuel Owen of the Lion Inn on Canal Road was noted in the census as an 'Inn Keeper and Timber Merchant employing eight men'.

Welshpool

A similar picture of a settlement housing a population in fairly mixed employment emerges at Welshpool. Severn Street was the thoroughfare leading from the main crossroads at Welshpool to the public canal-wharf. Some canal-workers lived on that road, as might be expected; they were a wharfinger and a boat-builder (twenty-one year old Richard Jones). David Hughes, 'Lime Burner', lived at Holly Cottage alongside his six canalside kilns on the Salop Road—some 550m from the centre of town. However, some of the canal-workers not resident on the canal wharves did live at some distance from the waterway. One wharfinger, John Williams, and a boatman, Thomas Pake, lived in their houses near St. Mary's Church, 250m from the nearest section of canal.

The cottages on Welshpool Canal Wharf (Fig. 94), somewhat contrary to appearances, were not always residences, and the occupants of two of the three cottages lived in by 1851 appear to have had only tenuous business connections with the canal (see chapter six for more details). In addition, the occupant of 'Canal Cottage, Severn Street' at the time of both the 1851 and 1861 censuses was Evan Evans, a septuagenarian wood-turner. Somewhat surprisingly this seems to suggest that the lock cottage at Welshpool was not occupied by a lock-keeper. In the 1861 census the two heads of household resident at the wharf were Jane Williams (a boatman's wife—thirty-eight years old with three children and a lodger living in) and Kate Roberts (a stone-mason's wife—fifty-five years old with three children living in).

Garthmyl

Garthmyl was the terminus of the Montgomeryshire Canal from 1797 until 1819-21, and even when the canal was extended to Newtown it still continued to grow and develop as an inland port. The resulting complex of wharves, buildings and limekilns will be discussed in chapter six.

In 1841 there were only six houses specified as being at Garthmyl besides the Nag's Head Inn. There were twelve wage-earners in these houses, a majority of whom seem *not* to have worked on the canal or in any closely connected trade. However, two-thirds of the six heads of household were probably employed in the canal trade. These consisted of one lime-dealer, a lime-burner and two labourers. The household of the lime-dealer was as follows:

Occupants	Age	Occupation	Place of birth
Mary Davies	45	'Limedealer'	Montgomeryshire
Two children, two servants, two lodgers and a nurse			
Edward Hughes	30	'Limedealer'	Montgomeryshire
Wife and lodger			

Edward Hughes was one of two Garthmyl traders who went bankrupt in the 1840s but in 1840 he was still the possessor of a large part of the port.[5] He occupied all three coal wharves opposite the Nag's Head (Fig. 85). The warehouse, its adjacent wharves and the southern Garthmyl kiln-bank were all his business property.

In 1859 it was recorded that Mary Davies was in possession of the fourth of the several wharves north of the southerly bridge at Garthmyl, the field and saw-pit to the north of the southern limekiln-bank, the yard to the north of the junction of the main Welshpool to Newtown Road, with the road leading to the northerly bridge at Garthmyl, and the terrace of four houses to the west of that bridge.

At the northern end of Garthmyl was the outlying kiln-bank at Redgate. Both households there seem to have been directly concerned with the operation of the adjoining kiln-bank:

Occupants	Age	Occupation	Place of birth
John Hughes	57	'Labourer'	Montgomeryshire
Wife			
Jonathan Meredith	57	'Lime burner'	Montgomeryshire

It is hard to evaluate other evidence for Garthmyl: the township of Garthmyl in the parish of Berriew covered quite a large area. However the 'Chain Bridge' at Garthmyl is the southerly of the two stone-arched bridges still standing there and in 1841 at 'Chain' were living:

Occupants	Age	Occupation	Place of birth
Edward Hammonds	50	'Lock-keeper'	Montgomeryshire
Wife and four children			

Hammonds may have been the lengthsman in charge of the busy section of canal at Garthmyl for the nearest locks were at Berriew village to the north and at Brynderwen some 4km to the south-west. The latter had its own lock-keeper's cottage.

An entry under the heading 'office' given between those for Redgate and Garthmyl also has the following living there:

Occupants	Age	Occupation	Place of birth
John Owen	50	'Labourer'	Montgomeryshire
Wife and daughter			

Corfield's Green is the area immediately west of the northerly of the stone-arched bridges at Garthmyl and was the site of a number of cottages including a terrace of four houses alongside the canal. In 1841 at Corfield's Green lived:

Occupants	Age	Occupation	Place of birth
John Bevan	49	'Lime burner'	Montgomeryshire
Wife and three children			

This then was the third most populous of the canal settlements. The other main waterways settlement to be discussed in chapter six is that at Pool Quay which was largely associated with the Severn River Navigation. In the 1841 census only one boatman was resident near there, and he lived at the scattered hillside settlement of 'Rhallt' on the valleyside above Buttington canal wharf.

Belan

The present limekiln cottages (Fig. 66) adjacent to Belan Locks and Limekilns were probably built some time after 1859. Earlier cottages are shown on the same site but to a different plan-form. These cottages were built on Powis Castle Estate land and their deliber-ately picturesque appearance may owe much to their being on one of the routes to the castle.

In 1840 the operator of the Belan Limekilns, a John Franks, was living in the south-western cottage.

The 1851 census returns recorded three 'Limekilns Cottages' by name, one at that time was uninhabited and the rest were lived in by:

Occupants	Age	Occupation	Place of birth
1. Thomas Humphreys	40	'Lime Burner'	Montgomeryshire
Wife and mother-in-law (born Newport, Shropshire) and four children (one son a 13 year old agricultural labourer) and a lodger.			
John Davies	23	'Lime Burner's Labourer'	,,
2. Thomas Jones	75	'Retired Agricultural	,,
Wife and daughter ('Dress-maker').		Labourer'	
3. Richard Jones	33	'Canal Boatman'	,,
Two daughters and three servants.			
Richard Samuel	14	'Boatman'	,,

The 1859 plan shows that Humphreys lived in the south-western and Richard Jones at the north-eastern cottages. All the inhabitants were born in Montgomeryshire except where otherwise stated.

In the 1861 census the inhabitants of the 'Limekiln Cottages' were:

1. Thomas Humphreys	51	'Lime Burner'	Montgomeryshire
Wife, daughter ('Dress-maker') and two sons ('Agricultural Labourer' and 'Boot Maker')			
Thomas Humphreys	24	'Lime Burner'	,,
2. John Evans	45	'Agricultural Labourer'	,,
Two children and father-in-law ('Agricultural Labourer')			
3. David Williams	26	'Agricultural Labourer'	,,
Wife and two children			

In 1859 John Evans was the next-door neighbour of Thomas Humphreys at the south-western end of the cottages. The 1871 and 1881 census returns are less clear but the seventy-year old lime-burner Thomas Humphreys and his lime-burner son Thomas were still living in Limekiln Cottages in 1881.

A track formerly led from the limekilns at Belan towards the Powis Castle Estate home-farm at Coed-y-dinas (Fig. 38), and it seems highly likely that most of the inhabitants of Limekiln Cottages, in the later nineteenth-century at any rate, were employed as agricultural labourers based at the home-farm. The cottages built at Belan kilns and locks (some 700m from Coed-y-dinas) might have been sited there because this was an industrial site on the estate where houses could be constructed without intruding on views of the

[5] Tithe map and schedule of Berriew Parish, 1840 (N.L.W) and A. Spencer, P. Horsley and J. Cooper, *About the Montgomeryshire Canal....Towpath Guide. 3. Welshpool to Garthmyl* (Welshpool, 1981),9.

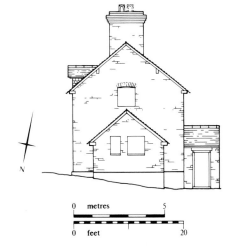
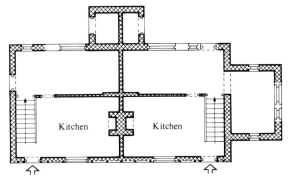

Fig. 66. Powis Castle Estate Housing at the Belan Limekilns. A 'veneer' of timber framing was added to new and improved brick-built late nineteenth-century accommodation for agricultural workers, lime-burners and boatmen of fairly humble status.

surrounding fields. Nevertheless it was also estate policy both to promote industrial growth and to improve the estate lands so that it can only have made sense to provide any accommodation necessary for workers to operate the kilns and the boat traffic generated by them.

Another house stood at the north end of the limekilns and here lived:

Occupants	Age	Occupation	Place of birth
John Thomas............................76		'Canal Lock Keeper'	Montgomeryshire
Daughter ('Dress-maker'), son-in-law ('Joiner') and three grand children (one of whom was a shoemaker)			

According to the 1859 canal map they shared the occupation of this building (now demolished) with the William Johnes who operated the adjacent limekilns and used the small garden surrounding the house. If he too had a family this house must have been rather crowded.

The 1859 map also shows a 'lock house' situated on the 'island' between the lock-chamber and by-pass at the Belan upper lock. This must have been replaced in the late nineteenth century by the lock-keeper's cottage that stands today alongside the lower lock at Belan. In 1840 the earlier lock house was described as the 'Office at Belan Kilns'.[6] The 1851 census records that living at the 'Lime-kilns Office' were:

Occupants	Age	Occupation	Place of birth
John Thomas............................41		'Canal Lock Keeper'	Montgomeryshire
Wife and three children			

This John Thomas was presumably the son of the elder John Thomas who may have been retired or at least semi-retired by this date. Jobs with the Montgomeryshire Canal Company may, in effect, have been hereditary. The younger John Thomas eventually had six children living in his lock-keeper's cottage and was still working when he was aged seventy-one in 1881.

Not all the people working at the limekilns lived in adjoining houses for the 1871 census of the surrounding area also records boatdwellers living at 'Little Vyrniew':

Occupants	Age	Occupation	Place of birth
Francis Evans 62		'Lime Burner'	Montgomeryshire
Wife			

Boat dwellers

Of considerable interest are the two boats with resident crews recorded at Belan in the 1851 census. Complete families living on boats only became the general rule after railway competition had seriously eroded the prosperity of canals and their dependent workers in the latter part of the nineteenth century. The number of canal boatmen living in houses at the Newtown basin is indicative of their land-bound domesticity in the pre-railway age. The frequent mention of the head of a household in mid nineteenth-century censuses as a 'boatman's wife' is also indicative of Montgomeryshire boatmen being away for long trips while their families remained at home. On a 'Canal Boat' at Belan in 1851 were:

Occupants	Age	Occupation	Place of birth
Edward Griffiths 18		'Canal Boatman'	Montgomeryshire (Welshpool)
Thomas Morgan........................13		'Servant'	Montgomeryshire (Guilsfield)

This entry upholds the generally accepted picture; indeed, railway competition did not begin to affect the canal's monopoly of cheap bulk carriage along the Severn Valley until the early 1860s. However the following entry given under the heading 'Belan' (next to that for 'Spout House') in 1851 does not appear to follow the general trend:

Occupants	Age	Occupation	Place of birth
Sarah Humphreys *Widow*...........39		'Canal Boat Woman'	Montgomeryshire (Llanbrynmair)
David Humphrys......................15		'Canal Boatman'	Montgomeryshire (Berriew)
John Humphreys......................11		'Canal Boatman'	Montgomeryshire (Berriew)
Mary Humphreys 6			Montgomeryshire (Berriew)
'Lives with them in the the Boat'			

The last comment is very revealing. It may have been the hardships of widowhood that drove Sarah Humphreys and her family from their earlier Berriew home.

[6] Tithe map and schedule of Poole Parish, Upper Division, 1840 (N.L.W.).

The Powis Castle Estate Timber-yard cottages.

Fig. 67. Cottages for workers at the Powis Castle Estate Smithy and Timber-yard. The gabled block to the right is an extension of 1880. (Ironbridge)

The architectural pretension of the Tudor-style chimney stacks and gothic porch of the timber-yard cottages (Fig. 67) indicate, as at Belan, that these houses were products of the polite architectural ideals of the Powis Castle Estate. The smithy behind the cottages (Fig. 57) serviced the timber-yard that processed huge amounts of oak either being shipped on the canal or being cut into serviceable timber for use on the estate and the surrounding area.

In 1841 one of the cottages (the 1859 map is unclear which, but probably the northern one) was lived in by:

Occupants	Age	Occupation	Place of birth
John Bullock	41	'Blacksmith'	*
William Bullock	32	'Blacksmith'	*
Wife			
Richard Bullock	15	'Blacksmith'	*
and six other children			

By 1881 one of William Bullock's sons had obviously taken over his father's work and tenancy:

James Bullock	41	'Blacksmith'	Montgomeryshire (Welshpool)
Wife, four children and two visitors			

The other cottage at this date was lived in by:

James Roberts	22	'Waggoner'	Montgomeryshire (Forden)

* born outside Montgomeryshire

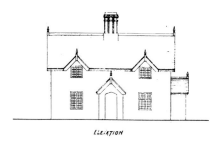

ELEVATION

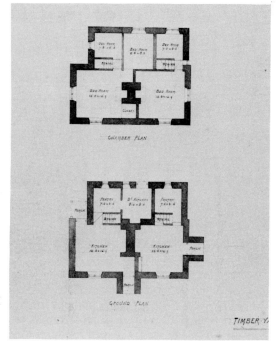

CHAMBER PLAN

GROUND PLAN

TIMBER Y.

Fig. 68. Estate plan of the canalside cottages for workers at the Powis Castle Estate Timber-yard, before the smaller of these two dwellings was extended in 1880. They provided comfortable accommodation when judged by contemporary local standards. (Powis Castle Estate drawings collection 182.1)

Roberts must have been one of the waggoners hauling the very large amounts of trees and wood to and from the timberyard. A three-bay waggon-shed at the yard (Fig. 55) indicates the scale of the traffic. The traffic on the Powis Castle Estate in timber to and from the yard, in farm products to and from Coed-y-dinas, and in lime from the Belan Kilns must have been so large by the later nineteenth century that a new settlement of waggoners' houses was built on a site between all three installations at Sarn-y-bryn-caled (literally 'the hard hill causeway').

Sarn-y-bryn-caled

This attractive settlement is sited on the main Welshpool to Newtown road some 2.4km south of Welshpool, adjoining the turning leading to the large bank of limekilns at Belan.

In the early nineteenth century the turnpike roads from Welshpool to Newtown and to Church Stoke divided at this point and a triangle of roads was created (on Powis Castle Estate lands). Two turnpike gates were built— 'the Brandyshop Gate' on the Church Stoke road and 'the Sarnybryncaled Gate' next to Belan Limekilns Lane on the Newtown road (both toll-gate houses still exist). This was the nucleus of a new settlement for estate workers.

By 1840 three cottages had been built facing the triangle of land between the turnpike roads.[7] The low semi-detached stone-built cottages at the north-eastern end of the present row may be the earliest. The only brick used in their good quality construction is on the rear wall of their back wings and in the chimneys. There are elegant Tudor-style drip-mouldings constructed of timber above the windows and doors. In 1881 these cottages were lived in by the Powis Castle Estate bailiff and the estate cowman. A large detached house also stood next to the modest brick toll-gate by 1840. This has a front wall of green-sandstone masonry but side and rear walls of red brick. In 1881 this was the estate groom's house. The land between these dwellings was used for gardens by the bailiff and cowman (or their predecessors) until four terraced houses were constructed there between 1851 and 1861. By 1871 two more had been added. According to the 1881 plan of the settlement (Fig. 69) five of these six houses were for occupation by waggoners.[8] In 1881 two similar houses were built to fill the remaining gap southwards to the groom's house. The waggoners' houses, like the earlier groom's house, have stone fronts and brick side and rear walls.

Information on the domestic water supply available for workers' housing alongside and near the canal is very limited. In chapter two it has been mentioned that there were agreements for people to obtain their drinking water

[7] Ibid.
[8] 1881 plan of Sarn-y-bryn-caled in the Powis Castle Estate drawings collection 218 (Powis Castle Estate Timber-yard). One house was for occupation by a 'pigman'.

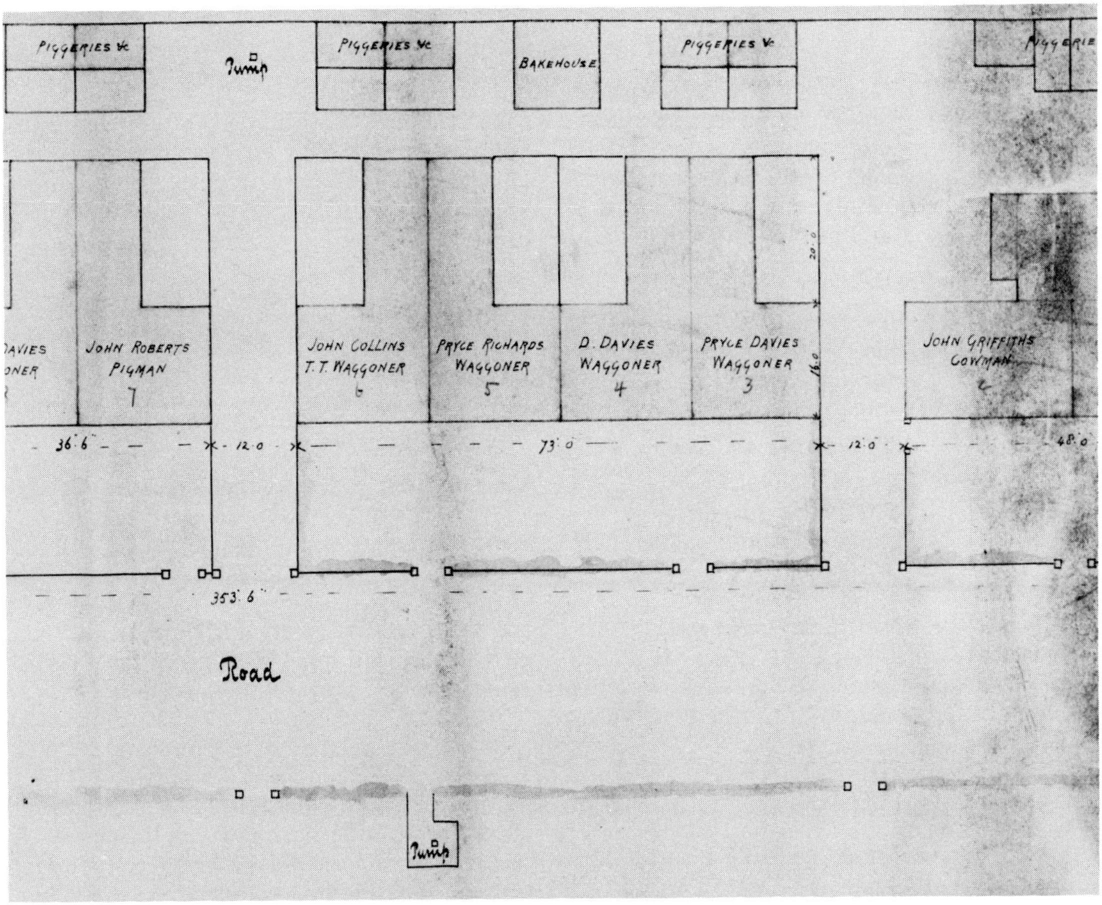

PIGGERIES &c
Pump
PIGGERIES &c
BAKEHOUSE
PIGGERIES &c
JOHN ROBERTS
PIGMAN
7
JOHN COLLINS
T.T. WAGGONER
6
PRYCE RICHARDS
WAGGONER
5
D. DAVIES
WAGGONER
4
PRYCE DAVIES
WAGGONER
3
JOHN GRIFFITHS
COWMAN
2
20.0
16.0
36'6"
12.0
73'0"
12'0"
48'0
353'6"
Road
Pump

Fig. 69. Plan of some of the Powis Castle Estate waggoners' cottages at Sarn-y-bryn-caled. The cottages lay between the Belan limekilns, the Powis Estate timber-yard and the estate home-farm at Coed-y-dinas. (Powis Castle Estate drawings collection 218)

from the canal; presumably many if not all canal workers would have done this without formal permission by 1881. At Sarn-y-bryn-caled (400m from the canal) there were two hand-pumps available for the use of the eleven households of Powis Castle Estate workers. The earlier pump was probably located on the far side of the Welshpool to Newtown road, the later between the piggeries (&c.!) at the rear of the waggoners' housing. The purity of that water in that situation can only be imagined. An additional pump for the use of the occupant of the toll-house still remains alongside Belan Limekiln Lane.

Other canal-workers' housing

Many other small settlements of canal workers existed up and down the canal especially where there were limekilns. One such was Tan-y-fron or 'Fron' (2km south-west of Garthmyl) where in 1841 lived:

Occupants	*Age*	*Occupation*	*Place of birth*
Richard Lewis	40	'Boatman'	Montgomeryshire
Wife and six children			

The evocatively named Bunkers Hill Bridge at Tan-y-fron (No. 137) was also near the similarly named residence of:

Richard Parry	30	'Limeburner'	Montgomeryshire
Wife, three children and a 71 year old pauper			

However appearances can be deceptive and not all canalside settlements had a preponderance of canal workers. Such was the case with the small collection of houses alongside the canal at Buttington limekilns (mentioned in chapter three). The house next to the limekilns was presumably built for the operator of the kilns and was certainly occupied by successive lime-burners throughout the nineteenth century:

Date	Occupants	Age	Occupation	Place of birth
1841	Bryce Jones 29		'Lime Man'	Montgomeryshire
	Mary Jones 64			,,
	Harding Jones 35		'Blacksmith'	,,
1871	William Owen 53		'Lime Burner'	Montgomeryshire (Berriew)
	Wife and two children			
1881	Samuel Benyon................51		'Lime Burner'	Montgomeryshire (Berriew)
	Wife and four children			
	Samuel Edwards 16		'Labourer Lime Burner'	Montgomeryshire (Llanfair)
	Stepson			

However, the four 'Canal Cottages' on the far side of the canal appear not to have had any strong connection with the limekilns or with the canal trade generally. In 1871 they were occupied by a labourer, a bricklayer and two platelayers, and in 1881 the cottages were mainly occupied by railway workers.

C The Canal Houses

The accompanying table gives an idea of the development of nineteenth-century workers' housing on and around the Montgomeryshire Canal and how this compared with houses built elsewhere.

House size and the numbers of ground-floor rooms and of bedrooms provided in a dwelling obviously considerably affected the quality of life of the working-class family of the period. It can be shown from this and other studies of workers' housing in the Industrial Revolution that these factors were largely dependent on the background of the house builder rather than the locality of building which was so much more important in the vernacular architecture of the post-medieval but pre-industrial period.

Table of Canal-trade and Comparable Housing

Name	Date	Builder	Internal Floor Area	Ground-floor Rooms	Bed-rooms	Grid Reference
a. Lock-keepers' houses						
1. Cilfynydd Lock Cottage	c.1794	Glamorganshire Canal Company	55.2m²	3	2	ST 0850 9310
2. Goetre-coed Lock Cottage	c.1794	Glamorganshire Canal Company	52m²	2	3	ST 0902 9599
3. Y Glyndrys Lock Cottage	c.1794	Glamorganshire Canal Company	50.6m²	2	3	SO 0515 0467
4. Tŷ-banc, Lengthman's Cottage	c.1796	Neath Canal Company	57.4m²	2	2	SN 8300 0325
5. Cae'r-lan, Lengthman's Cottage	1810	Swansea Canal Company	49.2m²	2	2	SN 8028 1212
6. Aber-fan Lock Cottage	c.1830?	Glamorganshire Canal Company	78.6m²	2	2	ST 0729 9910
7. Pool Quay Lock Cottage	c.1820	Montgomeryshire Canal Company Eastern Branch	58.2m²	2	3	SJ 2561 1059
8. Pool Quay Cottage extended	b.1845	Montgomeryshire Canal Company Eastern Branch	64.7m²	3	2	SJ 2561 1059

Name	Date	Builder	Internal Floor Area	Ground-floor Rooms	Bed-rooms	Grid-Reference
9. No. 2 Welshpool Canal Wharf	c.1870	Montgomeryshire Canal Company Eastern Branch	53m^2	2	2	SJ 2261 0738

b. Model housing plans and estate housing built on land adjoining the Montgomeryshire Canal.

Name	Date	Builder	Internal Floor Area	Ground-floor Rooms	Bed-rooms	Grid-Reference
10. No. 1 Timber Yard Cottages	c.1830	Powis Castle Estate	56m^2	3	3	SJ 2217 0592
11. No. 2 Timber Yard Cottages	c.1830	Powis Castle Estate	41.8m^2	2	2	SJ 2217 0593
12. Sarn-y-bryn-caled Groom's House	Before 1840	Powis Castle Estate	95.6m^2	3	3	SJ 2193 0505
13. Sarn-y-bryn-caled Waggoners' Cottage	1851–1861	Powis Castle Estate	71.6m^2	2	2	SJ 2197 0510
14. Upper Cottages Garthmyl	1860	Garthmyl Hall Estate	52.4m^2	3	3	SO 1862 9852
15. Model Labourers Cottage, No. 4	1872	Inclosure Office	58.1m^2	3	3	
16. Model Labourers Cottage, No. 6A	1879	Inclosure Office	74.3m^2	3 (incl. bedroom)	3 (1 on g. floor)	
17. Belan Limekiln Cottages	After 1859	Powis Castle Estate	69.5m^2	2 —	3	SJ 2168 0525
18. No. 2 Timber Yard Cottages. Extended	1881	Powis Castle Estate	72.6m^2	3	3	SJ 2217 0593

c. Private traders and manufacturers workers' housing

Name	Date	Builder	Internal Floor Area	Ground-floor Rooms	Bed-rooms	Grid-Reference
19. Bunkers Hill, Bersham (Iron Industry)	After 1785	John Wilkinson	25.5m^2	2	on g. floor	SJ 3120 4926
20. Bunkers Row, Blaenafon (Iron Industry)	1792	—	21.4m^2	2	2	SO 2521 0943
21. Ladywell Street Newtown (Woollen Industry)	c.1810	—	47.4m^2	1	2	SO 1085 9144
22. Cnel Bach Blaen-gwrach (Colliery Wharf)	c.1817	Cwmgwrach Colliery Company	49.5m^2	2	2	SN 8545 0459
23. 2-5 Chapel Street Penygloddfa, Newtown (Woollen Industry)	Early nineteenth century	—	34.4m^2	1	2	SO 1078 9192
24. Pump Court, Commercial Street, Penygloddfa, Newtown, (Woollen Industry)	1825–1830	—	26.4m^2	1	1	SO 1074 9191
25. Warehouse Cottage Garthmyl (General Warehouse)	c.1830	A canal trader	11.9m^2	1	beds on g. floor	SO 1943 9922
26. 65-73 Plymouth Street Merthyr Tydfil (Iron Industry)	Early nineteenth century	—	13.3m^2	1	beds on g. floor	SO 0537 0546
27. 6-9 Union Street Penygloddfa, Newtown (Woollen Industry)	1830–1833	John Matthews	33m^2	1	1	SO 1069 9198
28. Warehouse Cottage Garthmyl (Extended General Warehouse)	Before 1845	—	21.3m^2	2	beds on g. floor	SO 1943 9922

Name	Date	Builder	Internal Floor Area	Ground-floor-Rooms	Bed-rooms	Grid Reference
29. Pen-y-bryn, Cwmystwyth (Lead Mining)	c.1855	—	35.3m^2	2	1	SN 8292 7535
30. 1-4 Union Street Penygloddfa, Newtown (Woollen Industry)	1835–1841	—	23m^2	1	1	SO 1065 9196

d. Pre-canal housing

Name	Date	Builder	Internal Floor Area	Ground-floor-Rooms	Bed-rooms	Grid Reference
31. House No. 3 Barry	thirteenth century	—	46.5m^2	1	beds on g. floor	ST 1031 6719
32. House No. 2 Barry	late thirteenth century	—	21.7m^2	1	beds on g. floor	ST 1030 6730
33. House No. 1 Barry	thirteenth-fourteenth centuries	—	67m^2	3	beds on g. floor	ST 1027 6722
34. House No. 3 Merthyr Dyfan	thirteenth-fourteenth centuries	—	47.1m^2	1	beds on g. floor	ST 1171 6939
35. Old Cottage at Strata Florida	still standing in the nineteenth century	—	25.4m^2	1	beds on g. floor	
36. Rose Cottage Llandough	Later seventeenth century	—	61m^2	2	2	ST 1674 7320

Entries nos. 1, 14, 19, 20, 21, 23, 24, 26, 27, 28 and 29 are taken from information in J. B. Lowe, *Welsh Industrial Workers Housing 1775-1875* (Cardiff, 1977) and J. B. Lowe, *Welsh Country Workers Housing 1775-1875* (Cardiff 1985). Entries 31-34 are drawn from information in *An Inventory of the Ancient Monuments in Glamorgan, Volume III: Medieval Secular Monuments, part ii: Non-defensive* (Cardiff, 1982), 231-34. Entries 35-36 are drawn from information in *An Inventory of the Ancient Monuments in Glamorgan, Volume IV, part ii: The Farmhouses and Cottages* (1988).

Lock-keepers' houses

The first lock-keepers' houses on the earlier Eastern Branch of the canal may not date from before 1819 when the canal company's agent stated that, *'I am clearly of the opinion that unless there are some able stout men to look after and take care of the locks they will soon all be destroyed.'*[9] Certainly, the canal minutes indicate that something of a campaign of house building took place in the 1820s. Pool Quay lock-keeper's house (Fig. 70) may date from about this time and compares well in size with lock-keepers' houses built in the 1790s and shortly afterwards on other Welsh canals. All have internal floor areas of between 49 and 59 square metres. By 1845 the Pool Quay lock-keeper's house had been considerably enlarged by the addition of a lean-to extension and at 64.7 square metres was then much larger than the lock-keepers' houses on other Welsh canals (one exception on the Glamorganshire Canal is considered below), although the house created at Welshpool by the conversion of a salt-warehouse ('9' on the table) between 1851 and 1871 conformed to the size of the original canal houses built in the 1790s. Other Montgomery-shire Canal houses were extended in the same period. As already noted, this was a canal that had much greater provision for the housing of its employees than the Neath and Swansea Canals. The Glamorganshire Canal had a greater density of lock-keepers' dwellings than all these other canals, but out of the sample of four houses along the Glamorganshire Canal shown on the accompanying table three were in fact smaller than the Montgomeryshire Canal lock-keeper's house at Pool Quay. Con-

[9] A. Spencer, P. Horsley and J. Cooper, *About the Montgomeryshire Canal....Towpath Guide. 2. Welshpool to Llanymynech* (Welshpool, 1981), 5.

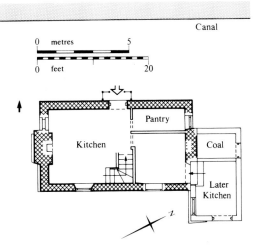

Fig. 70. Plan of the Pool Quay Lock-keeper's cottage. The Eastern Branch of the Montgomeryshire Canal built many more lock-keepers' cottages in 1819 and before the completion of the Western Branch in 1821, including this particular example which was enlarged again during the early nineteenth century to provide accommodation that was generous in comparison with that provided on other Welsh canals.

versely the Aber-fan lock-keeper's house on the Glamorganshire Canal at 78.6 square metres in area is the largest of all the Welsh lock-keepers' houses recorded. It may have been the residence of a more important lengthsman on that busier waterway for the houses of employees of a higher status (the engineer-managers) on the Neath, Swansea and Glamorganshire Canals were all double-pile dwellings twice the size of the houses of the ordinary lock-keepers.

The general uniformity in size of the Welsh canal companies' housing may well have been influenced by the common employment of two families of engineers during their construction. Thomas Dadford, father and son, and Thomas Sheasby, father and son, were together and sometimes individually responsible for the construction of the Glamorganshire, Monmouthshire, Montgomeryshire, Neath, Swansea, and Brecknock and Abergavenny Canals.

There were doubtless other factors determining the size of these dwellings. The majority of the Montgomeryshire Canal shareholders were the very wealthy landed gentry of the rich

Fig. 71. Pool Quay Lock-keeper's cottage.

Severn Valley farmlands and the surrounding area. They provided a considerable stock of housing for tenants, a good proportion of which was for workers engaged in the trade along the canal. Even if these estate houses did not influence the size of the canal company housing, it is highly probable that the high standard of design used in the model cottages of the local great estates did contribute to their pleasing appearance.

Mongomeryshire landed-estate housing

There is no doubt that the Mongomeryshire gentry took a paternalistic pride in providing housing for their tenants. The ornamental appearance of their workers' dwellings is clear evidence of this. The Limekiln Cottages at Belan have structurally superfluous timber-framed fronts in a stylistic tradition that was used well into the twentieth century by the Powis Castle Estate. The same estate used ornamental Tudor-style chimneys stacks on the estate timber-yard cottages and at Sarn-y-bryn-caled; features complemented by a gothic porch at the timber-yard and Tudor-style drip-mouldings (executed in timber) over the windows and doors at Sarn-y-bryn-caled. Additionally, in an age of brick-building in the later nineteenth century, the estate still maintained the use of green-sandstone ashlar masonry for the facades (but not the sides and rear) of its cottages at Sarn-y-bryn-caled.

The local use of ornamentation on tenants' housing was not confined to the large landed estates. The canal company's houses and warehouses, such as those built at Pool Quay (Fig. 71) and Welshpool (Fig. 94), had corbel tables of alternately projecting bricks supporting the eaves. Another decorative feature was the elegant gabled timber porch that is so common in Montgomeryshire building and must have

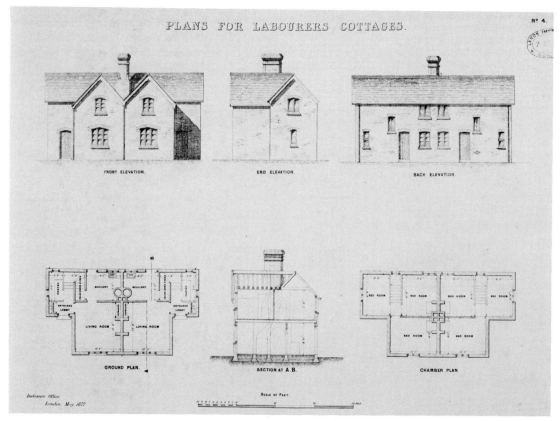

Fig. 72. The Powis Castle Estate drawings collection contains sheets of 'Inclosure Office' designs for the construction of model 'labourers' cottages. In fact the provision of housing on the estate matched or even exceeded the standards recommended in these plans which eventually reached the Powis Estate in 1891, nineteen years after the initial drawings were produced.

been produced in the local joiners' workshops, such as those on the canal wharves at Newtown and Welshpool. The use of these porches was not confined to the local landed estates; the canal company used a particularly elegant and larger timber-framed gabled porch with side-bays that can still be seen at Number 2 Canal Yard at Welshpool and on the Pool Quay Lock-keeper's House (Figs 71 & 94). They may well have been produced in the Welshpool Canal Maintenance yard by the company carpenter.

The estate houses show an interesting progression in size throughout the nineteenth century. The earliest houses shown on the table (entries 10 and 11) were built at the Powis Castle Estate Timber-yard in *c.* 1830, and the first of these at 56 square metres in area largely conforms in size to that of the lock-keepers' houses built in the 1790s along all the Welsh canals. The provision of three rooms on both

the ground and first floors is in fact superior to that made in contemporary canal company houses. Conversely cottage no. 2 at the Powis Estate timber-yard has a considerably smaller floor area at 41.8 square metres than any of the contemporary canal-workers' cottages and this may reflect a lower status for the occupant in the sharply hierarchical nature of contemporary society (the estate blacksmiths probably lived here). Certainly the near-contemporary Powis Estate groom's house was twice as large and this must say something about perceptions of status and the valuation of relative activities by contemporary aristocratic society. By the middle of the nineteenth century the accomodation for even fairly lowly workers had improved considerably. The Powis Estate waggoners' houses at Sarn-y-bryn-caled were begun to standard designs between 1851 and 1861 with an internal floor size of some 71.6 square metres. This was then larger than the extended

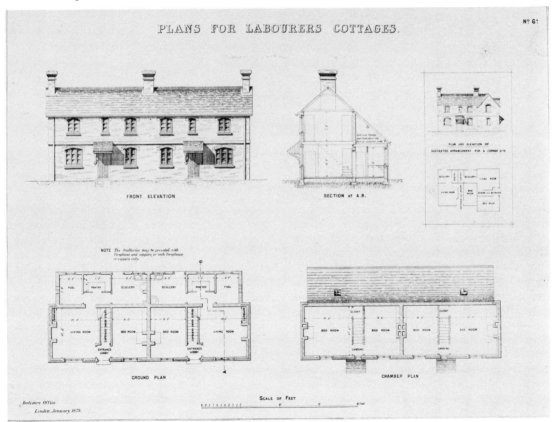

Fig. 73. Plans for model 'labourers' cottages produced in 1879.

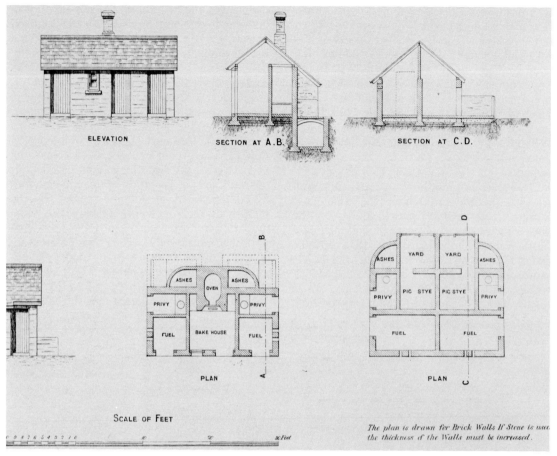

ELEVATION

SECTION AT A.B.

SECTION AT C.D.

ASHES OVEN ASHES

PRIVY PRIVY

FUEL BAKE HOUSE FUEL

PLAN

ASHES YARD YARD ASHES

PRIVY PIG STYE PIG STYE PRIVY

FUEL FUEL

PLAN

SCALE OF FEET

*The plan is drawn for Brick Walls If Stone is used
the thickness of the Walls must be increased.*

Fig. 74. Plans of model outhouses (drawn in 1872) found in the Powis Castle Estate drawings collection. The Sarn-y-bryn-caled houses certainly had pigsties for the Powis Estate tenants to keep their own animals. In addition the lock-keepers' cottages all along the Montgomeryshire Canal had beautifully built late nineteenth-century piggeries often with food-stuff stores built over them.

Montgomeryshire Canal lock-keepers' houses which had a floor size of 64.7 square metres. Such accommodation shows the paternalism felt for long-term (often hereditary) employees who were provided with houses that were deemed to be an ornament as well as an investment for the estate proprietor and his heirs. By the end of the nineteenth century the size of such generous accommodation was even increased for fairly menial workers. The smaller cottage at the Powis Estate Yard was extended to give 72.6 square metres of floor space, and the Belan Limekilns Cottages were built from the first as quite large houses (with 69.5 square metres floor area) for workers of fairly humble status: agricultural labourers, lime-burners and boatmen. Interestingly enough the Powis Estate drawings collection contained a number of 1870s design sheets (Figs. 72-4) of model dwellings and outhouses. These were date-marked by the 'Lands Improvement Company' on the 7th December 1891 and so did not directly influence the Powis Estate house designs until after the period considered. Nevertheless the housing on the vast rich lands of the Powis Estate matched and even exceeded the 'model' accomodation provided by the 'Inclosure Office' designs.[10] The provision of sufficient sleeping space was one concern of the Enclosure Commission of 1845 who probably produced these plans and such model examples were an effective influence. Nearly all Powis Castle Estate cottages were provided with three bedrooms whilst most

100

Fig. 75. Some of the canal-workers at the Newtown Basin lived in these tiny houses on the landward side of a timber wharf (C.3); nos. 10 and 11 Lower Canal Road. These twin dwellings are apparently conversions of open storage sheds.

canal houses only had two. The provision of adequate sanitation was another concern of this Commission and its plans of out buildings for labourers' cottages included combined units of privies (with earth bins or cess-pits), ash dumps, fuel stores and bake-houses. All or some of these features could be found mirrored in the design of workers' houses on Montgomeryshire landed estates. Water-pumps were also provided in locations near the houses. By the late nineteenth century it is also noticeable that the Shropshire Union Canal was also providing pigsties alongside all its lock-cottages.

Generally, though, the canal companies were commercial institutions more concerned with short-term profits than the proprietors of large landed estates. Even more preoccupied with the rapid accumulation of working capital and the restrictions of small building sites were the operators of small canalside wharfages.

Private traders and manufacturers workers' housing

A glance at the accompanying table shows how consistently smaller were the workers' housing provided by private proprietors than either those dwellings provided by the canal companies for their employees or those larger and more imposing habitations erected by the proprietors of the surrounding landed estates. The single-storey brick dwelling attached to the side of the Garthmyl warehouse (11.9 square metres in floor area) was only one-sixth of the size of the contemporary lock-keeper's dwelling at Pool Quay. By 1845 this warehouse-keeper's dwelling had been more than

---

[10] The 'Enclosures Commission' (presumably the originator of these 'Inclosure Office' designs) was formed to encourage the improvement of standards used in working-class housing on landed estates. It was established in 1845 and empowered to lend money for estate improvement and its inspectors encouraged cottage building while imposing certain minimum standards. Amongst its concerns were the use of properly seasoned timber and good quality bricks for construction purposes. L.Caffyn, *Workers Housing in West Yorkshire* (London,1986), 85.

Fig. 76. *Alongside the canal at Newtown (the canal was to the immediate right of the houses on the photograph) were a number of three- and four-storey workers' housing that seem to have had occupation split by storey as a 'dual row' or 'stacked housing'—often found where precipitous building sites allowed the provision of access doors from both higher and lower levels. No. 28 Llanllwchaearn Road and 'Riverside Cottage' have access at the lower ground level whilst a gable-end door gives a separate entrance to the third-storey level of the building from the Llanllwchaearn Road.*

doubled in size to 21.3 square metres. However, one-roomed cottages of a similar period and type still survive on the former wharves at the Newtown canal basin. No.10 Lower Canal Road, a dwelling some 21 square metres in area, seems actually to have been converted from former open sheds, as was its neighbour, No.11. In original size these tiny dwellings are equivalent to such abodes as the cellar dwellings in Merthyr Tydfil (see '26' on the table).

What is particularly striking is the way in which these miniature houses are so much smaller than the average houses of medieval peasants (31-34 on the contemporary table), poorly built and draughty as these must have been. The extended house at Garthmyl closely resembles the late eighteenth-century ironworkers' cottages at Bersham (near Wrexham) in size and type, but this is still no more than half the size of the usual late eighteenth-century lock-keeper's cottage.

Private traders with their restricted working sites and capital in fact evolved new house types to help reduce construction costs and to save land. On the table nos. 19, 21, 23, and 27 belong to one of these new types, all being back-to-back houses. Three are in the Welsh textile centre of Newtown; some of the houses around the Newtown canal basin seem also to have been back-to-back houses. However these houses, Nos. 5 and 6 Dolafon Terrace, were rebuilt in Victorian times and neither they nor their neighbours bear any structural evidence of this former multiple occupation.

The precipitous slopes found in Wales and other areas, such as the West Riding of Yorkshire, allowed for the construction of 'dual rows' in which housing was stacked on top of each other with the upper dwelling of one or two storeys giving onto the uphill part of the site and the lower dwelling of one or two storeys entered on the downhill side. Both three- and four-storeyed versions of this type of 'stacked housing' survive at the north-eastern end of the Newtown canal wharves. The structural evidence for this in the four-storeyed stone-fronted terrace of six units to the north of the ornate Victorian terrace on the Llanllwchaearn Road has disappeared with the wholesale rebuilding of the four-storey riverside (former canalside) elevations. However the attractive neighbouring three-storey block, at right angles to the road, comprising No. 28 Llanllwchaearn Road and 'Riverside Cottage' does retain structural evidence of probable multiple occupation. There are doors to the two semi-detached cottages down at the former canal level and a door leading from the gable-end of the third storey of the structure facing onto the Llanllwchaearn Road.

Some of the housing built by the wharfingers at Newtown provides a living area approximating to that provided by the canal company for its own workers. However, much of this larger housing was provided for the lessee and operators of the wharves themselves. Much of the housing for the ordinary workers on the canal wharves, as elsewhere in private industry, would have provided a living space approaching two-thirds the size of that given to employees of a canal company. The Montgomeryshire Canal employees were some of the best housed of any canal workers in Wales, but lucky indeed was the menial worker who was employed on one of the rich landed estates of the surrounding area!

5

Canal-generated Industry

It can be demonstrated in many cases that waterways were catalysts in the setting up of new industries or the spectacular expansion of established industries in the areas that they served. Markets and raw materials were made economically accessible. In some cases, as has been stated, the canal company actually encouraged the growth of dependent industry by letting new industrial installations use water surplus to the needs of navigation. The development of such industries in turn gave a marked impetus to the growth of related housing and settlements.

Immediately alongside the Montgomeryshire Canal were two flannel factories, one foundry, five maltings (and brew-houses), one gas works and two corn-mills, and four other canalside installations driven by canal or canal-feeder water. Four joiners' workshops also adjoined the canal to make use of the wood supplies brought along or to the waterway for loading. Most of these installations were based at the main canalside settlements of Newtown and Welshpool. In both places there were groups of coal-fuelled industries sited to the north of the main canal wharves. The huge

Fig. 77. Old canalside maltings built into the side of the canal above Pool Quay Lock. Good malting barley from the Severn valley supplied the poorer upland districts of Montgomeryshire and Merioneth and some was transported along the canal. Coal to fire the barley-kilns also came to the maltings by canal.

Fig. 78. The cast-iron fire basket removed from the barley-drying-kiln at the Garthmyl Maltings. (Community Programme)

amounts of limestone and coal carried also stimulated the more distant canalside extractive industries at Llanymynech and Porth-y-waen lime quarries and at Ruabon Collieries further north. Standard (or Stondart) Stone Quarry at Welshpool also made use of the canal and a nascent brick and tile industry was stimulated by the canal's northern line at Cabin Lock, Wern (Fig. 106) and Arddleen. The barytes mines of the upper valley were also given easier access to the grinding-mills near the canal at Pool Quay.

Of course, all the manufactories were in turn serviced by their own settlements. Two of the most interesting and attractive are the green-sandstone and brick terraces that served the Welshpool Flannel Company's Mills alongside the main Oswestry and Shrewsbury road in north Welshpool and the gothic green-sandstone houses adjoining the Powis Estate Yard one mile south of Welshpool (see Fig. 67).

It might be asked just what was the exact relationship of these industries to the canal: whether the canal was responsible for bringing whole new industries to the area or whether it was just the cause of superficial changes to the industrial infrastructure that already existed?

The gradual nature of the industrial changes generated by the canal were reinforced by a number of factors. It is true that the Carreghofa Junction had been made between the Llanymynech branch of the Ellesmere Canal and the Montgomeryshire Canal in July 1797, but the former canal did not as yet either connect directly with the coal-supplies and iron-works of the Ruabon area, or indeed with anywhere on the canal system at large.[1] It did, however, provide the vital short water link to the Llanymynech Limestone Quarries, and the lime-trade was the initial reason for building the two canals and would always remain the

---

[1] C. Hadfield, *Canals of the West Midlands*, 190.

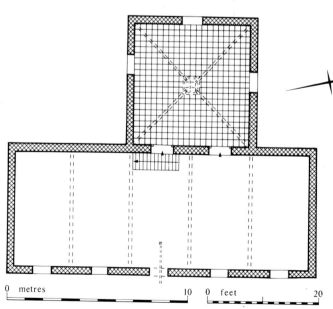

Fig. 79. Plan of the first floor of the Garthmyl (Nag's Head) Maltings showing the central loading-hoist in the front of the building. A barley-drying kiln stands at the rear with a floor made up of 1ft (0.3m) square perforated tiles to allow the heat through from the fire that was formerly situated below. A cross of beams supports the central roof ventilator. An associated brewhouse formerly stood between the maltings and the Nag's Head Inn.

0 metres 10   0 feet 20

mainstay of trade. However, even the coal to calcine the limestone had to be brought a considerable distance by road; the 5km railway from the Llanymynech branch to the small coalfield at Morda was probably not completed until c.1813. Coal from the main Ruabon coalfield had to be transported the considerable distance by road to the end of the Llanymynech branch at Frankton until the delayed completion of the Chirk Aqueduct in 1801. This also directly opened up the Chirk coalfield and in 1805 T. E. Ward leased the Black Park Colliery there from the Chirk Castle estates. Ward was also a main developer of the Newtown Canal Wharves as a user of his raw materials and between 1805 and 1825 spent some £20,000 developing the Black Park Mines, employing about 300 men there.[2] In 1802 the great declivity of the Dee Valley still separated the larger Ruabon coalfield from the canal, and this obstacle was only overcome with the much delayed dual opening of the great Pontcysyllte Aqueduct and the double-track Ellesmere Canal Company Railway to William Hazeldine's collieries at Plas Kynaston on the 26th November 1805.[3] From then on the wharves of the Ruabon coalmasters, William Hazeldine and Exuperius Pickering, senior and junior, burgeoned along the line of the Montgomeryshire Canal and were followed by a number of coal-fuelled industries.

Perhaps the industrial installations most dependent on the canal for raw materials (Ruabon coal and pig-iron) and almost certainly created as a result of the opening of the

---

[2] Bye-gones, 5 August 1931, 279.
[3] C. Hadfield, Canals of the West Midlands, 173-76.

Fig. 80. The late nineteenth-century canalside maltings at Garthmyl.

waterway were the local Montgomeryshire foundries. The Newtown Foundry was situated right alongside the canal to the immediate north of the main terminal wharves at Newtown. The Welshpool Foundry was so sited so as to use the water-power resources available on the old Domen Mill site at a little distance from the canal. Some of the buildings on the Welshpool site still remain in industrial use. Foundries were also sited at Ruabon itself and more elaborate castings continued to be transported along the canal as those of 1844 at the Powis Estate Timber-yard show.

The best-known contemporary industry along the canal was the woollen trade. By 1835 Newtown was described as 'a flourishing little town and from....being now the principal seat of the flannel manufacturing in the Principality has acquired the appellation of 'the Leeds of Wales''.[4] The exact role of the waterway in this ascendency (which coincided with the canal age) is very difficult to assess. Wool and cloth are both lightweight goods, not the heavy bulk loads for which the new waterways were the ideal, and indeed often the only possible means of transport. For this reason cloth did not, and indeed could not, constitute a major part of the tonnage carried on the canal. On Sunday evenings, for example, a heavy carrier's waggon left Llanidloes to travel down to the Welshpool Flannel Market, and this service continued until the railway reached Llanidloes in 1859.[5] However the canal extension to Newtown was largely the creation of William Pugh of Brynllywarch, the greatest Newtown textile entrepreneur of his day, who had to face bankruptcy and exile as a result of his endeavours. In 1821 the canal to Newtown was fully open and in 1832 the flannel market was moved to Newtown from Welshpool. Buyers came from London, Manchester, Chester, Shrewsbury and other parts of the kingdom. There had been a regular canal (and road, for there was a 16km gap between the Ellesmere and Trent and Mersey systems that was not filled until 1833) service between Newtown and Manchester from 1825; the journey took six days at a cost of 35 pence per hundredweight. By 1831 there were eighty-one flannel manufacturers in Newtown, and a local contemporary poet had this to say about the connection between the canal and the textile trade:

To London great, in short by the canal,
Thy flannel goes, as quick as one can tell,
And thence from there, the Flannel's quickly hurled,
To every part of Britain, and its known world.[6]

From this one would conclude that the Newtown textile industry sent nearly all its output along the canal, although a certain amount would have gone by cart travelling along the Severn Valley and down to south Wales. Even so there must have been some problems in carrying out this early long-distance trade for the Ellesmere did not link up to the Chester Canal until the end of 1805, and then it only gave access to the outside world via the Mersey or Dee until the opening of the Middlewich Branch on 1 September 1833 and the Birmingham and Liverpool Junction Canal on the 2nd March 1835 which gave the Montgomeryshire Canal direct canal access to the northern, midland and southern industrialised heartlands of England.[7] Even then a more general trade was slow to develop—the first boat, direct from London, arrived in the canal basin at Newtown on 25 June, 1839. It left again on the eve of the following day and was expected to arrive in London on the 30 June after a journey taking almost four days.[8] It is not surprising, then, that the Severn river-port at Pool Quay continued to function throughout this period.

The population of Newtown rose from 990 in 1801, to 2,025 in 1811, reaching 4,550 in 1831 as its textile industry was created and grew.[9] The local industry was characterised both by small-scale factories and an abundance of water-power resources. The dominant factor in determining the location of the industry was therefore the available water-power source rather than the immediate proximity of the transport outlet for its lightweight output. This situation changed only when a factory was steam-powered as a site close to a convenient means of transporting the coal was then an important consideration. Very few Montgomeryshire factories were steam-powered be-

[4] J. Geraint Jenkins, *The Welsh Woollen Industry* (1969, Cardiff), 129.
[5] Ibid., 128.
[6] Ibid., 143-44.
[7] C. Hadfield, *Canals of the West Midlands*, 178, 181, 186.
[8] *Bye-gones*, 1 September 1915, 177.
[9] Jenkins, *The Welsh Woollen Industry*, 143.

Fig. 81. The canalside mill of 'The Welshpool Company for the manufacture of flannel by steam', built by local 'gentry' in 1834 and extended and reopened by the Newtown entrepreneur Sir Pryce Pryce Jones in 1883. These 'Powysland Tweed and Flannel Mills' closed in 1900 and were demolished in 1930 except for the walls of the factory yard and the terraces of workers' housing remaining along the Welshpool to Oswestry Road. (Powysland Museum Collection)

fore the coming of the locomotive railways in 1859, and only two were built on canalside sites—one at Newtown and another at Welshpool (Fig. 81). There were a dozen textile factories in Welshpool in 1828 but the town did not grow spectacularly like Newtown, possibly because it was more remote from the sources of upland wool. Conversely other former centres of cloth production near the uplands seem to have lost out to Newtown's improved communications. Web production had been exported through the seaports of the Dyfi in the eighteenth century but from the 1820s the main manufacturing centre at Machynlleth was said to be 'stagnant alike in its manufacture and in population.'[10]

Other coal-fuelled industries were attracted to the canal-bank; at Newtown on the same plot as the first canalside factory in the town (wharf 'C.15' in chapter six) were a malthouse by 1842 and a bakehouse by 1845. These installations would have used coal brought along the canal. The high walls of both the Welshpool Gasworks and the 'Welshpool Company for the manufacture of flannel by steam' (Fig. 81) remain just north of the

former borough boundary of Welshpool as reminders of the former importance of the Montgomeryshire Canal in the development of local industry. It has been suggested that the woollen industry at Welshpool failed to develop on the same scale as Newtown because of the unsympathetic attitude of the Earls of Powis to the large-scale industrialisation of the town at their castle gates. Indeed, in 1841 one handloom weaver commented, 'The pride of Newtown is trade and the trade of Welshpool is pride'.[11] Certainly, the site of the canalside gas works, just outside the borough boundary, was made available by Viscount Clive, later second Earl of Powis. The Welch Pool Gas Company had come into being on the 14 February 1832 when a meeting of townspeople, held in the vestry of the parish church, resolved to establish the company with a capital of one hundred and twenty shares at £25 a share. Viscount Clive was the largest shareholder. The parish vestry approved a tender for 23 lamps, and on 12 December 1832 *Eddowes Salop Journal* reported that:[12]

'On Tuesday and Wednesday evening last, the town was most brilliantly illuminated with gas from the handsome works newly erected under the skilful and scientific superintendence of Mr. Forrest, engineer of Manchester, ...'

The railway came to Welshpool in 1860 and a contract to supply gas to the station was negotiated. In 1864 the consulting engineer advised the abandonment of the canalside works for a new and modern railside installation complete with siding. This (the present gasworks near the railway station) was completed in 1865 and the old works left to return to their rural setting.[13] The walled compound is now a garden for the remaining house once used by the gasworks manager.

The transformation of the local industrial economy from a canal-based infrastructure to an economy based on the new railway network is clearly shown by the changing location of industry.

---

[10] Ibid., 152-54.

[11] Ibid.

[12] J. Elwyn Davies, 'When Welshpool's streets were first lit by gas', *The County Times and Express*, 25 December 1982.

[13] J. Elwyn Davies, 'St Mary's was gas lit until 1950's, *The County Times and Express*, 1 January 1983.

Fig. 82. *Boats near the head of the Severn River navigation at Pool Quay in 1798, the year after the opening of the Montgomeryshire Canal. The river continued to have considerable importance as a link, both from Montgomeryshire and the canal, to the greater part of the United Kingdom until the largely self-contained Montgomeryshire, Ellesmere and Chester Canals system was linked to the main inland waterways network at Middlewich in 1833 (British Library, Map Library, XLVII, folio 77b).*

6

The Waterway Settlements

The combined growth of trade and industry with related housing needs are likely to promote settlements at the head of any navigation. In Montgomeryshire this tendency is reinforced by the geography of the upper Severn Valley, and particularly by the way in which it naturally funnels trade longitudinally towards the limits of arterial communication. Here there exists a palimpsest of important settlements connected with each of three successive waterway termini. The earliest of these, the limit of navigation of the River Severn, produced the river port of Pool Quay (later to be served also by the Montgomeryshire Canal, which passed close by). The second terminus, the head of the earlier arm (Eastern Branch) of the Montgomeryshire Canal, caused the growth of two important settlements: Garthmyl, right at the head of the navigation, and Welshpool, the nearest large market town. Finally, the settlement at Newtown became the terminus of the completed Western Branch of the Canal and experienced significant development as a result.

The importance of the settlements in terms of housing has already been discussed in chapter four and can be further illustrated by reference to the known concentration of canalside facilities at these points in the 1840s and 1850s. Sixty of the eighty-five canalside wharf-houses were situated at these centres as were twenty-four of the thirty warehouses, thirty-six of the forty-four recorded stables, ten or eleven of the thirteen to fourteen docks and two of the four dry-docks. Both canalside joiners' shops and most canalside industry were also concentrated in these inland ports.

A Pool Quay

Pool Quay was already an important waterway settlement before the Montgomeryshire Canal arrived here in 1797. It was the head of the navigation of the River Severn, and therefore served the whole of the Severn Valley above this point as well as the nearby town of Welshpool, from which it derived its name. The river had never been improved, but was naturally navigable from the mouth of the estuary near Bristol, 190 kilometres away. Navigation terminated at Pool Quay because a change in slope of the valley floor caused the river to become notably wider and shallower upstream, and because a large weir at this point obstructed passage.

Dominating the present hamlet is a very large eighteenth-century brick house, until recently partly a post office. To the north a track slopes up to Pool Quay Lock on the west side of the main road (see the accompanying plan). Here is another attractive lock-side complex with the top storey of an old building flanking the towing-path above the lock. Though latterly used as a warehouse, it formerly housed an engine and drying-kilns which belonged to the maltings at Pool Quay. The maltster's residence and offices were the large brick house by the main A483 road (already

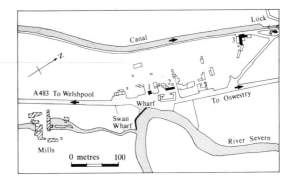

Fig. 83. A plan of the river and canal port at Pool Quay based on the local tithe maps of 1845-46. The infilled buildings on the plan show some of the remaining structures of importance: No. 1 is the remains of an eighteenth-century brick-built building that may have been a warehouse for river-borne goods; No. 2 is the Powis Arms (tradition has it that the river boatmen marked the beams for every day that they were stranded at Pool Quay by insufficient water for navigation); No. 3 housed the former drying-kilns and engine for the maltings at Pool Quay and No. 4 is the lock-keeper's cottage on the Montgomeryshire Canal at Pool Quay.

Fig. 84. A fragment of an eighteenth-century building, possibly a warehouse, remaining on the 'landage' of the river-wharf at Pool Quay.

mentioned) adjoining 'The Powis Arms'. The main road immediately south of 'The Arms' runs along the old 'landage' or wharf which was journey's end for the old Severn sailing barges from the seventeenth century into the canal period. The river-bank forms a precipitous edge to the main road and its nettle-covered cliffs show no traces of the wharf that lay here. A cart-ramp led down to the water at the south end of the cliff, while the smooth green field to the south was the 'Swan Wharf', once strewn with great timbers awaiting shipment to the naval dockyards.

On the opposite side of the road is a green flanked by two small red-brick buildings. This was probably a stack-yard for the main quay or wharf of (Welsh-) Pool. The more southerly building may have been an eighteenth-century warehouse. This is only a fragment of a once larger structure.

Navigation must always have been difficult to Pool Quay as the river has a small and irregular channel above Shrewsbury.[1] By the late seventeenth century, however, the 'New Quay' had been built and there was enough traffic to provoke disputes about the maintenance of 5 kilometres of road (presumably on the line of the A483) from there to 'Pool' itself. By 1712 one vessel capable of carrying over 40 tons—the Duchess owned by George Bradley—was journeying once or twice a month to Bristol and back. This was one of the medium-sized vessels on the river at the time, and was

---

[1] Much of this section on the Severn River Navigation has been written by Peter Wakelin from his Ph.D. research on the river (carried out at Wolverhampton Polytechnic).

110

probably about 60ft (18m) long and 16ft (4.9m) wide with a flat bottom, a single mast, and a square sail. Like other vessels, it would have been sailed when the wind was favourable or towed by a gang of 'bowhauliers' scrambling along the river-bank—no towing-path for horses was ever built on this part of the river. Smaller vessels trading over shorter distances must have been more usual at Pool Quay however. By 1756, when a list of vessels on the Severn was made, there were seven boats based there (owned by four merchants), compared with nineteen at Shrewsbury and 146 in the Ironbridge Gorge. Navigation was certainly difficult at this time, with frequent and lengthy delays due to low water. Lead pigs shipped from the smeltery nearby, for instance, were held up for over two months on their journey to Bristol in 1761. These difficulties seem to have become greater, probably due to changes in the flow of the river, and though it was still possible for vessels to reach Pool Quay well into the nineteenth-century, trade was declining. However, the Montgomeryshire and Ellesmere Canals did not obtain an outlet to the main canal system until 1833 so that transhipment from the canal must have been a fairly frequent occurence. A Mr. Edward Jones (1820-1905) of the Bank Farm remembered barges lying in the river at Pool Quay and the Landing Place completely covered with Montgomeryshire oak waiting to be loaded into barges.[2] At this date return cargoes of general goods on the river were still brought upstream for transfer to the canal and sale in the Welshpool area; in 1818 it was noted that 'Welshpool trades principally with Bristol for English commodities'.[3] The scene at Pool Quay in this period was so depicted by one writer passing along the Welshpool to Oswestry road who noticed several vessels at anchor in the river. The late continuance of a thriving transhipment trade is indicated by the Welshpool entry in Pigott's Directory of 1828-9.

'Conveyance by Water'
'To London, Birmingham, Wolverhampton, Worcester, Gloucester,
Bristol and all intermediate places. Richard Goolden, from the Union Wharf, and Thomas Groom from the Commercial Wharf, every Tuesday and Friday.'

In 1833 flannel, from Montgomeryshire, and lead and limestone, from Llanymynech on the Vyrnwy, were recorded as being carried down the Severn.[4] Indeed, until that year the only water-transport outlet from Montgomeryshire to most of the rest of Britain was via the River Severn to Stourport and so into the greater canal system. Lead and zinc, for instance, were shipped from Llanymynech to Birmingham and Macclesfield in *c.* 1800 by entering the greater canal system at Stourport.[5] Lead ore and slates from Bristol, originating inland at Llangynog, were shipped from the Clawdd Coch Wharf on the River Vyrnwy in the winter months. Trade on the Vyrnwy, as on the Severn itself, must have continued after the building of the Montgomeryshire Canal as it did not become a significant general carrier to central and southern Britain until linked to the main canal system in 1833. The Clawdd Coch Wharf on the Vyrnwy was not far upstream from the canal aqueduct on the east bank, and there must have been a period when sailing barges on the River Vyrnwy were passing under the aqueduct itself. However, with competition from the railways trade from places even further downstream on the River Severn, like Shrewsbury and Ironbridge, was virtually dead by the 1880s. The last barge to use the Montgomeryshire portion of the river was owned by Shropshire County Council carried road-stone from the Belan Bank, and the outcrop of rock on the riverside by Criggion. The barge plied the river until about 1890, by which time the Belan Bank was completely quarried away and consequently the trade ceased[6].

Before the canal was built the River Severn must have been the main route for the region's imports and exports. These can be illustrated from the Gloucester Port Books, the customs records for the port at the mouth of the River Severn (the entries from these records are at present being put on computer at Wolverhampton Polytechnic). One of the most

---

[2] A. S. Davies, 'The River Trade of Montgomeryshire and its Borders', *The Montgomeryshire Collections* XLIII. 1 (1933), 33-46, 35.
[3] Ibid, 43.
[4] Ibid, 41.
[5] Ibid, 42.
[6] Ibid, 35.

important exports of the region was timber, especially oak, which had been carried on vessels or floated in rafts down the river at least since the thirteenth century. Lead pigs from the Pool Quay smeltery were a major export from the 1690s to the 1770s, and agricultural produce of the valley, such as cheese and grain, must also have been carried. Many vessels would have collected other goods on their way down the river, such as Staffordshire pottery at Shrewsbury and Bridgnorth, ironware at Coalbrookdale and Bewdley, and salt at Worcester. The goods they carried back included commodities made or traded at the port of Bristol, such as wines and tobacco, oil, shot, brassware and soap. Other parts of the Severn Valley would have returned goods such as ironware, textiles, earthenware, cider, salt and coal. All these goods must have been seen piled on the quay itself or stored in the yards and warehouses nearby. After the canal was completed the character of trade must have changed: there would no longer be demand for coal hauled hazardously upriver from east Shropshire and transhipped as it could pass straight by on the canal from Denbighshire; and salt could be brought more easily by canal from Northwich than by river from Droitwich. Some more local trade must have continued, however. The settlement provided a convenient wharf for its immediate rural locality and the Pool Quay water-power site, and some transhipment from river to canal must have taken place of goods going to and from Shrewsbury and Ironbridge or the west of England. The trade in large quantities of Montgomeryshire oak for the royal dockyards continued to go down river. The small print on the poster illustrated (Fig. 52) concerning the timber trade clearly explains how in 1808 (and presumably through much of the first half of the nineteenth century) timber was felled, conveyed to the nearest turnpike road and thence to the nearest wharf on the Montgomeryshire Canal or to the River Severn at Pool Quay. 18. Feb. 1808.

'Oak Trees ..... of large Dimensions ..... and calculated for the Navy, or for other Purposes ..... The situation of the Timber to Purchasers, is most desirable, lying close adjoining an excellent Turnpike Road, about midway between the Wharfs on the Montgomeryshire Canal at Berriew and the White House [i.e. where the Powis Castle Estate timber-yard is], *from each of which it is only about a Mile and a Half distant, and within four Miles of the River Severn at Pool Quay'.*

The remains of the former water-powered mills lie 200 metres further to the south along the main road from the old quay area and are reached down a short track to the left (east— see plan). The small red-brick building on the right (south) of the track was once a corn-mill; the cottage straight ahead was probably the woollen-factory owner's house, and the foundations lying between the track and the tail-race pool to the left are those of the saw-mill. The water to power the complex was drawn from the Severn by a high weir to the south; this effectively prevented navigation of the river above this point. There was a lead-smelting works here from about the 1690s. By 1779 the site was used by an iron-forge while a new corn-mill and dye-house had been built by 1750. The woollen-mill was rebuilt in 1802 and was in use until 1858. Later came a saw-mill and a barytes mineral crushing mill.

B Garthmyl

Garthmyl is a canal port that came into existence by accident: the original Montgomeryshire Canal Company ran out of money here in 1797 before completing their intended waterway to Newtown. Between 1815 and 1819-21 the earlier plan to continue the Montgomeryshire Canal to Newtown was actually completed and the former terminus at Garthmyl never became a major settlement like that at the later Newtown terminus. By the mid nineteenth century one of the kiln-banks at Garthmyl had fallen out of use; the only kiln-bank on the canal to do so before the beginning of the twentieth century. The remains gradually became the fascinating and fossilized canal port that still exists today.

The accompanying plan (Fig. 85) shows both present and vanished features of the former port. This description starts at the southern end of the port where the Montgomeryshire Canal emerges from a culvert under the Garthmyl to Montgomery road (B4385). On the opposite, northern, edge of this road is a late

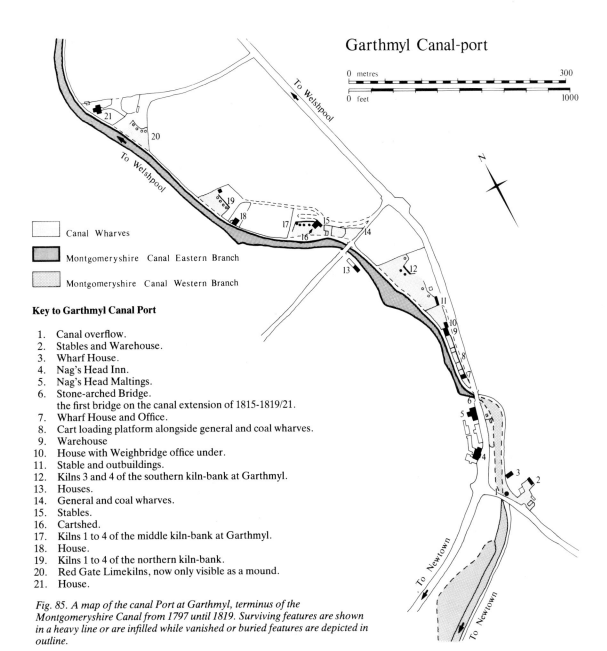

Garthmyl Canal-port

0 metres ————————— 300
0 feet ————————— 1000

Canal Wharves

Montgomeryshire Canal Eastern Branch

Montgomeryshire Canal Western Branch

Key to Garthmyl Canal Port

1. Canal overflow.
2. Stables and Warehouse.
3. Wharf House.
4. Nag's Head Inn.
5. Nag's Head Maltings.
6. Stone-arched Bridge.
    the first bridge on the canal extension of 1815-1819/21.
7. Wharf House and Office.
8. Cart loading platform alongside general and coal wharves.
9. Warehouse
10. House with Weighbridge office under.
11. Stable and outbuildings.
12. Kilns 3 and 4 of the southern kiln-bank at Garthmyl.
13. Houses.
14. General and coal wharves.
15. Stables.
16. Cartshed.
17. Kilns 1 to 4 of the middle kiln-bank at Garthmyl.
18. House.
19. Kilns 1 to 4 of the northern kiln-bank.
20. Red Gate Limekilns, now only visible as a mound.
21. House.

Fig. 85. A map of the canal Port at Garthmyl, terminus of the Montgomeryshire Canal from 1797 until 1819. Surviving features are shown in a heavy line or are infilled while vanished or buried features are depicted in outline.

nineteenth-century canal overflow ('1' on the map) consisting of a wooden flume carrying the surplus water of the canal through a sunken ovaloid chamber. The long sides of the flume would have formed an extensive overflow weir in times of heavy rainfall.

To the east (right, when viewed from the road) of the flume is what now looks like an ordinary farmyard ('2' on the plan) but which

by 1859 formed the buildings of a coal-wharf.[7] When the Montgomeryshire Canal was extended through this point between 1815 and 1819, this southern part of Garthmyl became the focus of later activity at the port. The

---

[7] The dates 1845 and 1859 given in this section refer to information given on the maps and schedules of the 'Shropshire Union Railway....Plan' of 1845 and 1859.

Montgomery road and its bridge over the Severn gave access to Montgomery, Chirbury, Church Stoke and the lowlands of the Camlad valley.

The farther building in the yard still has old stables on the ground floor and was described in 1859 as stables and a warehouse in the occupation of Thomas Evans. A second warehouse stood in the yard and the rendered modernised house adjoining ('3' on the plan) is the early nineteenth-century house of the Thomas Evans who operated the wharf.

The short section of canal that lay opposite the Nag's Head Inn is, at the time of writing, buried under the Welshpool-Newtown Road and an adjoining lay-by. (When the canal is re-opened there will be a new section of waterway on the east side of the road here.) There used to be two further wharves alongside the main road at this point. By 1845 there was a warehouse on the southernmost of these and a stable and shed on that to the north.

The Nag's Head Inn ('4' on the map) was the only building near the main road at Garthmyl before the coming of the canal. The present building is probably early nineteenth-century. To the north was a late nineteenth-century brewhouse and also a maltings ('5'—Fig. 85) which still stands. The kiln floor with its perforated tiles for drying the local barley is still intact but the ground-floor stoking room has been converted into a chapel of rest.

Fig. 86. The kiln at the Nag's Head Inn Maltings, Garthmyl.

Fig. 87. The Garthmyl Canal Port. The basin on the left was the original terminus of the Eastern Branch of the Montgomeryshire Canal until the Western Branch was extended under the arched bridge in the foreground. The road on the right was low enough to facilitate easy loading of water-borne goods from boats floating at a higher level on the canal to the left. The conservatory in the foreground stands in front of a late eighteenth- or early nineteenth-century stone-built wharf house and office which later had a brick-built extension added towards the canal. In 1859 this was occupied by an employee of the 'Westminster, Brymbo Coal and Coke (Limited)'. A series of wharves extended along the strip of ground, between the road and canal, that lies behind the house.

Just north of the Nag's Head Inn is the first stone-arched bridge (no. 131) over the canal extension of 1815—1919-21 ('6'—Fig. 85). The present main road branches off to the east and the old main road goes over the bridge and rejoins the new road alongside the first of the old limekiln-banks. When the canal is made navigable once again the main road will be re-aligned for the second time

The original terminus of the canal lay to the north of the bridge and for ninety metres the end of the old canal ran and still runs parallel

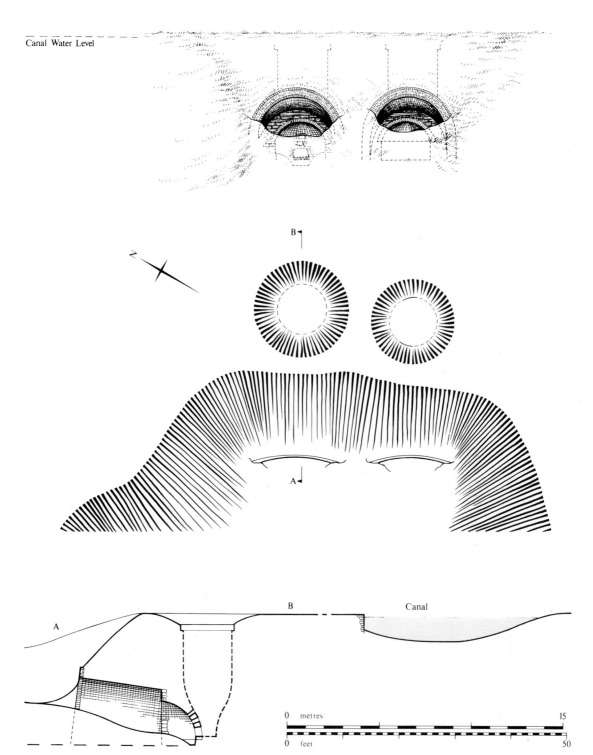

Canal Water Level

Fig. 88. Elevation and plan of kilns 3 and 4 in the southern kiln-bank at Garthmyl. The bowl of kiln 4 on the section is 21m from the canal.

to and at a higher level than the old road (Fig. 87). There were five separate wharves on this twelve-metre wide strip, and a convenient wall descending from canal level on the roadside provided a useful cart and waggon loading platform. The new canal-line will go through the middle of these wharves and under the main road, passing between the two wharf buildings.

The first of the two buildings north of the bridge ('7'—Fig. 85) is a small stone-built early nineteenth-century house with a brick extension. In 1859 this was described as 'house, outbuildings, office, yard and garden' and was occupied by the 'Westminster, Brymbo Coal and Coke (Limited)' who also had the weighing-machine and wharf to the north.

An early nineteenth-century warehouse, house and weighbridge office beyond this ('9-10'—Fig. 85) are discussed in the sections on houses and warehouses. To the north of this again is a much patched shed ('11' on the plan), described in 1859 as a stable. Two large nineteenth-century limekilns ('12' on the plan—Fig. 88) remain from a five-kiln-bank. At the time of writing this land is being cleared for building, but it is proposed to retain the kiln-mouths as features of interest.

Both warehouse and southern kiln-bank at Garthmyl were occupied by the trader John Dickin in 1845 but were unoccupied by 1859; an illustration of the relative decline in importance of the old northern part of the port. The trading depression of the 1840s also resulted in

Fig. 89. Students from the Ironbridge Institute in the large brick vault over the mouth of the drawing-hole at kiln no. 3 in the southern limekiln-bank at Garthmyl.

117

Fig. 90. Typical brick-arched bridge on the Eastern Branch of the Montgomeryshire Canal at Garthmyl (Bridge no. 130).

two of the other Garthmyl traders—Joseph Mansfield and Edward Hughes—having their boats seized for non-payment of tolls.[8]

A side-road to the north of the first kiln-bank leads to the first bridge (no. 130) of the original part of the Montgomeryshire Canal, and a track to the east leads onto the extensive remains of two kiln-banks, each having the remains of four kilns. At the first bank—the middle kiln-bank at Garthmyl ('17' on the

plan)—it is possible to see the charging-holes of the kilns. A mid nineteenth-century structure on top of the kiln retaining-wall may have been a cart-shed. A lean-to built against the revetment wall is on the site of the kiln-bank stables.

To the north is a bank of early nineteenth-century kilns with an adjoining house of

[8] *Towpath Guide, 3, Welshpool to Garthmyl,* 9.

Fig. 91. The two-period brick-built cottage (the oldest part is the smaller block nearer the canal) of the northern limekiln-bank at Garthmyl.

contemporary date which was much enlarged in the nineteenth century ('18-9'—Fig. 85). The early decline of the port is again suggested, as has already been mentioned, because these were the only Montgomeryshire Canal kilns not indicated on the 1859 map of the waterway.

Further north, the Red Gate Limekilns ('20') were reached via a separate access but a much altered early nineteenth-century house ('21') and a mound where the kilns stood are the only remains of this economic activity today.

The historic interest of this port might well justify the incorporation of all the remains into a conservation area.

Fig. 92. A view looking south-west from Severn Street Bridge in Welshpool at the beginning of the century. The large water-wheel of the corn mill on the Town Lock by-pass is visible beyond the canopy of the Welshpool Canal Wharf Warehouse, as are the cast-iron gates (now at Stoke Bruerne Museum) of the lock itself and the then new maintenance yard of the canal in the left background. (Community Programme)

Fig. 93. The remains of a water-wheel pit alongside the Town Lock at Welshpool. An axle-box for the large diameter breast-wheel is visible on the left and the corn-mill driven by the wheel stood on the right.

C Welshpool

Welshpool was the only town on the original line of the Montgomeryshire Canal and became the administrative centre of the waterway. Strangely, much of the canalside industry was built some way from the town and to the north of the borough boundary. This may have been due to the deliberate policy of the Earls of Powis, as has been discussed in chapter 5.

The Canal Wharf at Severn Street was the first site for managerial work and general mercantile activity. The wharf may also have formed the original base for maintenance work on the waterway but this by 1845 was sited on an adjacent area to the north-east.

The wharf was enclosed by a green-sand-stone wall and during the early nineteenth century a long row of buildings was constructed against and on this wall to service the commercial needs of the wharf. The accompanying drawings show the surviving buildings in this range. These were constructed in piecemeal order from south-west to north-east, and by 1851 were numbered in an order running in reverse to their age. The history of these buildings, as recorded on the 1845 and 1859 railway deposited plans and on the censuses carried out from 1841 to 1881, illuminates the changing fortunes of canal trade at Welshpool:

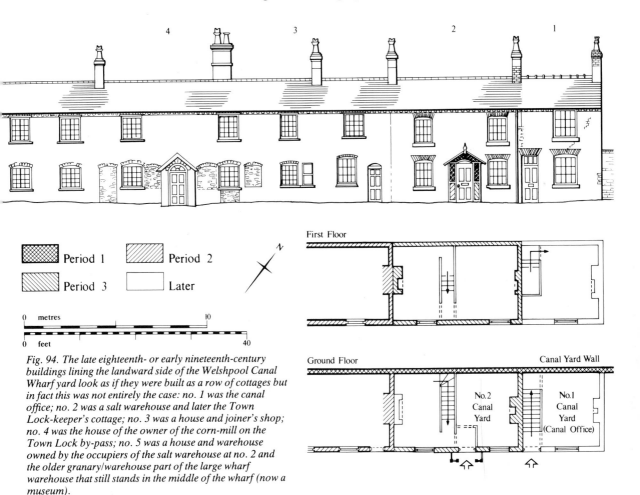

Fig. 94. The late eighteenth- or early nineteenth-century buildings lining the landward side of the Welshpool Canal Wharf yard look as if they were built as a row of cottages but in fact this was not entirely the case: no. 1 was the canal office; no. 2 was a salt warehouse and later the Town Lock-keeper's cottage; no. 3 was a house and joiner's shop; no. 4 was the house of the owner of the corn-mill on the Town Lock by-pass; no. 5 was a house and warehouse owned by the occupiers of the salt warehouse at no. 2 and the older granary/warehouse part of the large wharf warehouse that still stands in the middle of the wharf (now a museum).

Number 5 Welshpool Canal Wharf

Most of this large block was rebuilt in the late nineteenth century and the building illustrated is only a gutted remnant. The occupiers in 1845 (the 'representatives of Jane Jones deceased') also rented the large wharf in front of this property, including the 'warehouse and granary' standing independently on the wharf (now part of the large late nineteenth-century warehouse—Fig. 64) and Number 2 Canal Wharf which was then a salt warehouse. The whole of this property was described as 'house, stable, warehouse, outbuildings, wharf, yard and road'.

The trading function of this area seems then to have entered a decline and the property used as dwellings by various people not directly involved in the trade of the canal, as clearly revealed in the census returns for 1851, 1871 and 1881 (the 1861 returns are not very helpful in specifying who lived where on the canal wharf):

(Number 5 Welshpool Canal Wharf)

Date	Occupants	Age	Occupation
1851	David Dolby 21		Tallow Chandler
	Wife and servant		*(wife a milliner)*
1871	James Powell 49		Labourer
	Wife and three working children		
1881	Martha Edwards..................................60		Dressmaker
	Niece aged 8 and lodger aged 27		*(the lodger was a printer)*

All the residents came from Montgomeryshire except for David Dolby.

Number 4 Welshpool Canal Wharf

In 1845 this property was the house of Hannah Jones, 'Coal, Salt and Corn Dealer'. Hannah owned the end of the wharf nearest to Welshpool Lock that included the corn-mill driven by the by-pass water. An early nineteenth-century building survives at the south-western corner of the wharf and probably had stables on the ground floor with a store above. A late nineteenth-century former stable is attached to one side of this block. The layout of Number 4 Canal Wharf has been completely altered by conversion into a printing works. The later history of this building and those noted on Number 5: is similar.

Date	Occupants	Age	Occupation
1851	Hannah Jones 56		Salt and Corn Dealer
	Son and niece		
1871	Fredrick Roberts 40		Carpenter
	Wife, four children and a 62 year old lodger		*(the lodger was a nurse)*
1881	Empty		

All the residents were born in Montgomeryshire.

Number 3 Welshpool Canal Wharf

In 1845 this building was the 'House and joiner's shop' of Thomas Pierce. The internal arrangements of this building have been largely altered during its conversion into a printing works. The occupants seem to have remained involved with the trade of the canal until the coming of the railway in the 1860s; the 1871 census records a 'porter' in residence, but in 1881 the tenant seems to have once again been working on the canal wharf.

Date	Occupants	Age	Occupation
1851	Thomas Pierce 43		Carpenter
	Wife and two children		*(wife a seamstress)*
1871	Henry Cobb..40		Porter
	Wife, three children and lodger		
1881	George Clarke 39		Warehouseman
	Wife and two boarding children (scholars)		

It is only with the railway age that the first large influx of labour from without Montgomeryshire started: Henry Cobb came from Stafford and George Clarke from Hadley in Shropshire.

Number 2 Welshpool Canal Wharf

In 1845 this was a 'Salt Warehouse' occupied by the executors of the Jane Jones who had lived at Number 5 Canal Wharf. In 1851 it was still a warehouse but by 1871 was lived in by a lock-keeper and then a blacksmith.

The interior of this warehouse cum house has been recorded and is illustrated above. The handsome wooden gabled porch with finial, wooden arch and side-bays is identical to that on the lock-keeper's house at Pool Quay (Fig. 71). This suggests that these timber-framed structures were prefabricated at the canal company workshops. The abundance of Montgomeryshire woodlands spawned a multitude of joiners' workshops, as noted in the general sections on the waterway settlements at both Newtown and Welshpool.

Date	Occupants	Age	Occupation
1871	James Powell	65	Canal Lock Keeper
	Wife, daughter and two grandchildren		
1881	Edward Jones	27	Blacksmith
	Wife and twin daughters		

Number 1 Welshpool Canal Wharf

A 'canal office' is mentioned in the church-rate book for Welshpool from 1798 onwards (Powysland Club Library). At what date Number 1 Canal Wharf became the office is unknown. This building was the last part of the range of buildings to be built against and on the landward boundary wall of the Welshpool Canal Wharf. It is of brick and was probably built in the early nineteenth century. In 1845 it was noted as a canal 'Store House', in 1859 as an office; it is noted in the 1871 census as 'uninhabited' but in the 1881 census as 'offices'.

WELSHPOOL. THE CANAL.   61283.

Fig. 95. View north-east from the Severn Street Bridge in Welshpool at the beginning of the century. A family resident on the narrow-boat 'George' are moored alongside a warehouse with access both from the canal and Severn Street itself. (Community programme)

A 1922 lease-plan of the canal wharf still notes the building as an 'office' with a cart-shed adjoining to the north-east.

The canal company gradually took over more land between the Severn Street Bridge at Welshpool and the Lledan Brook Aqueduct. In 1845 and 1859 it was noted that the sheds and yard opposite the towing-path side of the canal were in the occupation of the canal company and were used probably as a maintenance yard for the canal until the construction of the large yard on the south-eastern edge of Welshpool late in the nineteenth century.

In 1845 the handsome green-sandstone warehouse with its external crane (Fig. 1), yard and house adjacent to the Lledan Brook Aqueduct on the towing-path side of the canal had belonged to the canal merchant Thomas Groom. By 1859 the canal agent was living in the house, and the yard, warehouse and an office were occupied by the canal company.

Above Welshpool Town Lock are further remains of canal installations. Several buildings remain from the Hollybush Coal Wharf on the opposite side of the canal from the towing-path. On the towing-path side of the canal most, if not all, the buildings of the late nineteenth-century canal maintenance yard remain, now used by a builders'-merchant. The narrow-gauge railway that led from the yard and over the towing-path to the canal-bank has recently been exposed to view.

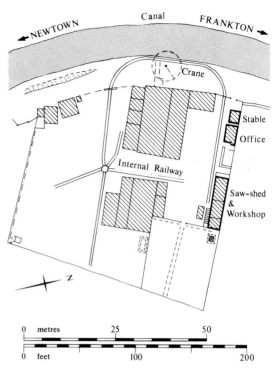

Fig. 97. Plan of the late nineteenth-century canal maintenance yard at Welshpool. The buildings are now used by a builders' merchants (B. M. S. S. Ltd.).

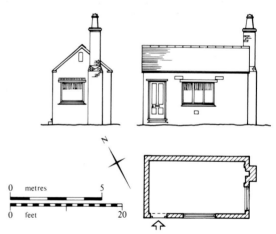

Fig. 98. Office at the canal maintenance yard.

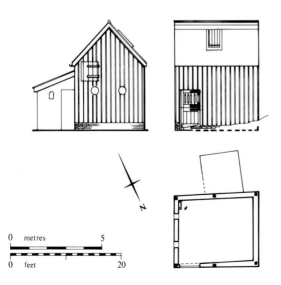

Fig. 96. Timber-built stable at the Welshpool Canal Maintenance Yard. Such simple structures built using both vertical timber planks and corrugated iron were characteristic of Shropshire Union Railways and Canal Company work and are still to be found all along the Montgomeryshire Canal.

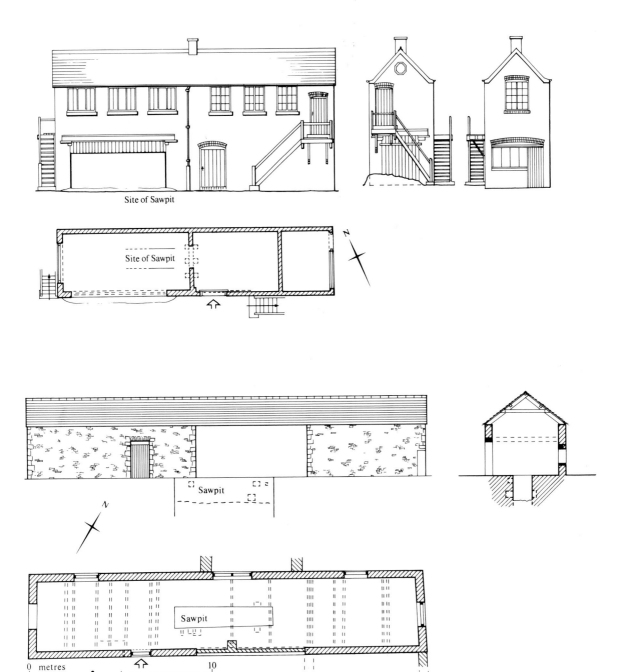

Site of Sawpit

Sawpit

Sawpit

0 metres 10

0 feet 40

Fig. 99. An important component of canal maintenance yards appears to have been the covered saw-pit. The two-storeyed example shown is at the former Welshpool Maintenance Yard on the Montgomeryshire Canal and the single-storeyed building with excavated saw-pit is at the former Tonna Maintenance Yard of the Neath Canal. In such pits a long double-handled saw would have been used vertically with the top sawyer standing above the pit and the unfortunate bottom sawyer standing below the timber being sawn.

Fig. 100. Welshpool; a section of the internal railway of the canal maintenance yard is visible in the foreground, the Welshpool Town Lock beyond, and the Welshpool Wharf Yard Warehouse in the background.

D Newtown

The last of the four main waterways settlements began to develop at Newtown after the Montgomeryshire Canal reached its final terminus there in 1821. The medieval core of Newtown is occupied by the present centre around Broad Street, enclosed by a northward loop of the River Severn. Its growth in the early nineteenth century under the allied stimuli of the canal and the local woollen industry produced three new and distinct suburbs. To the south-east on the Pool Road sprang up a minor new woollen manufacturing and tannery suburb. However, the main new woollen industry suburb lay between the old town and the canal on the north bank of the River Severn at Pen-y-gloddfa. The third of the new suburbs lay on the north bank of the river, due east of the old town, and centred around the canal basin. The large number of canal facilities noted here in the 1840s and 1850s demonstrate its importance in relation to the rest of the Montgomeryshire Canal. It had forty-five of the eighty-five wharf-houses on the canal, twenty-three of the twenty-four outbuildings, with two shops and a pub attached to these dwellings, at least sixteen of the twenty-four sheds, at least six of the thirty warehouses, one of the three granaries, at least twenty-one of the forty-four stables, one of the four dry-docks, eight of the eleven or twelve purpose-built docks, one of the two canalside flannel factories, and one of the two canalside foundries.

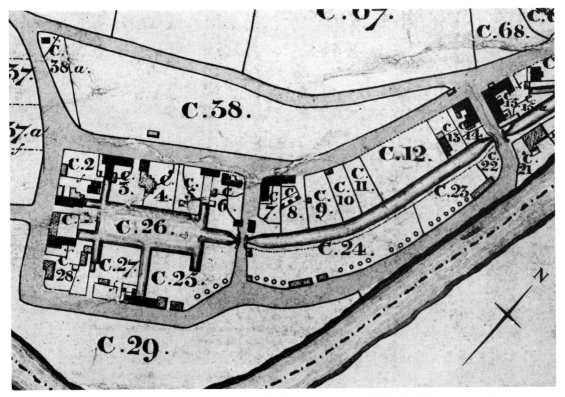

Fig. 101. The Newtown Canal Basin as shown on the Llanllwchaearn tithe map of 1842. The circles represent the charging-holes of limekilns. A full description of the numbered wharves shown lies in the accompanying text. (National Library of Wales)

Much of this inland port remains to be seen. Its terminal section will be discussed with reference to the plan of the site on the tithe map of 1842 (Fig. 101).[9] The site of the canal basin is approached from the centre of Newtown via Canal Road which leads onwards to the village of Llanllwchaearn. At 'C.38a' on the top left-hand corner of the plan ('Canal Villa') Lower Canal Road leads onto the circle of roads ('Dolafon Road') constructed by the canal company around the erstwhile canal basin. This former port merits the status of a conservation area and it is a great shame that very recent development has demolished the largest of the houses on wharf 'C25' and replaced it with an incongruous pseudo-Victorian copy. However, most of the blocks represented by dark solid shading on the plan represent early nineteenth-century wharf-workers' cottages in Georgian style which do, at present, survive in use as dwellings. The buildings on the plan represented by lined

diagonal shading were generally stables, warehouses and other ancillary buildings of which fewer survive. The cart-shed, stable and granary on wharf 'C.27' has been another very recent casualty of the infill development made to create 'Cwrt Dolafon'. The canal basin was until very recently an area of dry waste-land, but is now accessible via 'Cae Camlas' (literally 'Canal Field'), a road that cuts through the old wharf 'C.2' and gives onto a new residential development built in the old canal basin. The rectangular boundary of hedges and wooden fences around the development mark the course of the old wharf walls enclosing the main canal basin. The sunken hollows around this leading into various back gardens are the last vestiges of the seven dock arms that served the various wharves around the basin.

The small, square dark-shaded block shown

---

[9] Tithe map and schedule of 'Llanllwchaiarn', 1842 (N.L.W.).

Fig. 102. *Some of the remaining wharf-workers' housing around the site of the old canal basin at Newtown. The houses illustrated (Dolafon Terrace) stood on Wharf C.25 and those in the foreground may have been back-to-back housing prior to rebuilding. The road in the foreground was part of a system encircling the terminal canal wharves.*

on the plan to the upper right of Wharf 'C.3' represents Numbers 10 and 11 Lower Canal Road. These are minute early nineteenth-century brick cottages of virtually one large room each (a type common in poorer west Wales). Careful observation of their wall structure reveals that the wall-plates are supported on what were originally free-standing brick columns—they may well have been an early conversion from open timber-storage sheds. At their rear, in the hatched area bordering on the wharf 'C.4', are two stables of a similar date with much later patching. Further east, the left-hand (western) block of 'C.7' is an early nineteenth-century rebuilding of the 'Waggon & Horses' pub. The row of stone buildings adjoining were originally a block of five early nineteenth-century houses. Unfortunately the

Fig. 103. A double cartshed with haystore above and stable added alongside. This stood until recently on wharf C.27 at Newtown.

road sides of these properties have very recently been white-rendered. The two nearest the pub were lived in by employees of Charles Jones who operated the Wharf 'C.7' at their rear.[10] The three dwellings further east were lived in by employees of Thomas Edward Ward (also a large coal-owner at Chirk) who operated Wharf 'C.8' at their rear and the great limekiln-bank at 'C.24'.[11] The recent flood-bank works have destroyed the canal road that ran below 'C.24', 'C.23' and 'C.22', and also the remains of most of the eighteen limekilns that stood on those wharves. A bungalow named 'Severn Lea' is sited on the western entrance of this old road and in its garden (at the bottom-left corner of wharf 'C.24' on the plan) are two limekiln drawing-tunnels which penetrate beneath a second bungalow sited on the hump above. Further west at 'C.14' was the fine neo-Georgian block of the 'Commercial Inn'. The Inn included a shop, of which the early nineteenth-century frontage remained until very recently. Unfortunately the building has been replaced by a large modern shed.

Further west on 'C.27' and 'C.28' stand a block of very attractive early nineteenth-century houses built for further employees of Thomas Edward Ward who operated the wharves and kilns on those two sites. These extant houses (Fig. 102) ascended from east to west in order of social status; the most easterly three houses were in double occupation and were probably back-to-back dwellings. On the east (right when viewed from the road) are two terraced houses with single-room frontages, then three with double frontages, and at the western end stood the long, broad house presumably for the wharf manager. This has been demolished to make way for Cwrt Dolafon. To the east of this, and sited in a garden (below the 'C' of 'C.27' on the plan), was the early nineteenth-century double cart-shed, stable and hay-store mentioned earlier.

The canal-port and settlement at Newtown was a unique concentration of trading activity producing the associated settlement patterns that are found all along the Montgomeryshire canal. Fortunately a combination of source materials allows a detailed examination of the Newtown Port in the canal's hey-day to be made and hence an evaluation of the remains that survive can be attempted.

Newtown Canal Settlement in 1842.

The reference numbers in the following section (i.e. C.1-C.37) refer to the accompanying plan of the canal port at Newtown (Fig. 101). The descriptions of the various wharves have been taken from the Llanllwchaearn tithe map schedule of 1842 and the reference book of the 1845 deposited plan of a Shropshire Union scheme to build a railway along the canal. The dwellings of the contemporary inhabitants of the canal settlement have been located from the latter source, and detailed information on them and their households has come from the 1841 and 1851 census returns for the township of Gwestydd in the parish of Llanllwchaearn (the ages of the people given is that correct in 1842). Some indication of the early growth of the settlement has been given by referring to the 1833 plan of the 'Canal Basin and Wharfs at Newtown' as a source of information.

---

[10] The 'Shropshire Union Railway....Plan' of 1845.
[11] Ibid.

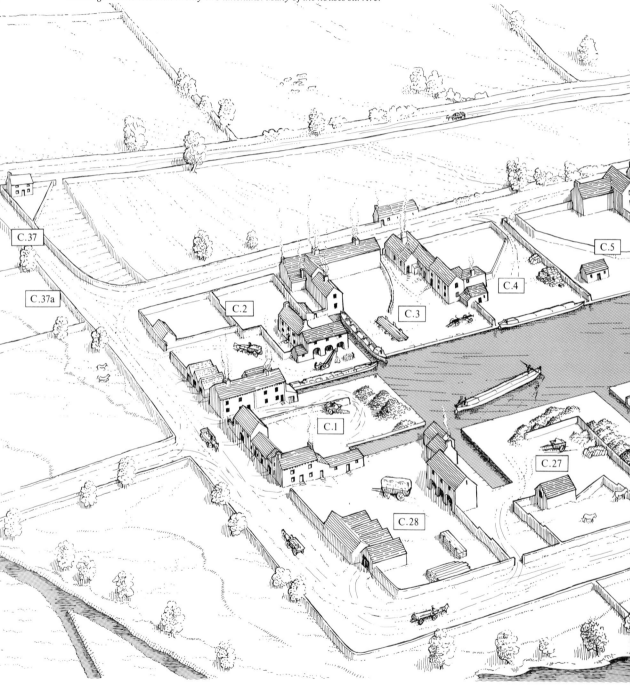

Fig. 104. An impression of Newtown Canal Basin in its mid-nineteenth-century hey-day. A large rectangular terminal dock was surrounded by some seven boat-loading arms, each large enough to take two narrow-boats. The canal company built two circuits of roads around their terminal wharves and the landward sides of these were lined with workers housing, ancillary buildings and no less than twenty-two limekilns. Many of the houses survive.

C.15 C.15a C.21 C.14 C.13 C.12 C.11 C.10 C.9 C.8 C.7 C.6 C.22-23 C.24 C.25

131

C.1 House, warehouse, stables outbuildings, garden, yard and wharf; cottage.

This wharf was originally owned by the iron-master and coal-master William Hazeldine and was almost certainly established to sell coal from his Plas Kynaston Collieries on the Ellesmere Canal at Ruabon. By 1845, with his death, it passed into the occupancy of David Lloyd who lived in a house on the north-eastern side of the wharf:

Occupants	Age	Occupation	Place of birth
David Lloyd	61	'Lime and Coal Agent'	Montgomeryshire
Sharlot Lloyd	56		,,
Margaret Lloyd	21		,,
Mary Davies	21	'Servant'	,,

The end of this house towards Dolafon Road had a cottage attached in which lived:

Occupants	Age	Occupation	Place of birth
Elizabeth Jones	61		Montgomeryshire
Thomas Peter	16		Shrewsbury

The roadside of the wharf had one small building erected on it by 1833, and by 1842 this had been extended into a range of 'warehouses, sheds, outbuildings' covering the whole landward side of the wharf except for one small access way.

Present Remains

The wharf itself is now an open garden whilst the wharfinger's house and the cottage form a single block of housing now called Number 1 Dolafon Road. This stands at right-angles to the road, and has been rendered and largely refenestrated.

C.2 Two warehouses, office, sheds, stables, outbuildings and wharf; house.

A house in the centre of the wharf was occupied by:

Occupants	Age	Occupation	Place of birth
David Morgan	31	'Timber Merchant'	Montgomeryshire
Susannah Morgan	36		,,
David Morgan	15		,,
Cate Morgan	13		,,
Jane Morgan	10		,,
Susannah Morgan	8		,,
Charles Morgan	6		,,
Harriet Morgan	1		,,
Mary Williams	16	'Servant'	,,

David Morgan also had a yard on the opposite side of Dolafon Road at 'C.37a.' for the stacking of his timber.

Present Remains

This wharf is now totally devoid of all old buildings. An access road—Cae Camlas—has been very recently driven across it to give access to a new housing development in the canal basin and a new block of houses has been erected alongside Dolafon Road.

C.3 Joiner's shop, stable, outbuildings, yard and wharf; house, outbuilding and yard; kitchen and houses.

Here, as elsewhere on the terminal canal basin, the landward frontage of the wharf and its sides were occupied by ranges of ancillary buildings and workers' houses. The range extending back from the canal company roadways encircling the basin towards the dock and basin was lived in by the occupant of the wharf and his family:

Occupants	Age	Occupation	Place of birth
Arthur Howells..........................56		'Carpenter'	Montgomeryshire
Sarah Howells 66			,,
Jane Roberts.............................16		'Servant'	,,

All the buildings on the road frontage of the wharf had been completed by 1833 and in 1842 they were occupied as follows:

No. 4	Lower Canal Road	'Kitchen'	John Baxter Owen
No. 5	,, ,, ,,	'House'	John Baxter Owen
No. 6	,, ,, ,,	,,	William Francis
No. 7	,, ,, ,,	,,	George Pugh
No. 8	,, ,, ,,	,,	Margaret Jones
No. 10	,, ,, ,,	,,	Mary Griffith
No. 11	,, ,, ,,	,,	David Hamer

The 1841 and 1851 censuses apparently only give information on three of these households.

No.6	William Francis.................46	'Carpenter'	Montgomeryshire
,,	Elizabeth Francis 46		*
,,	John Francis.....................21	'Carpenter'	Montgomeryshire
,,	Ann Francis 16		,,
,,	Elizabeth Francis 15		,,
,,	William Francis.................12		,,
,,	George Francis 10		,,

* *born outside Montgomeryshire*

No. 10	Mary Griffith...................51	'Pauper'	Montgomeryshire
No. 11	David Hamer 60	'Coal Dealer'	,,
	Margaret Hamer 20		,,

This information on the occupants of the terrace at 4 to 8 Lower Canal Road is incomplete but may suggest that the heads of the various households worked for the occupier of the wharf.

Present Remains

Numbers 4 to 8 Lower Canal Road are now one terrace of early nineteenth-century houses although Number 4 was originally only a kitchen and not a dwelling. The terrace was built in two phases, as indicated by a straight joint in the masonry between Numbers 5 and 6. Numbers 4, 5 and 8 are single-fronted, and Numbers 6 and 7 are double-fronted houses. All the houses have attractive late nineteenth-century wooden porches.

Numbers 10 and 11 Lower Canal Road are small single-storey brick cottages (a type common in west Wales—although made there using clay or rubble-stone walling). It is not perhaps inappropriate to find that a single pauper occupied one; the occupation of the other by a coal-dealer or merchant seems more surprising. They seem to have been converted from open storage sheds.

The operator of the wharf—Arthur Howells—lived in a house sited where the present late nineteenth-century backs of Numbers 4 and 5 Lower Canal Road now stand. Other nineteenth-century wharf buildings including stables survive at the rear of Numbers 10 and 11 Lower Canal Road.

C.4 Stable, yard and wharf; house, outbuilding and yard; garden.

The area of land enclosed by the quadrant on the landward or roadside of the wharf was a garden used by Richard Jones, the farmer and lime-burner who owned the wharf by 1833. In

1842 Richard Jones was recorded as living elsewhere at the basin—on the landward side of wharf 'C.15.'.

The house centrally located on the wharf (to the left of 'C.4.' on the plan) was occupied by:

Occupants	Age	Occupation	Place of birth
Richard Evans	41	'Boat Man'	Montgomeryshire
Mary Evans	31		,,
Elinor Evans	6		,,
Edward Evans	3		,,
Jane Evans	1		,,

Richard Evans was the boatman apparently employed by the operator of the wharf—a John Herbert—who used the stable, outbuilding and wharf on the water frontage of C.4.

Present Remains

Richard Evans's house and its early nineteenth-century outbuildings remain reasonably intact and a modern shed stands on the site of the canalside loading-wharf.

C.5 Stable, outbuilding, yard and wharf; house, shop outbuilding, yard and garden; garden.

As on 'C.4.' the quadrant of land on the roadside of the wharf was a garden (used by a Lewis Davies). The canalside wharf with its stable and outbuilding was tenanted by John Lewis—a forty-one year old lime-burner who lived elsewhere at the basin with his two teenage sons (thirteen and fifteen) who were both boatmen.

To the right (north-east) of 'C.5.' on the plan was a long narrow strip of land running from the terminus of a canal dock to the road. This was the garden and yard of the 'house and shop' occupied by:

Occupants	Age	Occupation	Place of birth
Joseph Mansfield	64	'Inn Keeper'	Shropshire
Mary Mansfield	34		Denbighshire

It seems likely that the 'shop' was also one of the canal basin's public houses.

Present Remains

A modern bungalow occupies much of the canalside loading-wharf and the roadside house/shop/ inn has been largely rebuilt (Number 13 Lower Canal Road) with a late nineteenth-century house added to the north-east ('Graford').

C.6 Elm Tree Wharf; warehouse, shed, yards; house, outbuilding, yard and garden; house, outbuilding, yard and garden.

This wharf had originally been leased by William Buckley Pugh who also operated wharves 'C.28' and 'C.22-23'. It was Pugh, of course, who largely initiated and financed the extension of the Montgomeryshire Canal to serve his large investment in textile manufacturing at Newtown.

The layout of this canalside wharf largely follows the pattern already seen with the other plots—the waterside open area allowed space for loading and unloading boats and carts, whilst the warehouses, sheds and/or stables were situated towards the middle of each wharf. A relatively narrow track gave access to the canal company roadways encircling the canal basin and the landward side of the wharves were occupied by the wharf operators, their employees and ancillary trades. Here at 'C.6' the layout of a corner plot allowed more room for domestic habitation on its longer road frontage.

The house above and to the left of 'C.6' on the plan was the 'house, outbuilding, yard and garden' occupied by:

Occupants	Age	Occupation	Place of birth
Richard Spoonley......................56		'Flower Dealer' (sic-more likely 'flour')	Montgomeryshire
Mary Spoonley 51			,,
John Spoonley 21		'Flannel Manufacturer'	,,
David Spoonley 16			,,
Ellen Spoonley 14			,,
Elizabeth Spoonley...................13			,,
Diana Spoonley 8			,,

Richard Spoonley was also the occupier of the 'warehouse, shed, yards and wharf' situated on the waterside of the wharf (below the labelling of 'C.6' on the plan).

The house on the corner of the basin-side roads was occupied by:

Occupants	Age	Occupation	Place of birth
Richard Owen 61		'Clerk per Lime'	Montgomeryshire
Ann Owen...............................51			,,

Present Remains

A large shed covers part of the wharf area and two post-war houses are sited close to the road whilst Spoonley and Owen's semi-detached houses survive in a much rebuilt form with a raised roof (Number 14 Lower Canal Road).

C.7 The Waggon and Horses Inn, stables, outbuildings, garden, yards and wharf; workshop, stable, outbuilding and building; houses.

By 1833 this wharf was under the occupancy of Charles Jones; the two houses on the landward side had already been built but the present Waggon and Horses Inn on the corner was constructed later.

The wharf area of the plot had a building adjacent to both the canal and road by 1842. The canalside of this building was a house probably occupied by:

Occupants	Age	Occupation	Place of birth
Thomas Reese 41		'Coal Merchant'	Montgomeryshire
Ann Reese...............................37			,,
Edward Reese 8			,,

The other side of this building was a 'work-shop, stable, outbuilding and buildings' occupied by the 'machine maker' William Jones who was the son of the lessee and occupier of the wharf, Charles Jones. The corner building on the landward side of the wharf was the Waggon and Horses Inn, stables, outbuildings, garden, yards and wharf' occupied by:

Occupants	Age	Occupation	Place of birth
Charles Jones 51		'Inn Keeper'	Montgomeryshire
Elizabeth Jones........................56			,,
William Jones..........................21			,,

The rest of the landward side of the wharf was covered by two houses occupied by a David Rogers and Evan Davies. These two households are fairly certainly identified in the 1851 census as follows:

Occupants	Age	Occupation	Place of birth
1. Sarah Rogers......................70		'Widow'	Montgomeryshire
John Rogers........................23		'Lodger'	,,

	Age	Occupation	Place of birth
2. Evan Davies	35	'Labourer'	Montgomeryshire
Jane Davies	—		,,
Edward Bird	9	'Stepson'	,,
John Davies	15		,,

Present Remains

All old buildings have now been cleared from the canalside of wharf 'C.7' and a large modern shed has been erected there—part of the premises of Central Dairies PLC. The main brick block of the Waggon and Horses public house was built sometime between 1833 and 1842. The attached terrace of five houses stretching back along Lower Canal Road is earlier. The first house in this terrace (the Rogers's house) is entirely built of green-sandstone rubble whilst the second has a green-sandstone street facade but a canalside elevation of red brick. The rest of the terrace occupied the landward side of the more northerly adjoining wharf 'C.8'. It is possible that the two houses fronting 'C.7' were the original Waggon and Horses public house. Unfortunately the Inn and the adjoining houses have recently been white-rendered.

C.8 Buildings and wharf; houses; pigcotes and gardens

Wharf 'C.8' was one of the wharves of Thomas Edward Ward, by far the largest of the wharfingers and lime-merchants operating at the Newtown Canal basin in the 1840s. As previously noted, Ward had been developing the canalside coalfield at Chirk from 1805 onwards. The occupants of the three houses fronting the landward side of the wharf were his tenants from at least 1833 and the houses were occupied by (in order south to north):

Occupants	Age	Occupation	Place of birth
William Bennett	46	'Labourer'	Montgomeryshire
Martha Bennett	41		,,
Moses Bennett (*Moses Bennett appears in the 1845 book of reference as head of the household, but does not appear in the 1841 census*).			
David Griffiths	46	'Labourer'	Montgomeryshire
Margaret Griffiths	46		,,
Margaret Griffiths	16		,,
James Jones	51	'Brick maker'	Montgomeryshire
Ann Jones	56		,,
James Jones	26	'Brick maker'	,,
Thomas Jones	21	'Shoemaker'	,,
Ann Jones	16		,,

Present Remains

The early nineteenth-century houses on the landward side of the wharf remain although the end one, Number 23 Lower Canal Road, is now derelict. The houses all had walls on their landward side built in green-sandstone rubble with canalside elevations in redbrick, and the gable-end of the terrace was constructed of stone. The attendant pig-cotes, shown on contemporary maps, and any other features of the wharf have disappeared under the premises of Central Dairies PLC.

C.9 and C.10 Wharf; office, stables, garden, road and wharf.

These two wharves were occupied by Joseph Mansfield, the publican/shopkeeper who lived on wharf 'C.6'.

Present Remains

Both former wharves are now occupied by the premises of Central Dairies PLC. and no original features remain.

C.11 Wharf.

This wharf was unoccupied in the 1840s.

Present Remains

None—part of the premises of Central Dairies PLC.

C.12 Unenclosed timber wharf and road.

This wharf was also unoccupied—'in hand'.

Present Remains

This wharf never had any buildings on it and the land it occupies is now also part of the large Central Dairies site.

C.13 House, stable, outbuildings, yard and wharf.

The land on the riverside of the wharf were unenclosed but the canalside was occupied by:

Occupants	Age	Occupation	Place of birth
Edward Humphreys	36	'Coal Dealer'	Montgomeryshire
Mary Humphreys	46		,,
Edward Humphreys	13		,,
Mary Humphreys	15		,,
Richard Humphreys	10		,,
Sarah Humphreys	7		,,

Present Remains

None.

C.14 The Commercial Inn—house, stable, outbuildings and yard; house and shop; cottages; pigcotes and yard and wharf and road.

As with wharves 'C.6' and 'C.7' the position of this wharf alongside a road over the canal provided ready road access directly to the water-frontage of the wharf and consequently released all the road-frontage of the site for building development. Covering most of plot 'C.14' was the Commercial Inn of the wharfinger Richard Lewis with its 'stable, outbuilding and yard'. The domestic part of the Inn was occupied by:

Occupants	Age	Occupation	Place of birth
Richard Lewis	26	'Inn Keeper'	Montgomeryshire
Ann Lewis	21		,,
Mary Thomas	21	'Servant'	,,
James Williams	41	'Engenere'	,,

(*sic*-John?)

On the north-western corner of the wharf were a 'house and shop' occupied by:

John Davies	46	'Labourer at Lime Works'	Montgomeryshire
Ann Davies	46		,,
Ann Davies	12		,,
Elinor Davies	9		,,
James Davies	7		,,

On the side-road leading over the canal from west to east lived the following heads of households:

1. David Davies   2. Hannah Evans   3. John Davies

It is impossible to say more with certainty about these households. A fifteen year old David Davies—a boatman—is noted in the 1841 census and a twenty-six year old 'labourer at lime works' of the same name in the 1851 survey: this may be the David Davies noted on the contemporary plan as living here. The occupants of all three of these cottages shared 'pigcotes and a yard' at the canal-end of their dwellings.

Present Remains.

In 1981 it was possible to record photographically the exterior of the early nineteenth-century brick block that once comprised the Commercial Inn and the adjoining shop. The cottages had already gone. Now all early features on wharf 'C.6' have been swept away and a large prefabricated shed erected there.

C.15 Flannel factory, outbuilding and garden; bakehouse, outbuilding and garden; house, granary, stable and garden; houses and gardens.

The early nineteenth-century manufacturing industries using coal brought along the canal were in effect segregated from the general wharves situated nearer the actual terminus of the canal at Newtown. The canalside factories at Newtown are in fact east of the two blocks of wharves completely encircled by the canal company roads at the canal head. A similar situation can be found at Welshpool where the early nineteenth-century suburb built immediately outside the northern boundary of the borough, including the area of *Waterloo* (a name evocative of the period and itself built near *Trafalgar House*), had its economic base founded on the only steam-powered flannel-mill in Welshpool and the town gasworks.

At Newtown the canalside of wharf 'C.15' was the site of a flannel factory (vacant in 1851 but later revived) operated by George Green.

In 1842 there was a malthouse on the adjoining piece of wharf but by 1845 there was apparently a bakehouse here operated by John Thomas and William Morgan—both these installations presumably would have used coal brought along the canal.

The fairly large house at the south-western roadside of the wharf was occupied by Richard Jones. In the 1841 census there are two Richard Joneses recorded—one a boatman and the other a 'Farmer of 300 acres [122 hectares] and limeburner employing 31 Labourers'. This fairly large house, adjacent to Richard Jones's six limekilns ('C.23') and sited quite near his large garden (the landward side of 'C.4'), seems more likely to have belonged to that Richard Jones who was the more substantial farmer/limekiln operator and who came originally from Kerry near Newtown.

This corner house was occupied by:

Occupants	Age	Occupation	Place of birth
Richard Jones	51	'Lime man and Farmer'	Montgomeryshire
Mary Jones	36		,,
Richard Lewis Jones	10		,,
Mary Ann Jones	4		,,
Edward Jones	7		,,

The next house along the landward side of the wharf was occupied by the John Thomas who operated the bakery with his neighbour William Morgan (on whom there is no census information available):

Occupants	Age	Occupation	Place of birth
John Thomas	66	'Labourer'	Montgomeryshire
Mary Thomas	36		,,
Hanna Thomas	8		,,

The house at the north end of the landward side of wharf 'C.15' was occupied by:

John Jones	36	'Labourer'	Montgomeryshire
Mary Jones	31	'Woolen Spiner'	,,
Mary Jones	5		,,
Elizabeth Jones	3		,,
Margaret Jones	1		,,
Margaret Jones	71	'Independent'	,,

Present Remains

The flannel factory called 'Kymric Mills' grew and prospered throughout the nineteenth century and for a good deal of the twentieth also. What look to be early twentieth-century buildings now cover most of 'C.15' and are used for other purposes. By the end of its working life weaving-sheds also covered most of the former wharves 'C.10-12'.

C.15a Graving dock, workshops, yard and road; sheds and yard.

The dry-docks of the canal ports at Newtown and Welshpool were both some way to the north of the main concentration of wharves. The Newtown Dry-dock was run in 1842 by forty-one year old Edward Jones who lived elsewhere at the basin with his wife and son. Edward Jones had been born outside the county.

Present Remains
None.

C.21 Foundry premises and yard.

The Newtown Foundry was worked in 1842 by John Onions. Pig-iron and coal would have been brought from Ruabon by canal.

Present Remains
None.

C.22-23 Limekilns, stable, office, yards and wharf; house and outbuildings.

These were used by the Kerry farmer Richard Jones who probably lived in the large house at wharf 'C.15'.

Present Remains
None.

C.24 Stables, office, outbuildings, limekilns, yard and wharf; house and outbuildings.

This wharf included twelve limekilns operated by Thomas Edward Ward—the largest wharfinger and lime-burner at Newtown in the 1840s (and developer of the Chirk coalfield along the Ellesmere Canal to the northeast). Between 1833 and 1845 a house was constructed on the north-eastern corner of the wharf and in 1842 was occupied by:

Occupants	Age	Occupation	Place of birth
Daniel Griffiths	51	'Labourer'	Montgomeryshire
Mary Griffiths	51		,,
William Griffiths	15	'Wool Sorter'	,,
Daniel Griffiths	15	'Woolen Sluber'	,,

Present Remains

The only visible remains on the wharf are two limekiln drawing-tunnels near Dolafon Road. These go under the bungalow named 'Dolafon' from the garden of 'Severn Lea' bungalow.

C.25 Cottages; stable, limekilns, yard and wharf.

From at least 1833 until 1842 this property had been occupied by James Hall and Co.; by 1845 it was part of the trading empire of Thomas Edward Ward. Four cottages fronted the wharf and two of the single-fronted houses now remaining were each described in 1845 as 'two cottages'—suggesting that these and the double-fronted house adjoining were back-to-back dwellings. In 1842 the occupants of the houses were as follows:

Address	Occupant	Age	Occupation	Place of birth
3 Dolafon Terrace	William Bennett	46	'Labourer'	Montgomeryshire
	Martha Bennett	41		,,
4 Dolafon Terrace	Thomas Price	46	'Labourer'	,,
	Martha Price	46		,,
	Edward Price	15		,,
	John Price	12		,,
	Richard Price	9		,,
	Susannah Price	7		,,
	Ann Howels	5		,,

The occupant of the other half of 4 Dolafon Terrace was John Thomas about whom no more is known. Numbers 3 and 4 Dolafon Terrace are double-fronted houses and a straight joint in the brickwork separates them from the later single-fronted houses at 5 and 6 Dolafon Terrace. All the houses had been built by 1833.

5 Dolafon Terrace	David Rowlands	26	'Labourer'	Montgomeryshire
	Margaret Rowlands	26		,,
	Mary Rowlands	8		,,
	David Rowlands	5		,,
	Jane Rowlands	1		,,
	Ann Owen	15	'Servant'	,,

The second half of 5 Dolafon Terrace was occupied by Morris Thomas of whom no more information is available.

6 Dolafon Terrace	Martha Breeze	51	'Widow'	Montgomeryshire
	Mary Breeze	18		,,
	Edward Breeze	15		,,
	Susannah Breeze	7		,,

The other part of 6 Dolafon Terrace was unoccupied.
The rest of this large wharf included a stable-block and six limekilns.

Present Remains

Numbers 4 to 6 Dolafon Terrace (Fig. 102) were rebuilt in the late nineteenth century and are now lived in by single families. The handsome gabled wooden porches that are so much a feature of houses alongside the Montgomeryshire Canal still remain.

C.27 Coal yard and wharf; stables, outbuildings, garden, road; house and cottage.

This coal yard was in the possession of Thomas Edward Ward by 1833. By that date the two houses on the road frontage of the wharf were already built. In 1842 the largest of these—

Number 1 Dolafon Terrace with its outbuilding and yard—was unoccupied.
Number 2 Dolafon Terrace was occupied by:

Occupants	Age	Occupation	Place of birth
John Ruff 31		'Labourer'	Montgomeryshire
Ann Ruff.............................26			,,
Ann Ruff.............................. 4			,,

Present Remains

In the mid-1980s a stable and double cartshed with granary above (Fig. 103), built between 1833 and 1842, were demolished, as was Number 1 Dolafon Terrace. Number 2 Dolafon Terrace remains inhabited but with a modern enclosed porch. Most of the wharf has been cleared for the building of Cwrt Dolafon.

C.28 Timber Wharf, yard; wharf and yard; shed and yard; cottage.

By 1833 the operator of this wharf was William Buckley Pugh who died between 1842 and 1845 and was succeeded by Evan Humphreys. A long narrow strip of land on the north-east of the wharf had been fenced off as a separate wharfage by 1842 and was tenanted by Richard Williams. Alongside had been added a shed and a cottage occupied by Richard Morris.

By 1833 a house had been added to the south-western, landward side of the wharf. In 1845 this was occupied by Evan Humphreys and had been extended back towards the canal dock with a warehouse also being added to the landward side of the wharf.

Present Remains

Two modern bungalows occupy the central part of the wharf with a semi-detached house—'South View' of 1905—built on the south-east area of the wharf. The original wharf-operator's house remains—now called 'Glen Dale'—and is rendered. No other early features survive.

C.37a Timber-yard.

This timber-yard would have been used for the storage of timber prior to shipment from the adjoining wharf 'C.2' which was also operated by the timber merchant David Morgan.

Present Remains

The road frontage of the property is now occupied by a mid nineteenth century house.

C.37 Timber-yard.

This would have served a similar purpose to the above yard, this time for Arthur Howells, the occupant of Wharf 'C.3'.

Present Remains None.

E Other Waterway Settlements

In addition to these major centres it was natural that smaller settlements should grow up and develop along the canal. In this way the Montgomeryshire Canal differed from its contemporary counterparts in south Wales, for it was a primarily agricultural waterway passing through a broad valley of fertile farmland, distributing lime and collecting produce from a large area. By contrast, the small canalside settlements of south Wales were few: the canals there passed through much poorer farmland in constricted valleys and aimed mainly to connect sporadic nodes of industry. The Montgomeryshire Canal, though, provides a number of good examples of lesser settlements; one particularly well-documented and preserved site is at Clafton Bridge.

Clafton Bridge

Clafton Bridge, the name of which is a corruption of Clopton's Bridge, is sited on the B4393, 13 kilometres north of Welshpool. It is 400 metres west of the crossroads at Four Crosses on the Oswestry road. At this point the growth of a trading settlement was facilitated by the existence of large basins on either side of the bridge. These basins had to be excavated here and at the next bridge further south in order to obtain material to build the large approach embankments to these two arched bridges on the level ground south of the Vyrnwy. These basins opposite the towing-path made ideal docks for unloading or 'winding-holes' for turning boats. At the time of building, this bridge was on the main Llanymynech to Welshpool road near its junction with the main

road up the Vyrnwy valley and was hence at a natural focal point for local trade distribution. The wharf on the south-east was probably originally the limestone wharf for Mr. Clopton Prhys of Rhysnant and Llandrinio Hall.[12] Over the bridge from Four Crosses can now be seen two early nineteenth-century houses on the left. The nearer, smaller house was probably one of two that were occupied by the lime-burners operating the four kilns that stood to the south.[13] 'Canal House', with its large garden bordering the humbler residence, was probably lived in by Mrs. Jones, the owner of the kilns, in 1838.[14]

In 1836, Richard Goolden, a trader and flannel-maker from Welshpool, built the warehouse with attached wharfinger's house that stands alongside the towing-path to the south

---

[12] *Towpath Guide, 2, Welshpool to Llanymynech*, 9.
[13] The 'Shropshire Union Railway....Plan' of 1845.
[14] *Towpath Guide, 2*, 9.

of the bridge. This was on the site of the old lime wharf opposite the kilns.[15] The two-storeyed rubble-stone warehouse has double loading doors with the remains of a timber support for a loading-hoist or crane.

Robert Rogers had rented or leased Hannah Jones's nearby kilns by 1841 and was living in 'Canal House'.[16] In 1844, he built the long row of white-washed buildings with attendant wharf next to the towing-path on the northern side of the road. These consisted of four houses, warehouses, and a barn with an office and weighing machine at the entrance to the yard at the bottom of the ramped approach to the bridge. The wharf was mainly for the sale of coal, and the field to the north was used to graze Rogers's boat-horses and cart-horses.[17] Sometime during the later nineteenth century a dry-dock was added to the north of the yard in order to service Rogers's boats. In 1863 one warehouse was converted into two cottages,[18]

and today the yard has a long row of occupied cottages built into the road ramp with a barn at its eastern end where a garage, probably the converted office and weighbridge house, flanks the entrance to the old coal-yard.

The creation and growth of these new settlements during the working life of the canal graphically shows the dynamism and import-ance of the 'canal economy'. Many of the kiln-banks and other sites mentioned in the gazetteer acted as the nuclei of other settle-ments of differing sizes which reached various stages of development before the 'canal eco-nomy' was succeeded by that centered on the local railway and later road networks.

---

[15] Monts. Canal Reports Bks., 7 February 1842.
[16] Tithe map of Llandysilio, 1841 (N.L.W.).
[17] The 'Shropshire Union Railway....Plan' of 1845.
[18] Monts. Canal Reports Bks., 1863.

Fig. 105. Clafton Bridge, showing the warehouses and canal-workers housing built into the approach ramps of an earlier canal bridge.

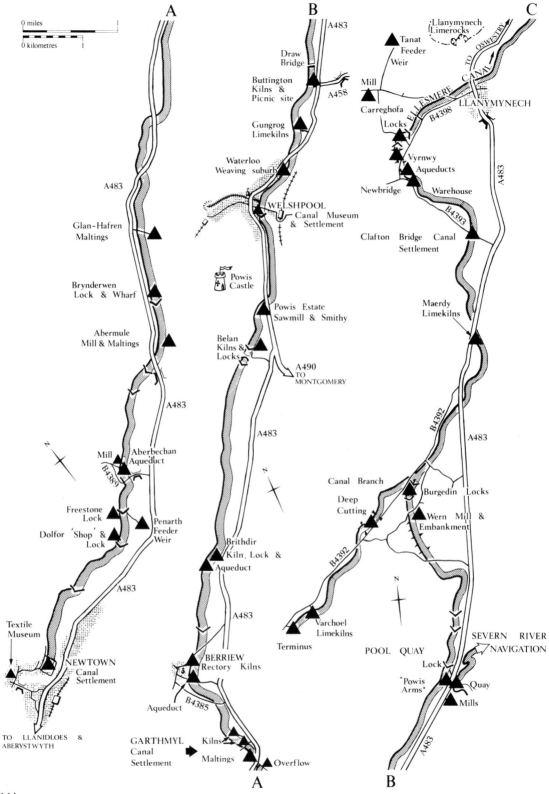

A

0 miles 1

0 kilometres 1

A483

Glan-Hafren
Maltings

Brynderwen
Lock & Wharf

Abermule
Mill & Maltings

A483

Mill   Aberbechan
        Aqueduct

B4389

Freestone
Lock

Dolfor 'Shop' &   Penarth
Lock   Feeder
                  Weir

A483

Textile
Museum

NEWTOWN
Canal
Settlement

TO LLANIDLOES &
ABERYSTWYTH

B

A483

Draw
Bridge

A458

Buttington
Kilns &
Picnic site

Gungrog
Limekilns

Waterloo
Weaving suburb

WELSHPOOL
Canal Museum
& Settlement

Powis
Castle

Powis Estate
Sawmill & Smithy

Belan
Kilns &
Locks

A490
TO
MONTGOMERY

A483

Brithdir
Kiln, Lock &
Aqueduct

A483

Varchoel
Limekilns

Terminus

BERRIEW
Rectory Kilns

Aqueduct

B4385

GARTHMYL
Canal
Settlement

Kilns

Maltings   Overflow

A

C

Llanymynech
Limerocks

TO OSWESTRY

Tanat
Feeder
Weir

ELLESMERE CANAL

Mill

Carreghofa
Locks

LLANYMYNECH

B4398

Vyrnwy
Aqueducts

A483

Newbridge   Warehouse

B4393

Clafton Bridge Canal
Settlement

Maerdy
Limekilns

B4392

A483

Canal Branch

Deep
Cutting

Burgedin Locks

Wern Mill &
Embankment

B4392

N

POOL QUAY

SEVERN RIVER
NAVIGATION

Lock

'Powis
Arms'   Quay

Mills

A483

B

Gazetteer

Gazetteer of selected remains along the Montgomeryshire Canal

Sites are arranged in order along the canal from south to north.

Key
** = most impressive and interesting sites (easily accessible);
* = sites of interest but not worth a special journey;
(**) = interesting sites (difficult access—i.e. the owner should be contacted);
(*) = minor sites (difficult access).

WALKS. Three short walks are recommended for those travelling by car between sites on the canal: a one and a half kilometre rural walk along the canal towing-path from Carreghofa Locks to Newbridge Warehouse (just south of the Vyrnwy Aqueduct) and back; an urban walk along the canal in the small market town of Welshpool, and a choice of longer rural walks from Aberbechan to Penarth Weir (3.4 kilometres) or to Dolfor Lock and back (6 kilometres). See the appropriate entries below for details.

Newtown Canal Settlement ** Reached from the A483 Welshpool to Llanidloes road by turning down the main shopping street of Newtown and over the River Severn into the northern suburb of Pen-y-gloddfa. Turn first right here into the old textile-workers' area with its interesting museum, and after 0.5 kilometres right again at 'Canal Villa' into Lower Canal Road. The old Georgian-style terraces beyond 'Canal Villa' surround the site of the large canal basin; the whole formed a substantial canal-port. See chapter six for a full description of the extensive remains.

A fine kilometre-long river-bank walk to the north along the floodbank that covers the site of the canal leads to the former steam-pump house (SO 1175 9222). This ornate stone building of 1860 is now a garage.

RECOMMENDED CANAL WALK 1.—A longer towing-path walk through the superb scenery next to the River Severn is recom-

mended to the more energetic. This leads from Aber-bechan Aqueduct to the three sites listed below. To the weir and back is a round-trip of 3.5 kilometres. An additional walk to Dolfor Lock may add a further two kilometres.

Dolfor Lock ** This can be easily reached if the towing-path has been cleared of undergrowth. On the near-side stands a lock-house (SO 1367 9273), much enlarged in the late nineteenth century (like many others) with a typical pretty 'Gothic' porch added. On a quay alongside the marshy canal-bed is the building that was once the storehouse and canal-'shop' (presumably a workshop—SO 1367 9269), a mid to late nineteenth-century brick building. Behind it stands another late nineteenth-century pigsty with granary above; built by the canal company (SO 1365 9268) into and taking advantage of the hillside for access arrangements.

Penarth Feeder Weir ** SO 1398 9266. A developed design of the middle of the Industrial Revolution, with two gracefully curved weirs crossing the Severn and an elaborate salmon-ladder on the canal or western side. The double weir was designed by Josias Jessop in 1813-1814 and built by John Williams in 1814-1818. The weir can be reached along a foot-path from Freestone Lock. Dolfor Lock can be reached along the one kilometre of towing-path (which may be overgrown) from Freestone Lock. In any case it is worth glancing above Freestone Lock in order to see the form of the (dry) canal-bed.

Freestone Lock ** SO 1389 9300—A kilometre from Aberbechan. This lock has a fine 'lock-tail' bridge; it was built over the end of the lock

---

Fig. 106. Map of the Montgomeryshire Canal with the major sites of interest indicated by triangles.

in order to save on the costs of building bridge abutments and constructing a large arch which elsewhere would have had to span the towing-path. A map of 1859 actually shows two other structures built over the lock-chamber: a house next to the bridge and a storehouse over the upper end of the chamber. No traces of these remain and maps of the 1840s give more conventional situations for these attendant structures. Derelict mid nineteenth-century semi-detached houses stand alongside the lock at the time of writing. A very pleasant riverside walk leads from below the lock for the one kilometre to Penarth Weir.

Aberbechan Aqueduct and Fulling Mill ** SO 1423 9351 and SO 1425 9357—Accessible by turning off the main A483 onto the B4389, then first right after crossing the canal. The half-timbered building on the rise to the left,

Fig. 107. Aberbechan Aqueduct, the only aqueduct to be found on the later Western Branch of the Montgomeryshire Canal.

Fig. 108. Aberbechan mill-house (nearer the picture) and fulling-mill.

just before the canal is reached, is the old Fulling mill-house. The mill-water ran under the adjoining timber mill-housing and into the canal below. The very pretty little triple-arched aqueduct over the Bechan Brook is reached by a short walk down the towing-path to the right (south).

Abermule Corn-mill and Maltings (*) SO 1605 9491 and SO 1603 9488—Two large and dilapi-

dated brick buildings visible from the new by-pass one kilometre north of Penarth Weir. The mill has *not* been demolished—both canal 'tow-path guides' are mistaken in saying this. The mill, maltings and an adjoining, but now vanished, kiln-bank were joined to the canal by a timber bridge over the River Severn.

Brynderwen Lock and Coal-wharf * SO 1628 9545—Alongside the main A483 road 0.7 kilometres north of the above site. A white-washed wharf-house, single-storeyed lock-cottage and a probable former weighbridge-house remain north of the lock. Alongside the lock and road is a late 'Shropshire Union Railway & Canal Co.' warehouse.

Glan-Hafren Maltings * SO 1678 9640—On the west side of the main road 3.7 kilometres south of Garthmyl. A fine whitewashed Georgian house has a warehouse-like building to its right which was in fact another maltings. However, the original fenestration has very recently been removed and the original character of the building largely lost.

Good malting barley from the Severn valley supplied the poor upland districts of Montgomeryshire and Merioneth and some was transported along the canal.

146

**Garthmyl Canal Settlement ** Directly along-side the main A483 road nine kilometres south of Welshpool.

Garthmyl was the terminal port of the Montgomeryshire Canal from 1797 until the canal was extended between 1815 and 1819-21. A map and fuller discussion of the remains are given in chapter six. Kiln-banks of three and four kilns survive (SO 1932 9939 and SO 1923 9947) attached to, respectively, an old cart-shed and a wharf-house. They are situated up a short track on private land.

A late nineteenth-century maltings (SO 1940 9905) with a barley-drying kiln at its rear stands immediately north of the 'Nag's Head Inn'— 300 metres to the south of the kilns. Between the kilns and the maltings are the scanty remains of another and later kiln-bank (SO 1940 9926), two wharf-houses and a former warehouse, alongside the main road. The southwards canal extension to the textile cen-tre of Newtown began from the bridge next to the maltings.

A short distance to the left up the minor road opposite the 'Nag's Head' can be found an unusual overflow (SO 1940 9892). The

Fig. 109. *The Brynderwen Warehouse was one of many built in the late nineteenth-century in order to encourage the traffic in agricultural feeds and supplies along the Montgomeryshire Canal.*

agricultural buildings behind formerly served as stabling and storage for a coal wharf on the canal.

To the south, the canal extension was fed with water by the Llifior Brook, after passing Pied Mill; another interesting element of the water-economy of the district.

Fig. 110. *The aqueduct over the Rhiw at Berriew.*

**Berriew Aqueduct ** SJ 1886 0060—Follow the riverside lane south-east out of Berriew in order to reach this structure—there is a picnic site alongside. This aqueduct has two nine-metre span river arches and is flanked by two smaller road arches. It was clad in blue brick in 1889. Until recently part of the ashlar stonework at the bottom of the central support could be seen resting on a horizontal timber beam or baulk. This was a rarely visible example of an early civil engineering practice. The beam itself would rest on timber stakes or piles driven vertically into the soft river-bed. The absence of solid stone bedrock at a shallow depth may partly explain why the Mont-gomeryshire Canal engineers had so many problems with the canal aqueducts.

Berriew Southern Kiln-bank (**) SJ 1901 0087—Access off the main road (B4390) to the village from the north. Remains of three limekilns situated in a private garden, one with its burning-cone intact. The weighbridge-house at the kiln wharf is now a garden shed. Unfortunately the front wall of what may have been the most complete early kiln on the canal has very recently collapsed at this site. These remains stand in the garden of 'River Whispers'.

Brithdir Kilns, Lock and Aqueduct ** Kilns at SJ 1996 0229—near the 'Horseshoe Inn', immediately west of the A483, six kilometres from Welshpool. The remains of three kilns and a whitewashed stone-built smithy (now a garage) back onto the public garden of the 'Horseshoe Inn'. Up a ramp lies a stone cart-loading platform, lock and lock-house. The iron aqueduct at Brithdir (SJ 1978 0221) was the prototype for that at Welshpool and can be reached by walking under the humped-back bridge and 200 metres south along the towing-path.

Belan Locks and Kilns ** SJ 2176 0535—2.4 kilometres south of Welshpool on the A483, accessible via a minor road turning to the west just beyond or south of the **Sarn-y-bryn-caled** houses at the A490 turn to Montgomery.

The painted Victorian black-and-white 'Limekiln Cottages' have replaced earlier cottages of the limeburners who toiled at the extensive kiln-bank (which is now a picnic-site). The locks here are also of interest. See chapter three for a fuller description of this site.

The Powis Estate Sawmill and Smithy ** SJ 2215 0590—Situated immediately south of the canal crossing when travelling on the main A483 road 1.6 kilometres south of Welshpool. A fascinating complex of features—permission to view should be asked for on entry to the sawmill yard. An artist-smith next to the sawmill yard accepts commissions for metal work. The sawmill machinery, formerly powered by canal water, is still in regular use. Just south of the sawmill and on the opposite side of the road are the extensive buildings of **Coed-y-**

Fig. 111. The remains of a huge 'bicycle-chain' drive (left foreground) from the water-wheel in the basement of the Powis Estate Sawmill. This replaced a more conventional pit-wheel that formerly engaged the toothed cog in the left background.

dinas Farm which used canal water both for drinking and for power-generation purposes.

RECOMMENDED CANAL WALK 2. An urban walk along the canal in Welshpool.

Welshpool Canal Museum and Settlement ** SJ 2261 1738—To reach the museum when travelling north along the A483, turn right at the traffic lights in the centre of Welshpool. After 150 metres and just before a humped-back bridge turn right into a canalside yard.

A canal exhibition is housed in the large late nineteenth-century wharf warehouse. Around the wharf is a row of old cottages. No. 2 was the canal office and No. 3 was originally a salt-warehouse that later became a lock-keeper's house.

Welshpool Aqueduct Warehouse * SJ 2270 0740—Access from the canal towing-path some 50 metres north-west of the Severn Street bridge (next to the Welshpool Wharf yard).

This is an early nineteenth-century warehouse built of green-sandstone and with the timber stubs, above the first floor loading-door on its canalside elevation, of the support from an external timber-built crane. (The house between the warehouse and aqueduct was the canal agent's house by the mid-nineteenth century).

Welshpool Canal Maintenance Yard (*) SJ 2260 0724—Access from the canal towing-path above Welshpool Town Lock.

A late nineteenth-century group of brick, timber and corrugated-iron buildings, built by the Shropshire Union Railways and Canal Company and now used as a builders' merchants. A section of its narrow-gauge railway system has recently been excavated on the canalside.

Welshpool (Lledan Brook) Aqueduct ** SJ 2271 0744—Situated next to the Aqueduct Warehouse.

The present aqueduct replaced an earlier masonry structure in 1836. A composite cast-iron trough is flanked by paths carried on masonry arches. There are fine cast-iron railings and the best view of the whole structure is obtained by crossing the canal on the old Welshpool and Llanfair Railway girder-bridge to the upstream side of the aqueduct. The plaque recording that J. A. S. Sword built it is visible over the arch as is the impressive circular weir, replacing the old Domen Mill-weir on the Lledan Brook.

Waterloo Weaving Suburb * SJ 2318 0788—The last two old terraces encountered on leaving Welshpool northwards on the main road, to Oswestry and Shrewsbury (A483). They lie to the east of the road: down the track

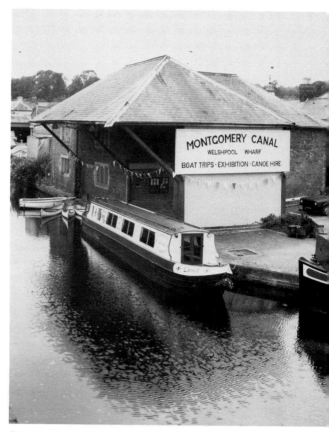

Fig. 112. The canal wharf at Welshpool in 1987 with the Wharf Yard Warehouse (c. 1880)—now housing a canal exhibition.

past the attractive stone facade of the shop lay the now vanished woollen mills that stood alongside the canal. These were built in 1834 for 'The Welshpool Company for the manufacture of flannel by steam' (see chapter five).

Gungrog Kilns * SJ 2370 0838—Access by a left turn 0.8 kilometres north of Welshpool on the A483. These may have been the only kilns owned and run by an individual farmer rather than by a lime and coal merchant. The scant ruins of one stone-arched drawing-tunnel remain in a field.

Buttington Kilns and Picnic-site ** SJ 2411 0891—Directly opposite the junction of the A458 Shrewsbury road with the A483 Newtown to Owestry route. A very attractive site; described in chapter three.

Pool Quay ** Quay site at SJ 2560 1130. This former industrial and waterways settlement flanks the main A483 and is described in chapter six.

Wern Mill and Embankment ** Mill at SJ 2517 1412. This complex of sites is reached via the web of side-roads between Deepcutting Farm and Bank. For notes on the interesting ruins of the mill see chapter two. Beware of the deep draught-tube of the turbine situated in the dry water channel. The beautifully executed over-flow weir provided water for the mill. Clay-pits to the east provided puddling-clay to make the canal watertight and bricks for the Eastern Branch canal company to build and repair its own structures.

The large Wern canal embankment to the immediate south was flanked by large square pits excavated by the canal company during the construction of the bank, and later rented to Welshpool basket-makers who annually harvested their raw material of osiers or young willows from them.

The Guilsfield Branch Canal—The three notable sites on its mostly dry course can be reached from Burgedin canal junction (see below) by continuing along the B4392 towards Guilsfield from the main Welshpool to Oswestry road (the A483).

Guilsfield Branch Terminus * SJ 2293 1252. This branch canal terminates three hundred metres before Guilsfield Village and is reached down a short cart-track leading to 'Tyddyn', a large rendered house converted from wharf labourers' cottages. A triangular pool remains alongside the Guilsfield brook from which this canal branch may originally have drawn water. A brick wharf-wall remains to the north on which stand a corrugated-iron store and a small warehouse of the later nineteenth century.

Varchoel Limekilns (*) SJ 2330 1272. There are the remains of two kilns; one with its charging-vent partly open. The parallel-walled drawing-tunnels are arched with stone and could be early in date. The kilns now stand in a knacker's yard.

'Deep Cutting' * SJ 2451 1402 to SJ 2464 1417. Visible from a road overbridge at the side of the B4392 opposite 'Deepcutting Farm', this was the deepest cutting on the waterway even though shallow by the standards set by later railway engineers.

Burgedin Locks and canal junction ** SJ 2530 1470 off the B4392 1.6 kilometres south of Arddleen.

This is a very pretty complex consisting of a large pool (where swans can usually be seen) above the locks marking the junction with the 3.6 kilometre-long Guilsfield Branch Canal. Here two locks exhibiting Buck's exceptional iron-gearing clearly bearing the name of the Coalbrookdale Ironworks flank one of the many remaining arched bridges on the canal. The inhabited lock-house is complete with storage basement, double stable stalls at the rear of the house, an office and the inevitable lock-keeper's pigsty. Everything about this complex, from original structures to the later outhouses and Victorian gabled porch, was carried out in the neat and attractive style that was characteristic of this waterway. The stub of the canal branch towards Guilsfield has a late overflow weir executed in fine brickwork which transforms the lock-house area into an island.

Maerdy Limekilns ** SJ 2639 1695—A fine bank of four stone-built kilns (Fig. 113) that are now situated in a scrap-yard just south of where the main Welshpool to Owestry road (A483) crosses the canal.

Here it is possible to walk into an almost intact kiln. The fused fire-bricks of the burning-cone can clearly be seen. These are at least the third successive lining to have been installed. The almost level terrain of the area meant that the charging holes of the kilns had to be well above ground level in contrast to the more usual expedient of sinking the kiln structure into a hillside below canal level. The terrain of Maerdy, Guilsfield, Varchoel and Newtown demanded far more effort in the barrowing of the coal and limestone needed to feed the kilns at these Border Country and flood-plain locations. An unloading dock survives on the canal immediately north of the kilns. The upper two metres of the kiln-stacks have been removed so

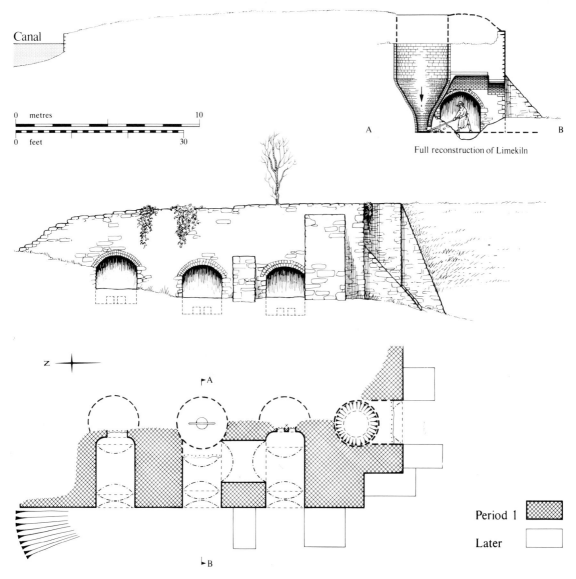

Canal

0 metres 10

0 feet 30

A

B

Full reconstruction of Limekiln

Z

⊢A

⊢B

Period 1

Later

Fig. 113. The kiln-bank at Maerdy is one of the most complete of the many that once existed at intervals along the line of the canal but is unusual in that the charging holes of the kilns were above the level of the canal. The section of kiln no.3 is reconstructed; an arrow indicates the iron-bar placed to stop the charge compacting.

that the present kiln-vents are now almost at canal level. In 1845 John Lewis and Samuel Williams operated the yard from what are now two ruined cottages at the yard entrance. The lessee of the yard, John Rogers, also operated the Bell Inn, a brewhouse and stables immediately to the north of the canal dock. (The Bell Inn now exists as a rendered building

called the 'Bell House'). Two stone-built loading-platforms (for carts) remain in the scrapyard (others are at Belan, Buttington and Brithdir).

Little remains of a second two-kiln-bank to the south. A small rendered cottage by the main road was almost certainly that of the kiln operator.

151

Fig. 114. Early cast-iron bridges with 'fish-bellied' beams (i.e. one edge of the supporting girder curves to a greater thickness at the point of maximum loading in the centre span of the bridge) are an intermittent feature of the canal as illustrated here on Bridge No. 97 at Newbridge (Pentreheylin).

Clafton Bridge Canal Settlement ** SJ 2646 1858—Accessible via the B4393 turn off the Llanymynech-Welshpool trunk road (A483) at Four Crosses.

An interesting complex of buildings, see chapter six for a full description of the extensive remains.

Newbridge or Pentreheylin Timber-wharf and 'Salt Warehouse' ** SJ 2553 1952—one kilometre from Carreghofa.

A very attractive structure—see chapter three for a full description (Fig. 63).

Newbridge Coal-wharf and Wharfhouse *
Wharf at SJ 2540 1957 and the Wharfhouse is at SJ 2542 1954—one kilometre from Carreghofa.

The old coal-wharf is situated on raised ground opposite the towing-path at the southern end of the Vyrnwy Aqueduct. A small modern garage abuts against its platform and on the opposite side of the road stands a small white-painted wharf-house: possibly built in 1831 by Mr. Turner of Pentreheylin Hall and Wharf.

The Vyrnwy Aqueduct ** SJ 2539 1967—Visible from the junction of the B4393 and B4398 2.5 kilometres west of Four Crosses. Access can be gained along the towing-path from the remains of Williams Bridge to the north of the aqueduct.

The bulk of this massive five-arched aqueduct (see chapter one—Fig. 6) is of puddled-clay surrounding the thin masonry

Fig. 115. The Vyrnwy Aqueduct.

walls and paved bed of the narrow water channel. The large and apparently frail outer walls rapidly increase in width as they proceed downwards within this huge core of puddling-clay.

The River Vyrnwy was originally navigable to a point just upstream of the aqueduct, but there is no evidence for any former interchange of traffic between river and canal as at the large river-port of Pool Quay on the River Severn.

Williams Bridge Coal Wharf * SJ 2535 1982— Immediately south of of the point where the

B4398 west from Llanymynech crosses the canal.

This former coal-wharf is situated between the two Vyrnwy Flood Aqueducts described below. The wharf itself sits on a high platform of made ground held up by retaining walls. Its somewhat inconvenient site is explained by its strategic position in relation to the Tanat and Vyrnwy Valleys and their respective markets. A wharf-house was built in 1814 by Mr. Pickering of Cefn Colleries, Ruabon. The adjacent bridge was given its name on 26 March 1844 when Mr. Edward Williams became the new tenant of the coal-wharf.

The wharf-house was unfortunately demolished in the early 1980s when the adjoining bridge was collapsed into this newly navigable section of waterway by order of the Powys Roads Engineer.

Vyrnwy Flood Aqueducts * SJ 2531 1997 and SJ 2537 1974—400 metres from Carreghofa and visible from the B4398 between Carreghofa Locks and the Vyrnwy Aqueduct.

These two aqueduct bridges (Fig. 4) are set in the large embankment built over the Vyrnwy flood-plain. They are probably original features although heavily rebuilt. The northern aqueduct is of squared stone with four (probably rebuilt) brick arches whereas that to the south has three arches and its original stone structure has apparently been completely refaced with blue brick. The internal waterproofing of puddled-clay (a mixture of kneaded saturated clay and sand) gives both these aqueducts their typically bulky shape. As a result such aqueducts have the appearance of tunnels burrowed under the vast bulk of the canal formation rather than that of a waterway carried over necessary arches. The channels of both structures are of full canal width but the southern one is separated from its leaky clay flanks by late nineteenth-century blue-brick walls which 'float' in the large mass of puddle-clay on the aqueduct deck.

RECOMMENDED CANAL WALK 3.—The walk from the Carreghofa Locks south across the Vyrnwy Aqueducts is one of two recommended rural walks along the canal. The return distance is about 1.6 kilometres.

Carreghofa Locks ** SJ 2539 2025—Access from Llanymynech via a right-turn 1.6 kilometres west along the B4398.

This very attractive site consists of a tollhouse, lock-keeper's and toll-collector's houses (the latter house is complete with an original as well as modern bay-windows for easy observation of the waterway), two locks with Buck's unique cast-iron sluice gearing, an arched overbridge, a feeder inlet and a toll-collector's pigsty. The quality of the buildings found along the Montgomeryshire Canal is well exemplified here. For instance, the sweeping curves of the brick overflow weirs at Carreghofa Top Lock are particularly fine and even the late nineteenth-century pigsty is well built.

Rising to the north of the locks is the great quarried cliff of Llanymynech Hill. This produced the limestone which stimulated the growth of the Montgomeryshire Canal.

Carreghofa Mill (**) SJ 2491 2101—Access as above but the mill stands on the minor road beyond the entrance to the Carreghofa Hall drive-way. The owner is Mr. G. Eyres of Aber-Tanat Hall, Shropshire.

The canal-feeder here has the appearance of a navigable canal-arm; often complete with resident swans. Below the bluff on which it runs is an attractive three-storeyed stone-built mill of the nineteenth century, clearly visible from the road. All its internal machinery has disappeared but the intake sluices and now dry head-race can be seen from the adjoining humped-back bridge over the water-feeder. One empty wheel-pit remains alongside the mill, but there was once a second water-wheel also fed by the canal-feeder.

A single-storeyed corrugated-iron shed alongside the mill still houses a water-turbine which replaced the two mill-wheels in June 1921. In addition to driving the old corn-mill this generated electricity for the Aber-Tanat estate. The turbine was made by Gilkes and Company of Kendal and the adjoining electrical generator, a 'Phoenix Dynamic' unit bearing the imprints of both 'M F K Ltd.' and 'English Electric', is a rare survival.

Tanat Feeder Weir (**) SJ 2535 2183—Access is by a right turning over the canal 0.4 kilometres west of Llanymynech on the B4398 and another right turn one kilometre further on into Carreghofa Hall drive-way.

This large and impressive weir in its present form probably dates mainly from about 1975. The uppermost step, however, (an elongated 'V' in plan) probably dates from 1821-22 when the weir was heightened with the intention of making the River Tanat and the feeder navigable for boats. This was in order to avoid the necessity for all traffic from the limestone quarries having to pay Ellesmere Canal tolls. The Ellesmere Canal Company opposed and blocked the Parliamentary approval for this

Fig. 116. The canal feeder from the Tanat at Carreghofa utilised the earlier headrace to Carreghofa Mill. This water-turbine and electrical generator (in the foreground) are still in situ at the mill. A belt-drive to power the older corn-mill was located behind the wooden boarding.

scheme but the Montgomeryshire Canal completed the new weir and re-aligned the feeder (Fig. 27) in order to have an independent water supply for their top lock at Carreghofa.

The original weir on the Tanat was used by the ancient manorial mill of Carreghofa (see above). Its water-leat had been originally continued on an inconvient level to a point half-way down Carreghofa Locks where the present side-pond was, in fact, the original mouth of the Tanat water-feeder. Its dry channel can be traced back towards Carreghofa Mill and the River Tanat.

A change in canal company

The main canal-line above Carreghofa Locks was built by the Ellesmere Canal Company as a completely independent business enterprise. In fact the two canals were originally intended not to meet at all but to have independent termini at the limestone quarries.

155

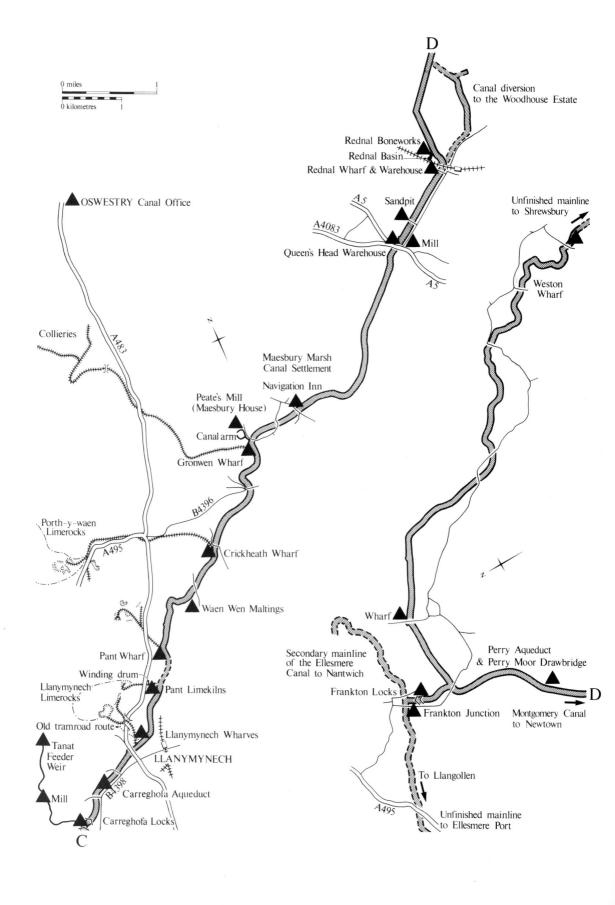

D

Canal diversion
to the Woodhouse Estate

Rednal Boneworks
Rednal Basin
Rednal Wharf & Warehouse

Unfinished mainline
to Shrewsbury

Sandpit

A5

A4083

Mill

Queen's Head Warehouse

A5

Weston
Wharf

OSWESTRY Canal Office

Collieries

A483

Maesbury Marsh
Canal Settlement

Navigation Inn

Peate's Mill
(Maesbury House)

Canal arm

Gronwen Wharf

B4396

Porth-y-waen
Limerocks

A495

Crickheath Wharf

Waen Wen Maltings

Wharf

Secondary mainline
of the Ellesmere
Canal to Nantwich

Perry Aqueduct
& Perry Moor Drawbridge

Pant Wharf

Winding drum

Llanymynech
Limerocks

Pant Limekilns

Frankton Locks

Frankton Junction

Montgomery Canal
to Newtown

D

Old tramroad route

Tanat
Feeder
Weir

Llanymynech Wharves

LLANYMYNECH

To Llangollen

Mill

B4398

Carreghofa Aqueduct

A495

Unfinished mainline
to Ellesmere Port

Carreghofa Locks

C

0 miles 1
0 kilometres 1

A Gazetteer of selected remains along the Llanymynech Branch of the Ellesmere Canal

by Graham Deamer

Introduction

As has been explained elsewhere, the waterway known popularly today as the 'Montgomery Canal' is in fact an amalgam of four waterways. The Llanymynech branch and the fragment of the original mainline of the Ellesmere Canal together form the English section of the canal (the Llanymynech branch also reaches for two kilometres or so into Montgomeryshire as far as its end on junction with the original Montgomeryshire Canal).

The bulk of the large industrial complexes attached to the Montgomery Canal lie in the Shropshire length. The place-names, however, remain largely Welsh. This is the curious result of some political sleight of hand in the sixteenth century. The national boundary runs down the main street of Llanymynech village.

Llanymynech limestone had long been prized for making fertilizer and the workings were extensive before the coming of the canal. These lime quarries were without doubt the principal *raison d'être* for the construction of waterways which met here.

The workings at Llanymynech and Crickheath Hills and the nearby Porth-y-waen quarries were linked to the canal by means of narrow-gauge tramroads. The one other feeder tramroad at Gronwen Wharf was a coal-carrying line.

Canalside communities were generated by these and other activities. The best example is the settlement of Maesbury Marsh which grew up at a strategic road crossing as a 'port' handling general cargoes. Possibly the most curious is the small community at Frankton Junction which grew up largely because of the needs of boatmen and boat-building.

Much of the English section runs through fairly remote countryside. For nearly fifty years after the disastrous breach of 1936 which precipitated the demise of the canal the waterway mouldered away quite unmolested. Little has changed, most of the original infrastructure survives and is every bit as attractive as the much lauded Welsh section.

Carreghofa Aqueduct * * SJ 2594 2067. Alongside the B4398 some 700 metres west of the centre of Llanymynech.

This aqueduct of the 1860s was added to carry the canal-line over the new cutting of the West Shropshire Mineral Railway. The aqueduct looks quite impressive from the now disused twin-line railway bed and is made up of rivetted wrought-iron plates supported on cast-iron columns. The original line of the canal lay to the north of the present structure.

Llanymynech Wharf and Tramroads (**) SJ 2672 2160—This was the most complex of the limestone shipment points. As is often the case on industrial sites the general layout was altered over the years. The canal was certainly here by 1796 but the precise date of the appearance of the tramroads is not known. The Canal's Act however specifically allows for the construction of such mineral lines and the tramroad here appears in local records by 1806.

The earliest 'rail road' from the quarries at the southern end of Llanymynech Hill was probably a 'plate-way'. It used a section of a pre-canal cart-road for part of its length, some of this can be seen today—a long narrow enclosure in which 'Rock Cottage' is situated. The line terminated at the smaller (northern) of the two canal arms.

Considerable alterations appear to have

Fig. 117. Map of the Llanymynech Branch of the Ellesmere Canal with the major sites of interest indicated by triangles.

Fig. 118. The Carreghofa Aqueduct.

been made later in the century. By 1858 at least the lines from the base of the inclines were being taken under the main road by means of a low bridge (SJ 2668 2130). A second, slightly longer canal arm had been added. Both arms take the form of a 'V', with transhipment on both sides. The grade of the horse-worked lower section seems to have been eased by means of a cutting which also allowed the 1863 route of the Cambrian Railway's Llanfyllin line to cross on an overbridge. This railway took much of the lime trade and the large rotary kiln with its tall chimney is associated with the rail-borne traffic.

The quarry inclines, canal arms, road bridge, stables and earthworks survive largely intact, as does the rotary kiln. They are on private land but much can be seen from the towing-path and the A483. The quarries themselves are criss-crossed by public rights of way. There were lead-smelting, iron-working and brick-making activities nearby of which little trace remains. Raised banks with some stone revetment can be seen alongside the canal arms (especially the southernmost). These carried tramroad sidings (one of which crossed the Cambrian line on the level) from which the larger unmanageable quarried rocks would be dropped to wharf level where they would be broken up by hand into more convenient sizes. This arduous task was apparently given to pensioners.

The canal wharf was probably disused by the turn of the century, while quarrying and

limeburning here ceased by the eve of the First World War.

Pant Limekilns * SJ 2744 2183—About a kilometre north of Llanymynech Wharf there is a quite well-preserved bank of limekilns at the canalside, albeit with a modern dwelling built on top. They are significant in that they are located above the canal level (i.e. the drawing-tunnels are at wharf level while the shafts are high above) suggesting that some burnt lime was loaded into boats here (although there is a road access). A now vanished bank of kilns 1.6 kilometres further north had canal access only via a short arm. The kilns were supplied by an inclined plane which led to the same set of quarries which supplied Llanymynech Wharf. This railway is commemorated in the nearby canal bridge (No. 90) 'Old Rail Road Bridge' (otherwise Kynaston's Bridge). A notable relic of the incline arrangement survives nearby at SJ 2730 2187 where the local community have preserved one of the old winding drums.

Pant Wharf * SJ 2773 2236—The Llanymynech limestone workings continue northwards to

Fig. 119. Llanymynech Limestone Quarries and Mines. (Community Programme)

Crickheath Hill. The Crickheath Hill quarries were linked to the canal by another tramroad/inclined plane arrangement. The construction date is not known, but it had passed its peak by the 1870s. The course survived intact until quite recently when building works took place close to the canal end. However, much can still be seen. The bridge by which the platforms and tracks of Pant railway station were carried over it survives, as does the wharf-side. The station is a matter of yards from the canal wharf and, upon emerging from under the bridge, tramroad sidings turned sharply northwards for a short distance straight on to an end-tippler, and also ran for some distance to the south where the bridge (No. 88) carrying the lane over the canal has another bridge built onto it to accommodate the tramroad. There was a

tramroad/railway interchange here too but the railway remains have suffered more than the canal.

The Malt House—Waen Wen (*) SJ 2842 2291—A large three-storeyed building with its gable end to the towing-path. Despite severe damage in recent years the ruins are substantial. Like many canalside structures on the Montgomery the upper storeys are red-brick extensions to an older random-stone-built lower storey.

Crickheath Wharf (*) SJ 2918 2343—This is the most northerly of the limestone transhipment wharves. A tramroad about four kilometres long, promoted by the Earl of Powis, linked the canal to quarries at Whitehaven (Porth-y-waen). Ploughed up stone-block and tramplate chairs and sleepers attest to its early vintage. The line seems to have been modernised in the 1890s (a 2ft. 6in. (0.76m) gauge edge-railway by now) and was still in use until the First World War.

A small community (Crickheath Wharf as opposed to Crickheath proper) grew up here.

The linear wharf was quite sizeable and still survives albeit covered by undergrowth. Waggons would appear to have negotiated the sudden fall from the field to canal level by means of a switchback arrangement. A platform for a waggon end-tipping arrangement is now the site of a greenhouse. The remains of two boats are to be found here in the silt of this drained section of canal.

Where the line crossed fields all remains have been ploughed out, and the bridge by which the line crossed the Cambrian has gone, but the bridge shared with the Cambrian's Porth-y-waen branch survive (SJ 2722 2428) and a field gate (SJ 2820 2405) marks the point at which the main road was crossed at Llynclys.

The cottage on the towing-path side opposite the wharf is well preserved.

Gronwen Wharf—Morda Colliery Tramway (*) SJ 3043 2468—This isolated wharf was the interchange place for horse-drawn coal from the long-disused Morda coalfield. The tramroad serving the Gronwen and other collieries near Trefonen was over five kilometres long, a plate-way, but little is known of its chronology.

159

It had certainly ceased to operate by the time of the large-scale Ordnance Survey map of 1874 although it had survived long enough to be crossed by the Cambrian Railway in 1860. Some slight earthworks still remain along its route and the bridge survives where the Cambrian Railway crosses the earlier line (SJ 2933 2554).

The cottages at the wharf belong to a post-tramroad period.

Peate's Mill (Maesbury Hall Mill) (*) SJ 3030 2500—This still-active green painted edifice has a long and continuous history. It was once dependent on corn brought by narrowboat from Ellesmere Port, indeed the Peates operated the last fleet of boats on the canal and were the only firm known to have experimented with motor boats. Canal traffic ceased in 1932. The sinuous and narrow but largely dry 0.4 kilometre arm of the canal to Peate's Mill can still be seen from the lane which runs parallel. Much of the early mill-leat system here can be traced too.

Maesbury Marsh ** SJ 3133 2500—An attractive little canal settlement almost a kilometre from Maesbury village. A large late nineteenth-century warehouse has gone but a number of interesting features survive. Foremost among these is the brick 'Navigation Inn' which is combined with a three-storey warehouse. The ground floor of the warehouse is of an older, stone construction. Some stables survive, as do relics of a bone-works (the red-brick chimney remains, with lozenge shapes picked out in yellow) a little to the north.

The large house 'Sycamore' near the 'Navigation' looks decidedly in the style of Thomas Telford. Of the dozen or so wharfside cranes which were latterly to be found throughout the length of today's Montgomery Canal, the 15 cwt (762 kilogram) example at Maesbury Marsh is the only (standing) survivor.

Queens Head Warehouse *SJ 3398 2681—Close to the old A5 crossing, the largest of the canal's late nineteenth-century composite blue-brick/ corrugated-iron warehouses can be seen in a good state of preservation. One of its main customers was the corn-mill across the lane.

It holds a curious secret. From the ground floor, which is somewhat below the level of the adjoining lane, there is a tunnel through which ran a little railway communicating with a sand-pit on the far side of the lane.

Canal Office, Oswestry * SJ 2912 2954—The nearest that the waterway gets to Oswestry town is a distance of over five kilometres. The wharves at Queens Head and Maesbury Marsh served this important market town, the latter place being slightly nearer. In a corner of the town's car park is a wooden shed which was the office at which freight bookings were handled.

Rednal (Heath Houses) * SJ 3511 2764—A pre-canal settlement served by a unique (as far as the canal is concerned) small, two-storeyed timber-framed warehouse with quite light-weight studding and brick fill. The wharf level is served by the warehouse's ground floor while its first floor opens to the road. A curious external roofed-in stair arrangement (of later date) has now gone.

Adjacent is the canal's only example of a true roving or turnover bridge which allows the towing-path and the towing horse to be transferred from one side to the other without any tiresome unhitching of ropes.

About a quarter of a km away from Heath Houses is Rednal station on the Shrewsbury to Chester line of 1848. For a brief period in the 1850s prior to the construction of railways in the Severn Valley, Heath Houses was the terminus of a packet (passenger) boat service from Newtown. The timetabled journey took nearly five and a quarter hours to cover the forty-eight kilometres. The passenger's ten-minute stroll to the station to catch connections for Shrewsbury or Liverpool probably came as a relief.

If passengers and parcels went by way of Heath Houses Wharf then heavy goods went via the nearby 'Rednal' basin (SJ 3502 2782). A short arm of the canal leads to a sizeable basin alongside the railway embankment. Remains of a railway jetty and a stranded boat are still to be seen. Sidings may have been quite extensive at one time but, whatever the case, this interchange facility was short-lived. The arm of the canal, however, attracted a bone-works which operated until the 1920s, the

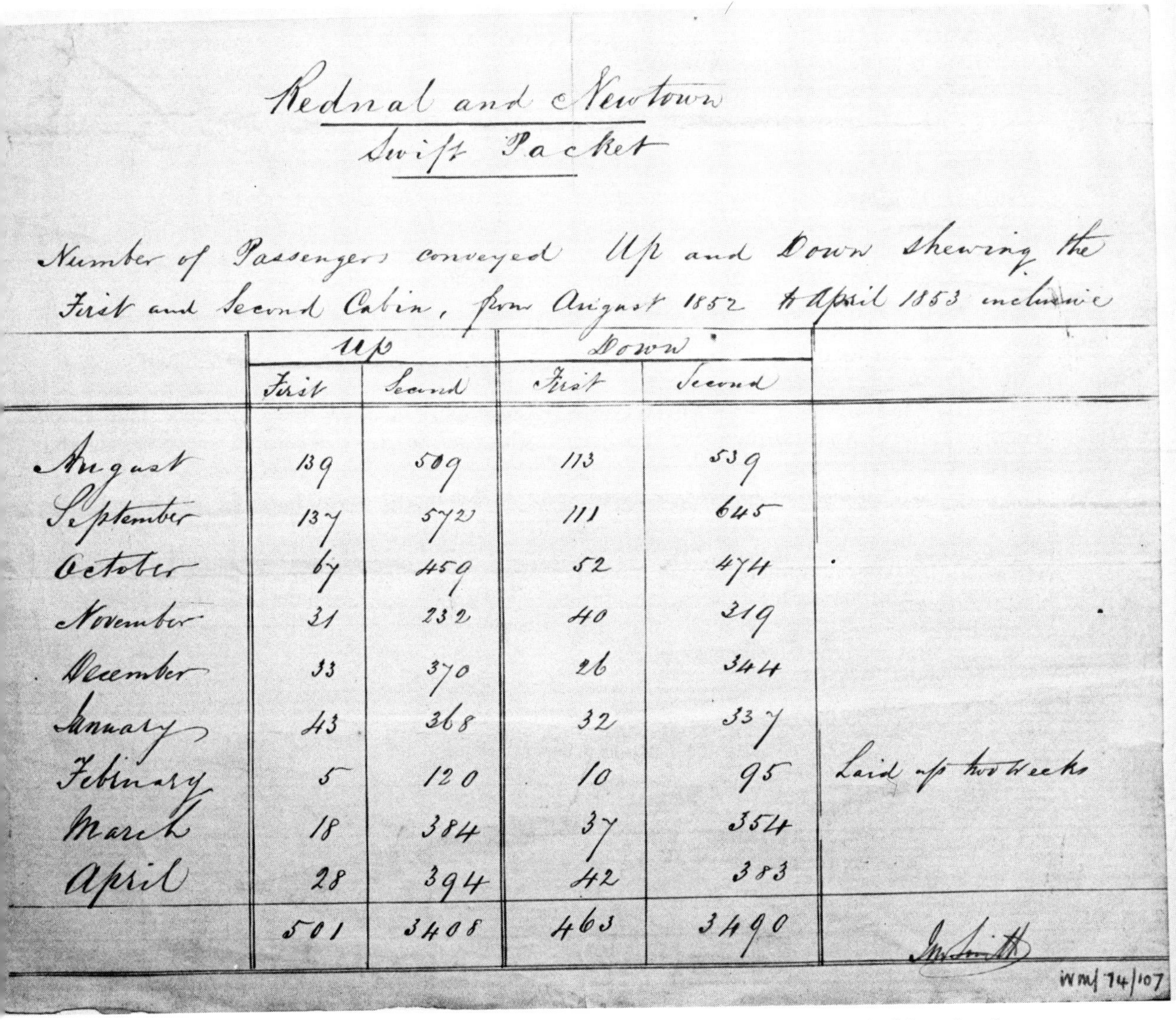

Rednal and Newtown
Swift Packet

Number of Passengers conveyed Up and Down shewing the First and Second Cabin, from August 1852 to April 1853 inclusive

	Up		Down		
	First	Second	First	Second	
August	139	509	113	539	
September	137	572	111	645	
October	67	459	52	474	
November	31	232	40	319	
December	33	370	26	344	
January	43	368	32	337	
February	5	120	10	95	Laid up two weeks
March	18	384	37	354	
April	28	394	42	383	
	501	3408	463	3490	Jno Smith

WM 74/107

Fig. 120. For a brief period in the 1850s the canal from Rednal Station to Newtown served as a branch of the main railway passenger network. (Community Programme)

derelict remains of which are still there.

Access is via the towing-path, but please note that the basin is now designated a nature reserve.

Perry Moor * ST 3600 2977—By means of some modest embanking and a three-arched aqueduct across the river (ST 3600 2977) the canal traverses this low ground. Extensive nineteenth-century field drainage here may have contributed to the infamous breach of 1936 which hastened the abandonment of the canal. This failure took place approximately one kilometre north of the aqueduct.

A curious diversion of the canal through the Woodhouse Estate was contrived by that estate's owner, Rev. John Lloyd, at the time of the canal's construction. Later the canal reverted to its authorised course to the west of the estate. A considerable length of this 'old canal' can still be followed on the 1:25,000 Ordnance Survey map.

Frankton Junction, Lower Frankton * SJ 3700 3185—Four locks, the top two being a 'staircase' drop the canal 9.4 metres from the level of today's 'Llangollen' canal. (The alterations to the water-table already alluded to above, will probably make the addition of a fifth lock (with slight fall only) necessary).

A glance at a map will show that the locks are on a short stretch of waterway linking two 'T'-junctions (roughly speaking lines to Trefor and Llangollen to the north-west, Llanymynech and Newtown to the south-west, Weston Wharf to the south-east, Hurleston Junction and the rest of the canal system to the north east). It must be remembered that the Ruabon line and the short length to Weston Wharf form the central section of the abortive Severn to Dee navigation which was the original aim of the Ellesmere Canal Company's promoters.

A small community sprang up at the locks. This minor bottle-neck attracted a pub, now a farm-house. An interesting opening in the towing-path wall, with an iron strap over the gap to guide tow-ropes, leads to steps which took the boatmen to the pub. On this short pound between the staircase and lock three there was a dry-dock, still faintly visible as a depression in the ground although the opening has been built across. Adjacent is a cottage.

The lock-keeper's house with stables are below the embankment.

Alongside the top lock is the toll-house. The small warehouse with crane at the actual point of junction has sadly gone.

Weston Wharf (*) SJ 4210 2569
The earthworks of the intended line to Shrewsbury peter out in the field a little to the south of the wharf. Boats went no further than this wharf as far as is known. The whole length from Hordley Wharf (visible at SJ 3811 3115) was abandoned after a breach in 1917 and is now quite dry. Since then Weston Wharf seems frozen in time. The warehouse, tavern, lime-kilns, stables, office, wharf walls, and even a cast-iron crane-base survive. Only the bridge and the water have gone.

INDEX

(All numbers in bold type refer to pages on which there is an illustration of the subject referred to)

163